DISCLOSURES

For

Ned, the youngest member of our workshops, Ruby and the new-borns: Dorothy and Vanessa Jade

Disclosures

Edited by
PAUL CORCORAN
and
VICKI SPENCER
The University of Adelaide, Australia

Ashgate

Aldershot • Brookfield USA • Singapore • Sydney

Published by
Ashgate Publishing Ltd
Gower House
Croft Road
Aldershot
Hants GU11 3HR
England

Ashgate Publishing Company
Old Post Road
Brookfield
Vermont 05036
USA

Ashgate website: http://www.ashgate.com

British Library Cataloguing in Publication Data
Disclosures
    1.Disclosure of information - Political aspects
    2.Self-disclosure - Political aspects 3.Disclosure of
    information - Philosophy 4.Self-disclosure - Psychological
    aspects
    I.Corcoran, Paul E., 1944- II.Spencer, Vicki
    320'.014

Library of Congress Catalog Card Number: 99-75549

ISBN 1 84014 796 2

Printed in Great Britain

Contents

List of Contributors

CAROL BACCHI, Associate Professor of Politics at the University of Adelaide, lectures in feminist theory and public policy. Her books include *Liberation Deferred? The Ideas of the English-Canadian Suffragists, 1877-1918* (1983), *Same Difference* (1990), *The Politics of Affirmative Action: 'Women', Equality and Category Politics* (1996), and *Women, Policy and Politics: The Construction of Policy Problems* (1999).

ANGELA CLARE has an M.A. in social and political thought from the University of Sussex and was recently awarded a Ph.D. in political theory at the University of Adelaide. Her main research areas are feminism and critical theory and she has published scholarly articles on Habermas and in the field of labour relations.

PAUL CORCORAN, Associate Professor of Politics at the University of Adelaide, has published widely in the fields of political theory, political language and rhetoric, and the history of political ideas. His books include *Political Language and Rhetoric* (1979), *Before Marx: Socialism and Communism in France, 1830-48* (1983), and *Awaiting Apocalypse* (1999).

MARION MADDOX, a lecturer at the University of Adelaide during the course of this project, is now an Australian Parliamentary Fellow. She has a Ph.D. in theology and has recently submitted a Ph.D. in political theory at the University of New South Wales. She has published widely on ethics and religion and is the co-author of *Myth, Ritual and the Sacred: Introducing the Phenomena of Religion* (1993).

GREG MCCARTHY is a lecturer in public policy and popular culture at the University of Adelaide. He has a Ph.D. from the University of Adelaide in comparative politics and has published widely on Australian public policy, cultural studies and post-modernism. He is the author of *Telling Tales About the State Bank of South Australia* (1999).

VICKI SPENCER lectures in political theory at The University of Adelaide. As a Rhodes Scholar she was awarded a D.Phil. in political theory from the University of Oxford. She has published a number of scholarly articles on J.G. Herder's theories of language, culture and community, and co-edited *Rethinking Nationalism*, a special issue of the *Australian Journal of Politics and History* (1997).

Acknowledgements

The idea for this book arose from a series of seminars held by the Language and Rhetoric Research Group during 1996 to encourage greater collaboration among colleagues in the Politics Department of The University of Adelaide. In 1997 we conducted a series of workshops on the concept of disclosure and early in 1999 we held a conference to present and discuss each author's chapter. Throughout this process our authors have contributed significantly to the thematic coherence of the book and the development of each chapter. We are grateful to all our contributors for their commitment to this project and for making our meetings a highly enjoyable and intellectually stimulating experience in which far more was disclosed than any of us ever intended.

We would also like to express our gratitude to the Politics Department for providing us with early financial support to conduct our research and to the Australian Research Council for awarding us a grant to bring the project to completion. Finally, thanks to our research assistants – Lauren Buchanan, Glenda Mather and Rachel Templer – for their valuable work.

Paul Corcoran
Vicki Spencer
June 1999

Introduction:
Revealing Disclosure

PAUL CORCORAN AND VICKI SPENCER

Disclosure is an act of communicating hidden things. It involves the risk of confiding in others, the responsibility of deeper awareness, and the danger that one's confidences may be breached. Disclosure, as an act of revelation, presupposes that something is unknown or covered up. Its disclosure may create intimacy or lead to personal betrayal, official scrutiny and public scandal.

Apart from private and personal matters, there are several formal kinds of disclosure. Statutes require politicians or other officials to disclose financial assets; parties at law must disclose evidence to each other; 'unnamed sources' disclose confidential or scandalous information about the actions or intent of others. Disclosure is a kind of transaction. It tips the balance of what is known by whom. The dynamic effect of revelatory communication gives disclosure, and certainly non-disclosure, a kind of tension or pressure.

The confiding of knowledge carries with it the potential for exposure, shifting perspectives, new confidences. It can also mislead, baffle or deceive us. That which is disclosed might be only part of the picture, a selective and even biased account, or just incomprehensible to most people. In these circumstances the disclosure is less than full, and yet the recognition of this incompleteness is itself a revelation. A mistake, an untruth, an enigma, whether intentional or unintentional, can also be disclosed. Disclosure is thus an act of power, in which a revelation, for example, may be a gift of love and trust, a legal duty of compliance, a confession of guilt, or an intentional betrayal of a confidence.

Disclosures occur at every level of human experience. They range from a slip of the tongue or an intimate avowal of passion to the carefully worded affidavit. The psychological intensity of disclosure resonates in the mythic words and deeds of ancient religion. In the Judæo-Christian Bible, the *Book of Genesis* tells how Adam and Eve's original nakedness was revealed to them by their first act of defiance against God's command,

1

while the ultimate final disclosure, the end of time, is prophesied in the closing *Book of Revelations*, titled *Apocalypse* in the original Greek.

The word *apocalypse* – 'disclosure of that which was previously hidden or unknown' – was also used to describe the sinful act of mothers and fathers appearing naked before their sons and daughters, an indiscretion prohibited in ancient Hebrew law. This early, the disclosure of the sexual organs was sanctioned by strict rules to govern desire and to forbid certain acts of men and women. The 'innocence' of children was thought to be preserved by covering up the sexually mature body, thus preventing its disclosure to youthful eyes. Disclosure and closure, avowal and disavowal, revelation and repression, efforts to uncover and cover up are always in tension with each other, inciting, resisting and limiting one another.

Disclosures come in many forms: a declaration, a confession, a discovery, a revelation, an uncovering, an opening up. To disclose is to make something known. It is an act that exposes, relates or reveals something to oneself and often to others. It may take the form of a voluntary disclosure of one's private self or a disclosure enforced by laws and regulations. One's private things may be revealed instead by someone else, an informant, an investigator or a disloyal confidant. Special explorations may also disclose previously unknown things about nature, human institutions and society. The act of disclosure is an unveiling, a display, an exhibition, a showing. At its most intense it is a shocking revelation between close friends. In the public arena, it is a moving, perhaps horrifying and extravagant spectacle.

The potential for disclosure is boundless, yet, from earliest times, societies have sought to bind, control and discipline this boundlessness. Human institutions, social norms and customs are evolving mechanisms to enclose, limit and order the unpredictability and extent of our disclosures. The flasher is designated a criminal for 'exposing' himself, but we may also blush when a friend, or even a stranger, surprises us with a deeply personal revelation. From childhood we are taught that there are appropriate places and times for different forms and levels of disclosure.

Speech itself is an act of disclosure. To speak is to act. And all human action is in some sense a disclosure. We may disclose more or less of ourselves when we speak by the tone, intensity or accent of our voice. Though in intimate settings we may reveal our most private secrets and innermost feelings we often seek to hide them, even, or especially, from our closest friends. Nevertheless, in this act of hiding we still reveal much about ourselves. Often what remains unsaid is more poignant than what is said. The persona we disclose to others may not be whom we believe ourselves to be. And yet even our masks betray revealing features. When we act out a role in our professional lives, whether in our capacity as teachers, doctors or mechanics, we publicise to others our skills, our knowledge and our abilities. Publicity, too, is a force of disclosure as well as non-disclosure.

To say that all human action is an act of disclosure is suggestive but it is true only in a trivial sense. The interesting and relevant point in trying to understand human interaction and social norms lies in the unravelling of the kinds and levels of disclosure which exist in the language games of different communicative contexts.

In this book the term *disclosure* resonates in its many connotations as we examine different forms and levels of disclosure, from publicity in the political arena, to the contemporary Western penchant for excessive public self-disclosures, and finally, its opposite, silence. Just as there are dangers and consequences in uncovering the human body, so we find there are issues of probity, honesty and responsibility in the disclosure – or non-disclosure, a disavowal – of one's actions, possessions, intentions, knowledge, emotions, aims and faith.

Disclosure leads inexorably from moral, religious and psychological concerns to legal and political affairs. Today, 'disclosure' is still understood as an act of uncovering private things. Disclosure and discovery – a term that only a century ago still meant 'uncover' or 'reveal to someone' – are formal procedures preceding a criminal or civil trial. The duty to disclose is formalised in insurance agreements, commercial contracts and company relationships with shareholders. A failure to disclose by one party results in the other interested party being released from contractual obligations. Among public officials, the disclosure of financial, personal and other interested ties is seen as a means of preventing private interests and corruption from distorting the administration of public policy. Party rules and statutory regulations are formalised to require politicians to disclose their private assets in the interests of the public good and as a way 'to keep people honest.' In all these instances of obligatory 'coded disclosure' information is elicited and disseminated within the boundaries of formal procedures.

Yet coded disclosures can be routinized to hide, mystify and lull us into thinking we know all that we need to know. We sign the fine print of a contract or formal declaration quite complacently. Pervasive realms of silence quietly endure beneath all that is open and above board in this contemporary era of relatively uninhibited disclosure. The redoubts of religion and familial patriarchy are cases in point. Often far more is left undisclosed than is disclosed as democratic governments present expedient, popular and ideologically driven policy solutions under the veil of a full, honest and neutral disclosure and examination of the issues. Away from the public show of accountability in the noisy 'debates' staged in the chambers of Parliament and Congress, we also discover that the deals and decision-making occur behind closed doors of Cabinet meetings and party caucuses marked 'Private – No Admittance.' And yet these attempts to conceal, silence and close off debate reveal, at the same time, significant features of our political system.

While silence and non-disclosure are viewed with suspicion in democratic societies, it is important to remember that privacy is highly valued in liberal conceptions of individual freedom and dignity. The moral worth, or indeed the legal necessity, of publicly revealing oneself and one's things requires political and ethical justification. In conflict with the values of 'openness' and disclosure are the rights of personal privacy, intellectual autonomy and free association. In procuring and exposing to all and sundry the most intimate fantasies and private acts of public figures such as the Prince of Wales and the United States President, journalists and editors justify their salacious disclosures by insisting that the 'public' – or more accurately their readers – have a right to know. The question of whether such stories nourish the hunger for knowledge, or whether they feed puerile and voyeuristic appetites, does not often make the climb of conscience to journalism's high moral ground.

We live in an age in which the most intimate facets of personal life are uncovered for public showing. Public confessions of individual behaviour flourish on high-rating television shows. The popularity of soap operas – ordinary life viewed, as it were, through a keyhole – reveals a hunger for gossip. In recent years the press has gone to extraordinary lengths to expose whatever can be captured by phone taps and telescopic lenses. Revealing pictures of royalty with their pants down attract huge fees in the fierce competition to sell newspapers. But despite their hyper-real images, disclosed by others in excesses once unimaginable in 'family newspapers' and prime-time viewing, neither the United States President nor the Prince of Wales is a fictional character. Their most intimate acts of self-disclosure with their lovers have been exposed to the public against their own volition. Here disclosure is an exposé.

In addition to these political and ethical implications, there are also important psychological and interpersonal dimensions to disclosure. Psychiatry, counselling and various types of psychotherapy are based on the assumption that individuals can and must disclose, essentially, themselves. Psychoanalysis, for example, involves an intensive procedure of stripping oneself bare: returning to, re-discovering and re-experiencing one's childhood, one's dreams and fantasies, one's most vulnerable and intimate moments, thoughts and experiences in a setting of individual confidentiality. This setting and the development of trust between patient and therapist are vital to the fostering of this profound personal disclosure. We know intuitively that such self-disclosure carries with it enormous risk to ourselves and sometimes to others. To reveal our innermost feelings in the face of distrust, antipathy or prejudice rather than understanding and acceptance is a dangerous and potentially soul-destroying experience. Yet neither understanding nor acceptance is possible without the disclosure of ourselves. We are forever walking a tightrope between disclosure and closure.

The act of intimate and profound self-disclosure can in itself be therapeutic. To confess a secret in total confidentiality to a psychiatrist or priest can lift a burden which lies heavily upon us. Confession and pain go hand in hand. When judgement is passed upon the painful disclosure of our sins in the confessional, this is accompanied by the knowledge that with repentance there is a closure of the matter and absolution is given. That is the deal. The sin has been paid for and life starts anew, unburdened by the past. The process of revealing oneself to a therapist is also fraught with anguish. It is a slow and difficult process which many cannot endure. The deal – redemption, healing, remission of pain – is less certain.

Words seem to escape us when we need to reveal what has never before been spoken. We may also have a sense about the way things have been, that something in one's life is wrong. But we have never before thought it in a conscious way because we have never known or experienced any other way of life with which to compare it. It is, in Christopher Bollas' words, an 'unthought known' (1987). Some people discover, in a crisis or at the moment of opportunity for intimate disclosure, that they lack the language to express their deepest emotions. Others are unwilling to take the risk. For once we reveal ourselves, as we do when we put these things into words for the first time, we open ourselves not only to the ears of a confidant but inevitably to a process of self-questioning, doubt and critical reflection. Psychotherapy is not only a process of intimate self-disclosure to another but, most importantly, to oneself.

In a no less profound and intimate way, friends, family members and sexual partners form close interpersonal bonds by revealing themselves, letting drop, as they do, their clothing of formality, public manners and social inhibitions. In this very process of getting to know one another we see again how disclosure becomes a force, a procedure, a carefully guarded mechanism that enables us to discover and confirm cherished values, special meanings and prized behaviour. Disclosure to another, accepting that other person into one's intimate realm, carries with it the potential for acceptance of oneself.

Yet there is always risk and uncertainty with the possibility of rejection. We might discover our partner has a host of irritating personal habits, thus producing a desire for distance rather than intimacy. A declaration of love and a desire for closer commitment can open the door to more intimate revelations and experiences between two people but, if one's love is not reciprocated, this disclosure only serves to bring the relationship to a painful and even premature closure. Once our feelings are disclosed to ourselves and to another, they can never be successfully hidden away again without significant cost to oneself. A life of pretence is a painful charade in which the self is suppressed and stunted.

Disclosures can also be used as a weapon to humiliate, hurt or disgrace others. We may reveal to a friend or lover an embarrassing secret only to have our confidentiality betrayed and find ourselves the brunt of ridicule from a wider community. Like so many other valuable possessions, the gift of intimacy through self-disclosure carries with it the risk of loss, intrusion and exposure by one's confidants to individuals or groups for whom this disclosure was not intended. Non-disclosure, too, can be injurious. Between intimates, a refusal to talk – the 'silent treatment' – is often used as a form of punishment. But revealing one's true feelings can just as readily be an act of cruelty as the guise of a candid disclosure is used to vent one's anger with the intention of causing maximum harm. The 'truth' disclosed in a vindictive statement is rarely, if ever, the entire picture.

Disclosure is not a good in itself, but always context-dependent. If, following Kant, we made the dictum to tell the truth an unconditional command, most of us would be plunged into serious 'hot water.' In the film *Liar, Liar*, Jim Carey comically portrays the trouble confronting a lawyer who, suddenly and uncontrollably, begins to reveal everything he thinks. According to national opinion polls, the American public were not overly concerned that President Clinton lied to keep his sexual liaisons hidden. Many, indeed, admitted they would do the same if questioned about their personal lives and especially about an extra-martial affair. Most of us have experienced moments when we cannot, or do not want, to live up to Kant's imperative. When a relative asks if we like her new dress, the newly redecorated lounge room or, even worse, whether we liked a recent gift, and our answer is 'No', we might feel compelled to lie. To do otherwise would be to break all the rules of polite society. Disclosing the truth would be gratuitous, a thoughtless act of hurting someone needlessly. Non-disclosure of our thoughts and feelings may, at times, be a necessary good.

Disclosures are not always intentional. Though at times requiring courage and a conscious effort in an open declaration, a disclosure may also take the form of 'letting something slip'. While striving to put on a brave face and hold back our feelings, in a fleeting moment we can reveal to another the pain beneath this facade through a quiver in our voice, a slip of the tongue or a look in our eyes. A partner might tell you a seemingly innocent story about meeting an acquaintance at a restaurant. Yet in listening you begin to realise what an unlikely coincidence that was. It dawns upon you that something is amiss. Then, like a movie projector on fast forward, images flash in your mind of similar tales you have heard about this person, your previous misgivings, combined with your partner's disclaimers and over-insistent protests of innocence. In a second, the pieces of the jigsaw puzzle have come together and you now know with absolute certainty your partner has been having an affair with this 'acquaintance'.

With this revelation your partners' words of denial also take on a new and more profound significance. The bond of trust created through your apparent intimate and mutual disclosures is broken as it is revealed that what you once believed were your partner's full and truthful disclosures were in fact deceptions intended to hide a betrayal. You begin to look on your partner in a new light, not only as an unfaithful and disloyal person but also as a liar and deceiver. The words which once appeared to you as the truth disclosed far more about your partner's character than you had ever before realised. The cynic, unlike you, may never have believed your partner's disclaimers. But while your partner's words originally deceived you, paradoxically this deception does not make these words any less revelatory. On the contrary, the act of deceiving – a non-disclosure in which things are covered up rather than uncovered – discloses far more levels of meaning, by virtue of its hidden depths, than a transparent and truthful statement of fact.

Revelations do not always, or often, provide us with absolute certainty. Christian theologians remind us that human beings can never know the divine plan for humanity, and that to aspire to such omniscience is a sin of pride. Great truths are only ever revealed partially, a word here, a glimpse there, by prophecy, intuition or miraculous good fortune. Truth cannot be captured and communicated as simple facts and logical statements. Often what is revealed is itself a mystery. One might rather aspire to the virtue of humility in admitting that the same is true for our knowledge of other human beings, the complex groups we form over time, and indeed the knowledge of our own selves.

Accepting this limitation does not oblige us to adopt the extreme view that no facts exist, making it therefore impossible ever to disclose the truth. If a politician has a million dollars in the bank, that is a fact that can be truthfully disclosed, along with the date on which it was deposited, the type of financial instrument presented and other factual matters that may be of relevance to statutory authorities. Despite attempts by some accountants and financial advisors to hide their clients' assets, truthful disclosures of fact are possible and necessary to fair dealing. But so are other kinds, no less important, that are far less certain. The uncertainty arises not because we are honest or deceitful, but because we are disclosing other kinds of truths: our loves and hatreds, our hopes and fears, our misgivings, our sorrow for events and remorse for misdeeds, our carefully laid plans that may turn out badly timed or horribly misconceived. Our perceptions of these things are subject to time and change, the adequacy of our knowledge, the deftness of our sensitivity, the tension between conflicting motives, the intervention of unforeseen forces and our capacity, or desire, to understand them from different perspectives.

Things that are *covered* or *uncovered* do not exist freely, uncontested, simply in and of themselves. Being covered or uncovered implies a reciprocal condition. The story of Adam and Eve in the Garden of Eden makes this as plain as can be. Indeed theirs is the paradigmatic condition of self-conscious human beings. Reminding ourselves of the ancient Judaic resonance, their dilemma of disclosure faces everyone both empirically and metaphorically in the question: 'Before whom may I stand naked?' As every child, lover or hospital patient knows, it is a question that may be answered.

When Adam and Eve ate the forbidden fruit of the Tree of Knowledge of Good and Evil, there was a disclosure. Revealed to them by this act was the knowledge that they could no longer stand naked before God, or each other, as they had done before. This disclosure was the first of tribulations, and initially involved the felt need to hide themselves in their own paradise and sew together the leaves of another tree for clothing, the badge of lost innocence. So that uncovering begat this covering. It was a separation from God and each other, a matter of shame and the disclosure of differences that, as the story tells us, passed down this fundamental alienation from God and between man and woman to all generations.

One of the many significant points of this story is that, for human beings, things are never simply what they appear to be. To our eyes all things are either covered or uncovered, hidden or revealed, clothed or naked, seen or unseen. These valences – the *impact* of what we see, the *desire* to uncover what is hidden – are full of meaning for our lives. They create necessarily, by virtue of our presence before these things, intimates and strangers; those who know and those who are ignorant; initiates *versus* novices; priests and the laity; the ones in whom things have been confided and those who have been excluded. The process of disclosure creates, in and of itself, an enclosure: the lovers' rendezvous, a circle of friends, the secret society of rebels, the cognoscenti's circle.

Just as the act of disclosure involves a certain force or power – to uncover and reveal – so the act of closure cuts across and severs disclosure. This cannot help but be willful, an expression of power and judgement, with enormous costs at stake. A closure changes the world of possibility. A novel, film, play, or life ended this way and not some other. The passage of an Act of Parliament or Congress, or a judgement by the highest court in the land, are disclosures which close off debate, alternative ideas, policies and procedures; they reduce the potential and narrow the range of alternatives for things to develop and change as they otherwise might have done.

In a sense, then, closure is something like a silencing, a suspension of what may be seen, said and done. This is the whole point, for example, of both overt and covert censorship. Censorship boards are established to prevent and limit the disclosure of highly 'immoral' and 'obscene' material. Yet social mores also operate to silence many minority groups through non-recognition, as well as direct condemnation. In the more extreme times of war or national unrest, governments tend to proclaim Official Secrets Acts and impose stricter regimes of censorship over publishing and what is produced in literature and the arts. Patriotic values and deeds are encouraged while other views are discouraged or prohibited. The public is incited to suspect and inform on those who ask questions or seek information. There is a tendency to close down or control spheres of political and cultural diversity, political opposition, or groups traditionally associated with dissent and foreign interests. Thus minority ethnic or religious groups, universities, unions and international societies may also be the object of official censure.

Authoritarian political systems strive to make these oppressive emergency measures the ordinary order of the day. Despotic governments rule, as it were, by silence. 'Closed' societies, however defined, exert power and impose policies according to unwritten or at least unpublished rules, secret orders and unappealable acts. Reasons may not be disclosed in advance and, as with the 'the disappeared' in Chile and elsewhere, certainly not afterwards. Eventually the burial pits are uncovered and the policy is gruesomely disclosed. Such is the politics of secret enclosures. Decisions are made *in camera*, the public may not hear or see, and the silence of the public forum corresponds eloquently to unspeakable actions under the cover of darkness.

What is evident, however, is that the politics of repression does not resolve the tension of the human presence inevitably surrounding atrocities any more than clothing suppresses sexual desire. The tension will endure and grow. The regime of official silence may initially succeed in dumbfounding and stupefying a population, but eventually even that regime begins to wait in desperation for a shattering response to the terror. Just as certainly, this explosion will lead to the disclosure of hidden truths, however tragic they may be. One need only think of the recent experiences of Afghanistan, Albania, North Korea or Yugoslavia to illustrate the oppressive closing down and the violent opening up of national cultures.

The dynamics of closure and disclosure do not only occur in the catastrophic circumstances of totalitarian meltdown and ethnic 'civil' war. It is argued in the pages of this book that closure and disclosure characterise the 'routine' process of any society that attempts to delineate, control and change aspects of its culture which are defined as problems and are subjected to strategies of reform. When commissions and legislative inquiries disclose society's hidden injustices – crime syndicates, patterns of discrimination, domestic violence and child abuse – policy makers respond with new policies and guidelines intended to 'redress' what has been shamefully revealed. The disclosure of something hidden unleashes a demand for closure.

Traumatic events can also reveal a nation's character. The murderous assault upon children in a local school, the phenomenon of children killing other children and the gradual unravelling of a one-party police state, as in Poland and East Germany, are dramatic instances of a community's self-disclosure: a revelation of what it has become, and a period of painful crisis in which difficult truths must be confronted.

There are other revelations to be considered besides the historic disclosures of national tragedies and the existential crises of individual life. No less important as a feature of humane self-understanding, disclosure is a feature of aesthetic as well as psychological and political experience. Closure in a novel, play or film brings action – the narrative motion and development of character – to a resolution. A cathartic response to the narrative disclosure enables us to accept the plot and imaginatively experience a world in which it could happen. A film that ends without this resolution leaves the audience with a disturbing sense of incompleteness. We feel uncomfortable when the director intentionally leaves us wondering what might have been. The conclusion – the film's disclosure – is incomplete and our yearning for closure is frustrated. Even novels that provide the reader with multiple endings – for example John Fowles' *The French Lieutenant's Woman* – enable the reader to choose how the characters' lives turn out. Unlike a work which is purposely unresolved, Fowles' provision of three alternative conclusions places the responsibility for final closure within the reader's domain.

Yet closure is always transitory. Every text is opened up again by new readers who find more possibilities, different tensions for disclosure between characters and new resistances to closure. Think, for example, of Iago, in Shakespeare's *Othello*. Every reader or viewer of this play sees that Iago has still not tipped his hand, still not disclosed his innermost drives and secrets – not even, one suspects, to Shakespeare. The text is still awaiting this additional disclosure. And when it comes, what will it uncover in the other characters, and in the play itself?

What is true of plays, films or novels – narratives which have at least traditionally aimed for coherence, stability, closure – is even more true of speech. It is through speech that we express ourselves, clarify our thoughts and feelings, and give some order to our knowledge and memory. Language is always an act of revelation both to ourselves and others. At the same time, speech is the skill which enables us to keep some of these things hidden, unexposed, while in the same instant disclosing others. We say, all at once, less and more than we consciously intend, less and more than we know.

Nevertheless we form our thoughts and feelings and speak within the enclosure of a native tongue. We share these crucial subtleties of language with some persons and not others. The accent of our native speech, with its unique semantic, grammatical and syntactic elements, imposes important closures of meaning and communal identity. 'Outsiders' simply cannot grasp the nuances of slang, jargon, rhythm and pronunciation. Nor are they meant to. In some neighbourhoods and gangs that is the whole point. The linguistic exclusion focuses the meaning and intensifies the message for those who 'speak the lingo.'

The desire for stability and closure is a powerful force. It is at the heart of the rationalist philosophical project in which Descartes searched for some fixed point of view from which all metaphysical and epistemological problems could be solved. Under the enchantment of modern scientific achievements, the belief that closure can be attained through the use of rational procedures to disclose the truth has held a central place in Western thought. The idea that there might not be one true solution to a philosophical problem is extremely unsettling for many, and was certainly repugnant to the optimism of the seventeenth and eighteenth-century Enlightenment. Rationalist philosophers have long insisted that such an idea could only lead to moral chaos.

Yet others realise that, despite our longing for the revelation of one right answer to serve as a final closure, when we are faced with a moral dilemma it is often necessary to sacrifice one ultimate principle for the sake of another. Whether we have made the best choice is a question left lingering in our minds. Nor are we altogether relieved to acknowledge that our answer is the product of moral self-examination – self-disclosure, a recognition of who and what we are – rather than rational or scientific, much less transcendent, authority. Though we yearn for certainty in closure, it is often elusive or, at best, fleeting. One path closes off some possibilities but opens many others.

Nevertheless, at least for a time, the passing of an Act of Parliament or Congress closes off debate. The act of disclosure, which occurs as these institutions enact a new law, is at the same time a momentous and sometimes a tragic and oppressive closure. Policies are notoriously opportunistic and provisional, but this is not to deny that the temporary closures reached by these institutions have real and even tragic consequences for people's lives. The introduction of the poll tax in Britain by Margaret Thatcher's government, to take only one example, affected every person enrolled to vote. But the passing of this Act was not a final closure. People took to the streets in protest until finally both Thatcher and the poll tax were defeated. Policy making bodies make decisions, but this is typically by way of changing previous decisions. In one decade economic rationalism was all the style; now John Maynard Keynes, an authority until recently unmentionable, is quietly being resurrected in the guise of the Third Way. Human society and history are never static, and the orthodoxy of one day is ever revealed as the perfidy of the next.

Disclosure and closure as we explore them in this study are not simply opposites, but rather alternate moments in a process of communication. The one leads to the other, and endows it with meaning, as surely as the surprising revelation in a detective story leads to 'solving' the crime and the closing of the plot with the scales of justice balanced. By way of analogy, the danger, pain and suspense of therapeutic disclosure are themselves necessary elements of a patient's recuperation. Yet we can never disclose everything about ourselves, any more than we can hide completely behind the most carefully constructed mask. Certain things about ourselves, perhaps painfully obvious to others, may be invisible to our conscious minds. Indeed at some point self-disclosure must stop, even if only for a temporary resort in silence, a still point to find, renew or catch up with some aspect of personal experience. Even when we do not choose silence, others may impose it on us. A closure motion, or 'gag', may silence us, just as it ends debate in Parliament and Congress.

Although the concept of disclosure implies openness, by choice, accident or obligation, it is typically attended by countervailing pressures to limit and control. Having disclosed something, we may then choose to hide and close off other parts of ourselves or our past. If our secrets are disclosed by others against our will, we may desperately want to put an end to this exposure. Even extroverts, such as publicity-seeking politicians and entertainment celebrities, nevertheless seek to put a 'spin' on what is disclosed. Governments employ public relations teams to help them disseminate only the information they want the public to hear. Disclosures are not always, or often, complete or entirely open as we are sometimes led to believe. It is a continual struggle to keep the curtain open against the ever-present pull of closure.

Yet against these attempts at closure, disclosure constantly resists. 'Leaks' from government departments are commonplace. Photographers do capture celebrities in compromising positions. We have a natural desire for intimacy with others, which can only be satisfied through self-disclosure. Eventually we find that we do need to take our clothes off. Dissidents and minority groups 'gagged' by powerful regimes and pervasive social mores are increasingly successful in their struggle to show themselves and to speak in their own right. And while the policy decision of one government might lead to a closure of debate and a suppressive cover-up, its successor may well resurrect the debate with the disclosure of new information and different perspectives. The contemporary Western world is replete with disclosures. Mass entertainment, telecommunications and the internet have shown themselves to be remarkably, even obsessively, committed to disclosures of all kinds. It is an extremely noisy world.

We are all eating the fruit of the Tree of Knowledge of Good and Evil, whether we like the taste of it or not. This of course draws our attention to many contemporary dilemmas. Publicity, mass media and political democracy are all, in their combined ways, forces of disclosure. Chapter one examines publicity as a spectacle of political performance. Vicki Spencer explores the political arena in ancient Athens and imperial Rome to establish a critical perspective on the theatrical artifice of political publicity and rhetoric in modern democratic forums. The ancient arenas are revealed as authentic sites of competition, persuasion and spectator participation in matters of life and death, whether in the precarious existence of the Athenian city-state or the Colosseum's bloody spectacle.

Angela Clare offers an illuminating analysis in chapter two of the role of disclosure in the thought of Jürgen Habermas, both criticising and, in effect, rescuing his theory of rational communicative action by reconciling its procedural aims with the broader and deeper forms of cultural expression and communicative disclosure.

In chapter three, Marion Maddox examines the use of personal disclosure in the moral discourse of two religious organisations. The experiential disclosures of children and other 'representative' voices of the world's poor and oppressed have been effective techniques to solicit charitable donations and, despite profound cultural differences, foster ethical dialogue and unite people in moral action. Maddox reveals the real-world paradox that in motivating listeners to moral action, these organisations reduce the storytellers to powerless victims.

Chapter four emphasises the difference between traditional and 'post-positivist' approaches to policy analysis. Traditional or positivist analysis,

Carol Bacchi argues, is a process of disclosure that seeks the closure of policy solutions by disciplining and constraining political analysis. By contrast, post-positivist analysis is a constant attempt to avoid closure by uncovering the narrative construction of problems.

Paul Corcoran examines the 'talking cure' in chapter five. Freud's psychoanalytic theory is reviewed within the context of self-disclosure as a prominent feature in the ancient Western philosophical and religious traditions no less than in the contemporary 'therapeutic culture' and the modern aesthetic.

In chapter six, Greg McCarthy offers an entertaining exploration of 'excessive personal disclosures' in popular culture. Cinema, sit-coms, comedy and cultural critique are shown to be politically and ideologically potent vehicles of disclosure, creating a hyperreality in which the distinction between sex scandals in the White House, or actual wars and movie scripts, becomes not just diffuse, but ironically ambiguous.

The final chapter entertains what at first might appear to be the very opposite of disclosure, silence. Paul Corcoran discloses the communicative complexities and powerfully expressive capacities of silence as a way to rebel as well as reveal. Silence is a force and a meaningful presence, whether it is heroically maintained or violently imposed. At the end of every disclosure, we feel the need for a moment of eloquent silence.

What we strive to do in the following chapters is listen for the closures, the regimes of powerful, subtly imposed silences that accompany the penchant for disclosure. A wall of sound is, always, a wall of silence.

Reference

Bollas, C. (1987), *The Shadow of the Object: Psychoanalysis of the Unthought Known*, Free Association Books, London.

1 Publicity in the Political Arena: Metaphors of Spectacle, Combat and Display

VICKI SPENCER

Introduction

The arena is a place of action, spectacular displays and dazzling exhibitions in which human courage, breath-taking feats, pain, disappointments and loss, as well as the glory and excitement of victory, are disclosed to and experienced by the audience. By definition it is a 'public space'.[1] The spectators are as necessary to the arena's very existence as the performers – whether orators, politicians, gladiators, football players, or wrestlers. The symbiotic relationship between spectators and performers in the arena is such that spectators can never be accurately described in the usual sense of the term as mere onlookers of action performed by others. Without the spectator as participant, the arena begins to crumble.

When strolling towards an 'arena' one cannot help but be impressed by its majestic edifice. The distinctive colonial architecture of parliaments throughout the Commonwealth; the grandiose white dome of the United States Congress; the sheer size of major football and other sporting stadiums inspire awe and admiration. Both ancient and modern structures emanate an aura of power demanding a certain reverence. One can only imagine now the splendour and extravagance once experienced by the Romans as they climbed the public stairways of the Colosseum, with its ceilings painted gold and purple, and its inside walls adorned with marble.

The arena is a place of spectacle, exhibition and performance which requires an audience for the fulfilment of its purpose. It is for them that the arena exists. At the same time, the audience is an active and essential part of the spectacle created within the confines of the arena's walls. Degrees of audience participation vary between types of arenas, but it is a central theme of this chapter that, with its wholly passive audience, the 'political arena' in modern representative democracies is no longer alive. The tradition of the arena, especially as a political metaphor, might survive, but it is in this case a dead tradition, a museum in which the spectators are reduced to voyeurs.[2]

The spectacle taking place within the dimensions of the arena is one of high drama. Whether the scene is an FA Cup final at Wembley Stadium, a major debate over the issue of war in the Athenian Assembly, or a gladiatorial contest of life and death in the Roman Colosseum, suspense is paramount and tragic consequences are always possible, indeed feared and anticipated. The link with the performative[3] and cathartic aspects of the theatre are immediately evident. Good performances in both the arena and theatre are achieved by directly effecting the audience, generating a sense of identification among the spectators with the scene before them.

Both theatre and arena are sites of self-presentation. Fame and glory can be attained by the individual actor, orator, gladiator or modern politician, whose skills of performance before the audience are a publicity of the self. Spectators in the arena, like the theatre, demand this performance. Nevertheless, performers in the arena do not re-present other characters as do actors in a play. In the arena, one's own courage and skills, strengths and weaknesses, are disclosed to the spectators – and yet, at the same time, a magnified public persona is displayed to hide the private self from the public gaze. The spectacle is thus a vehicle for disclosure, but in the exhibitionist form of self-publicity and boasting of prowess rather than as an authentic and profound self-disclosure of one's private self, which only occurs incidentally in the event of success or failure.

Unlike theatre, the drama of the arena is both inherently and actually competitive. The arena *is* a site for combat. The theatre can re-present winners and losers in the dramatic unfolding of a play, but the action of the arena *creates* winners and losers. Nor can it be likened to a meeting place where participants work cooperatively toward a common end as do the actors of a play under a director's guidance, or as the rule-bound participants in Habermas's 'ideal speech situation' are meant to behave. Rather, the arena is, by definition, a battlefield in which contestants vie for the prize of victory. Some contestants might cooperate among themselves as in the case of football teams or political parties, with the football manager or party whip approximating the theatre director's role. But the arena has its own distinctive moment of truth. Unlike the theatre, the arena demands competitors – whether as individuals, parties or teams – for the spectacle of victory and defeat.

Formal procedures govern the activity of the arena. Authorities and regulations stipulate the 'game' and determine who will take the part of performer or spectator, and their respective roles. Not all who might wish to may participate directly in the play of a football match. Similarly, the rule of law which lies at the heart of the Western democratic ideal demands that the legislative process be conducted for all to see. Yet not all can speak in Parliament or Congress. Rules of order and engagement are designed to restrict and contain the action and disclosures of both performers and spectators. Without them, the ambience of the arena would become more like the bedlam of the hordes hungry to consume the bargains at yearly sales, a jungle – wild and unconstrained.

The arena is a container. While it is 'open' to the 'public' so that spectators and performers must enter into it to breathe life into the proceedings, at the same time the door can be closed and may be closed permanently to some. Appropriate dress, tickets and security checks are common requirements of entry into this public-private domain. Once inside, we are simultaneously a part of the building's contents and surrounded by its structure. It is literally a marvel of contradiction, a 'public enclosure'. The 'public' spectacle of competition, display and exhibition occurs within a defined and confined space. Further enclosures within the arena are reserved in sporting grounds for spectators who are, in some instances, literally confined by cages.[4] Inside and outside, open and closed, public and private, disclosure and enclosure are not dichotomies, in any accurate sense of the term as is sometimes mistakenly assumed, but always two sides of the same entity.

This chapter examines four features of the arena – the spectacle of competition, publicity as a form of disclosure, the spectator-participant, and enclosure – in relation to the participatory democracy of the Athenian Assembly, the games of the Roman Colosseum, and the representative democracy of the British Commons and the United States Congress. It is commonly assumed that these latter two institutions are modern 'political arenas'. While they remain forums for exhibition and publicity, it is argued that the contemporary political performance is largely a ritual, a public mask which hides the struggles and processes of decision-making taking place behind the scenes. The combat of these 'arenas' is thus reduced to ritualised performance. With media-driven grandstanding now the main action, these forums of representative democracy have more in common with the theatre, at least in its gaudier forms, than the arena. Yet, with the simultaneous demise of the spectator-participant, these modern democratic 'arenas' are in essence museums. The rhetorical and architectural structures are expensively preserved, but they have been largely emptied of the content and meaning conveyed by the metaphor of the arena. Rather than a reality, the political arena of representative democracy is purely symbolic.

Athenian publicity and self-disclosure

The city-state during the second half of the fifth century BC, renowned as 'the golden era' of Athens, was a hub of intense activity and vitality. The empire was at the height of its power; artistic endeavour flourished as Pericles' immense public works programme created the splendour and radiant beauty of the great buildings on the Acropolis. The democratic reforms, commenced by Cleisthenes in 507 BC and completed by Ephilates in 462-61 BC, had stripped the aristocratic enclave, the *Areopagus*, of its power and established the Athenian *Ecclesia,* or Assembly, as the ultimate forum of political power. With political decision-making invested in an arena where oratory was the main spectacle and the spectators and performers were one, Athens also became, under Pericles' patronage, a place where professional teachers of rhetoric, known as Sophists, came from all over Greece. Athens was truly emerging as a cosmopolitan city-state in which political reform, prodigious artistic and philosophical genius blossomed amidst the turmoil and instability generated by the ever present preparedness for war. In this ancient scene of great turbulence and much talk, the amphitheatre was transformed into the first 'political arena' where speech was the main event.

Situated on the Pnyx, a gently sloping hill which formed a natural amphitheatre, the Assembly met forty times a year. All male Athenian citizens could, in theory, attend, speak and vote at its proceedings. Yet, in practice, the enclosure of the Pynx could accommodate only 6,000 of Athens' approximately 30,000 male citizens. Nor in the Periclean Age does there appear to have been a demand for a larger amphitheatre. While Ephilates' democratic reforms had instituted payment for jury service in the courts around 451-50 BC, payment for attendance at the Assembly was only introduced in 403-02 BC (Thornley, 1996: 30-32, 76). Participation of citizens was limited. Despite half of potential voters residing in town by 431 BC, many Athenian citizens worked for a living in the docks and city, and could only afford to attend for the most important issues. Those living in the countryside were restricted by the seasonal demands of ploughing and harvesting, and the tyranny of distance. From the farthest reaches of Attica, the journey to Athens took two days by foot (Starr, 1990: 35-36; Thornley, 1996: 32). Nevertheless, with 5,000 citizens typically in attendance, it must have been a formidable sight for anyone wanting to put on a wreath and speak from the podium.

With speech as the main action of the political arena and a show of hands as the accepted voting procedure, attendance at Assembly meetings was mandatory for participation. Politics, for Athenians, could not occur in isolation, for it demanded the existence of a community, a *polis* of speakers. As Gadamer indicates, speech belongs to the sphere of the 'We' rather than to the 'I': 'To speak means to speak *to* someone' (1976: 65), it is intrinsically public. Political action, that is, the spectacle of speech in the arena, required an audience. The concept of speech as action, implicit in the metaphor of the political arena, stems from the pre-Socratic Greek idea that action (*praxis*) and speech (*lexis*) are 'coeval and coequal, of the same rank and the same kind' (Arendt, 1958: 26). According to Arendt, with the experience of an expanding, increasingly sophisticated and civilised *polis*, combative action and commanding speech became increasingly independent with the emphasis shifting to words and persuasion: 'To be political, to live in a *polis*, meant that everything was decided through words and persuasion and not through force and violence' (1958: 26). Thus we see in Aristotle's classical definitions of human beings as both *zoon logon ekhon*, 'a living being capable of speech' (Arendt, 1958: 27),[5] and *zoon politikon*, political creatures, an essential link between language and politics. But, rather than speech *replacing* action as Arendt suggests, the democratic reforms which placed political power in the hands of the people and hence within the debating arena of the Assembly meant that speech *was* now the action of politics.

As a public event, speech *acts* upon others who are capable of their own reactions, responses and actions. These consequences are boundless; there is always a new action that affects others as each speech act causes a chain-reaction of new responses. Politics, in a sense, is an attempt to limit the unpredictability of this boundlessness. For Arendt, this is the case with both territorial borders and constitutional boundaries such as the Athenian *polis* (1958: 190-91). But we can also see this attempt to limit and confine action in the political arena of the Assembly. Great care was taken to channel its deliberations and thereby regulate permissible types and levels of disclosures. Much of this work was performed by the fifty standing committee members (*prytanies*) of the five hundred *Boule* or Council. As the executive wing of government, the *pryanties* prepared the agenda for the Assembly which was published four days before a meeting. The agenda included draft proposals (*probouleuma*) in the form of recommendations previously voted on by the *Boule* and questions for the Assembly to deliberate upon. The Assembly could decide that an item should be included on another agenda, but it would appear that the people never acted on a matter without a *probouleuma*. Nor would a citizen tend to put forward a proposal in wanton disregard of its consequences since, if it was later found to have been mistaken or unwise, its formal initiator could be sued by any fellow citizen and heavily fined by the courts (Thornley, 1996: 30; Starr, 1990: 15, 26).

Rules of engagement were issued to regulate and constrain attendants' behaviour from the time of Solon, when the Assembly had only a limited public role. Rituals were observed: meetings began soon after day-break with prayers and the sacrifice of a pig. In the Periclean Age, the daunting task of presiding over the 5,000 male citizens who typically attended the Assembly's proceedings lay with the chairman (*epistates*) of the *Boule*, who was chosen daily by lot from the *prytanies*. Once various *prytanies* had proposed the council's draft proposals on each agenda item, the chairman would ask 'Who wishes to speak?' It is said that any attending spectator could then become a performer by speaking on that item from the podium (Thornley, 1996: 32). The following passage from Aeschines' speech, *Against Timarchus,* summarises the rules of conduct for speakers in both the Council and Assembly:

> Speakers in the council or assembly must keep to the subject, must treat each subject separately, must not speak twice on the same subject at the same meeting, must avoid invective, must not interrupt another speaker, must not speak except from the *bema*, must not assault the *epistates*. For each offence the *poedri* may impose a fine of up to 50 drachmas, or for a greater penalty they may refer the matter to the next meeting of the council or assembly (cited in Starr, 1990: 51).

From this ancient age we thus see the emergence of 'coded disclosures' whereby speakers in the political arena were ordered and restrained within the enclosures of formal procedures.

With approximately 5,000 to 6,000 potential speakers, not all spectators could practically address the Assembly. Mechanisms designed to ensure parity of access to the podium are not entirely clear, and without them, the extent to which fairness was applied is open to question. According to Starr, in the fifth century BC, priority was given to citizens of fifty years of age and over (1990: 50). Also, if Socrates' account in Plato's *Protagoros* is accurate, Athenians would only tolerate the views of the general public on non-technical matters of government. In cases of an architectural or ship-building project, for example, those with no technical expertise wishing to speak were not only jeered at by their fellow participants but, at times, ejected by the police on orders of the *prytanies* (319c). Such controls are the other side of the arena's public dimension. All public places have regulations designed to define, constrain and discipline disclosures.

The Assembly was, relatively speaking, a place of 'equals'. Socrates tells us that on matters of government the speaker could 'be a builder or equally well a blacksmith or a shoemaker, merchant or shipowner, rich or poor, of good family or none' (*Protagoras*: 319d). But the Assembly was also a place to be noticed, a site of self-presentation. Male citizens could be heard and seen by an audience of their fellow citizens. To approach the podium was to seek attention and publicise oneself. One's views, as well as one's skills as an orator, were disclosed to others. Unlike actors who re-present the character of another, speakers in the Assembly presented themselves. This was an opportunity to make a mark, to distinguish oneself as an orator, and to become a part of the collective memory of the audience. Greatness could be realised though the act of speech. From its birth in this ancient arena, the democratic ideal not only assumed equality at the starting gate, but also rewarded those who excelled in the contest (Thucydides, 1960: II, 37). Power and influence were there to be won. Stars were created.

One such star was Pericles. Plutarch reports that he 'far excelled all other speakers' with the charm of his voice and 'the smoothness and fluency of his speech' (1960: *Pericles*, 7-8). The comic poets of the time depicted him as 'thundering and lightning when he addressed his audience and as wielding a terrible thunderbolt in his tongue'. And Plutarch further informs us that Thucydides, Pericles' long-time political opponent and leader of the aristocratic party, when asked by Archidamus, the king of Sparta, who was the better wrestler, him or Pericles, said: 'Whenever I throw him at wrestling, he beats me by arguing that he was never down, and he can even make the spectators believe it'(1960: *Pericles*, 8). Already in this ancient age sporting imagery was used to depict the competitiveness of the contest in the political arena.

The rewards were great for those, like Pericles, who excelled in the game. While the Athenian *demos* in the fifth century BC filled most public offices by lot and with limited tenure, the Assembly assumed the power of electing each year the ten generals who also acted as leaders of the Assembly. They did this by open vote and with no bar on repeated appointments. Thus the role of general became the key power base in Athenian politics and the Assembly the path toward its attainment (Starr, 1990: 18; Thornley, 1996: 37-39). Rising to prominence during the 450s, Pericles was re-elected general every year until his death in 429 BC (Fornara and Samons, 1991: 28, 34). According to the historian, Thucydides,[6] during the Periclean Age 'what was nominally a democracy became in his hands government by the first citizen' (1960: II, 65). Yet, while early in the Peloponnesian war Pericles once managed to prevent an Assembly meeting 'for fear that he might be forced to act against his better judgement' (Plutarch, 1960: *Pericles*, 33), this example itself shows that his power in the arena was never absolute. Despite his years of good service, in 429 BC the Assembly vented its anger on Pericles for the deprivations they experienced during the war with Sparta and, in Plutarch's words, 'made themselves the masters of his fate' by removing him from his command and punishing him with a fine (1960: *Pericles*, 35). Although Pericles was recalled to office shortly thereafter, it is clear that not even the greatest of all orators could always win his way. The Assembly, indeed, held ultimate power.

Despite the potential for greatness, loss and disgrace were always imminent. Athenian public life could be a game of chance and a hazardous sport. Politicians not only faced the possibility of the failure of re-election, removal from office, or being fined, but also the threat of ostracism[7] and the death penalty. Admittedly, as was tragically displayed with the execution of Socrates, these punishments were not only reserved for those actively engaged in politics. Yet, with the greater attention accorded one who regularly participated in Assembly meetings, the risk was also intensified. Plutarch's account of Thucydides' confrontation with Pericles, whom he accused of squandering public funds, dramatically demonstrates the fine line between winners and losers in the arena:

> ...so Pericles appealed to the people in the Assembly to declare whether in their opinion he had spent too much. 'Far too much,' was their reply, whereupon Pericles retorted, 'Very well then, do not let it be charged to the public account but to my own, and I will dedicate all the public buildings in my name.' It may have been that the people admired such a gesture in the grand manner, or else, that they were just as ambitious as Pericles to have a share in the glory of his works. At any rate they raised an uproar and told him to draw freely on the public funds and spare no expense in his outlay. Finally, Pericles ventured to put matters to the test of an ostracism, and the result was that he secured his rival's banishment and the dissolution of the party which had been organized against him (1960: *Pericles*, 14).

Thus, through his manifest brilliance at oratory, Pericles orchestrated a complete turnabout of the people's sentiments and the defeat of his adversary. As its critics lamented at the time, the *demos* had a tendency for 'emotionality and fickleness' which the politician could, with sufficient skill, fully exploit (Raaflaub, 1990: 57-58). With the spectators swayed by the more expert orator, victors and vanquished were created.

With so much at stake, it is no wonder that teachers of rhetoric were in demand at this time in Athens. The excitement generated by the Sophists' visitations to Athens amongst the Athenian youth eager to forge a successful political career is vividly portrayed by the earnest character of the young Hippocrates in Plato's *Protagoras*. In his exuberance, Hippocrates is willing to sacrifice both his own and his friends' fortunes to pay Protagoras, the leading and most famous of the Sophists, to tutor him (310e). Asked by Socrates what he thinks a Sophist is, Hippocrates replies, 'master of the art of making clever speakers' (312d). Although most of the Sophists also had their own speciality,[8] in common they taught the art of rhetoric, that is, the art of correct and persuasive speaking. Various rhetorical exercises were performed as part of their teaching methods, including the preparation of a lecture on a set theme, questions and answers to develop the ability to speak briefly and, most importantly, the opposing of one *logos*, or argument, against another (Kerferd, 1981: 29-34). It was this method of *Antilogik,* Kerferd notes, that distinguished the Sophist rhetorical style first developed by Protagoras who, according to Seneca, thought that it was possible to take either side of an argument and debate it equally well (Kerferd, 1981: 84).

What is or is not the case was not the central concern of the rhetorician. The Sophists were fully aware that rhetoric could be employed for either good or bad purposes. Nevertheless, success was the essential criterion for the rhetorician, and that was determined by the orator's skill in persuading his audience with his particular argument irrespective of its validity. For Gorgias, who specialised exclusively in the art of rhetoric, oratory was 'the greatest blessing', the means to freedom and 'dominion over others' (*Gorgias*: 452d):

> ...the power to convince by your words the judges in court, the senators in Council, the people in the Assembly, or in any other gathering of a citizen body. And yet possessed of such power you will make the doctor, you will make the trainer your slave, and your businessman will prove to be making money, not for himself, but for another, for you who can speak and persuade multitudes (*Gorgias*: 452e).

Indeed, in front of a popular audience, Gorgias contends, the doctor or trainer would be no match for the orator (*Gorgias*: 456b-c). In his view, the power of the word is such 'a mighty despot' that even if Helen of Troy were convinced to commit adultery through the skill of the rhetorician, she would be as lacking in guilt 'as if she had been abducted by force' (Guthrie, 1971: 188). The persuasive power of *logos* is thus likened to the effect induced by drugs. Rather than trying to appeal to the intellect through the disclosure of an objective truth, as rational argument claimed to do, rhetoricians sought unashamedly to evoke the emotions and to entertain with both boldness and wit (Guthrie, 1971: 42). The resemblances to techniques used in modern advertising are unmistakable. Both are designed to stir the audience to respond, not at the behest of their own volition or as the result of rational thought, but as the speaker or advertiser aspires (Kerferd, 1981: 82).

Sophists publicised their rhetorical skills by exhibiting them in public displays, which either took the form of a monologue on a set theme or answers to questions from the audience. At the great festivals at Olympia, Sophists competed for prizes like the poets, musicians and artists. They also performed in various public places and buildings around Athens, as well as at private houses like that of Callias, the dramatic setting for Plato's *Protagoras* (Guthrie, 1971: 42). Yet this publicity was not without a degree of precariousness. The Sophist's art, Protagoras reveals, 'is an ancient one but...those who put their hand to it in former times, fearing the odium which it brings, adopted a disguise and worked under cover' (316d). He proudly boasts that he was the first to confess to being a Sophist, although he makes it clear that this disclosure was a precaution against the distrust and hostility often exhibited toward them. In this way he explains his preference for conducting his display with Socrates in front of the entire company at Callias' house rather than in a private discussion. Plato nonetheless hints at the egocentric dimension of this penchant for exhibitionism when Socrates cannot resist the temptation to appeal amusingly to Protagoras' vanity by suggesting they might also invite the Sophists, Prodicus and Hippias, to listen to them (317b-d). Only later, is it revealed, when Socrates petulantly refuses to continue the discussion except on his terms, that, for Protagoras, this display is also a battle, 'a contest of words' (335a) where the objective is victory and the publicity which ensues from the defeat of a formidable opponent.

The Sophists' focus on the means of debate for the purpose of victory was, in Plato's view, both dangerous and illicit. Indeed, far from being an honourable pursuit, rhetoric is depicted as a perversion of argument. The result is a scepticism and distrust which threaten philosophy itself, that is, the pursuit and disclosure of truth. The notion that any side of a question can be argued with equal success, with no concern for its validity, can only yield the appearance of success (*Phaedo*: 90b-d; *Theaetetus*: 167d-68c). Thus, writes Plato, '[w]e must not let it enter our minds that there may be no validity in argument' (*Phaedo*: 90e). For Socrates, the purpose of argument is 'not to convince...[his] audience, except incidentally, but to produce the strongest possible conviction in...[him]self' (*Phaedo*: 91a). Oratory, therefore, is not an art, but 'flattery'. 'And having no thought for what is best, she [that is, flattery] regularly uses pleasure as a bait to catch folly and deceives it into believing that she is of supreme worth' (*Gorgias*: 464d). Oratory is to justice and popular lecturing is to legislation what cookery is to medicine and beauty-culture to physical training: the former of these pairs all create 'an illusion' of their respective arts but are, in fact, mere masks and counterfeits (*Gorgias*: 464b-65d).

The idea that oratory and deception were synonymous in the political arena was fully exploited for its comic potential by Aristophanes (1978) with his savage satire of Cleon in *The Knights*. Cleon, a prominent personality in the Assembly, rose to power during the Peloponnesian war and persuaded the Assembly not to accept Sparta's peace treaty. Aristophanes depicts him as villainous and corrupt, with the new champion, the Sausage-Seller, needing to surpass him '[i]n trickery and crime [a]nd sheer audacity' (300-45) to win the contest for power. According to Aristophanes, a speaker's disclosure of his good character in the Assembly was far from sufficient to secure his place in the collective memory of the audience. Nor did victory depend upon the most rational and well conceived argument. More than an attack on Cleon, *The Knights* is also a satirical portrait of 'Thepeople', a character who is easily duped by flattery and requires a boiling treatment to come to his senses (1277-1373). Far from a site for authentic disclosures, the Athenian political arena is here exposed as a place of duplicity where politicians were engaged primarily in a contest for power and self-aggrandisement.

A further irony lies in the revelation contained in a surviving speech, delivered by Cleon to the Assembly, that he was equally frustrated by its inconsistency and the need to resort to 'flattery, lies and mudslinging to prevail' in its midst:

> Such constancy…is imperilled, on the one hand, by competition among the politicians who vie for the favour of the masses with ever more ingenious proposals, and in their arrogance, forget the common good (37); on the other hand, such competition is enhanced by the masses themselves who enjoy those rhetorical fireworks, consider themselves experts in judging them and, in falling for novelty and appearance, disregard content and the common good (38) (cited from Thucydides in Raaflaub, 1990: 58).

The day before it was under Cleon's influence, however, that the Assembly mercilessly sent a trireme to kill every man and enslave the women and children of Mytilene as punishment after their failed rebellion in 428 BC. By proposing this motion, important aspects of Cleon's character were unmistakably disclosed to his fellow citizens. Similarly, the above speech displays his intense annoyance when the Assembly repented and reversed its decision by a small majority the next day (Thucydides, 1960: III, 36-49). That Cleon accused the Assembly of acting like 'slaves to the pleasure of the ear, and more like the audience of a rhetorician than the council of a city' (Thucydides, 1960: III, 38), perhaps more accurately discloses his incapacity to persuade the people to act as he wished, rather than their constant failure to consider the common good. Nevertheless, his holding sway for the initial vote reveals the dangers of the democratic arena where the spectacle of oratory, with its competitiveness and the vital need to persuade the audience for victory, reign supreme. There are no guarantees that the people's decision will be 'rational', 'good' or 'just', only that the audience determines the winners and losers. It is important to remember that Plato was just as critical of democracy as he was of oratory, both being means of securing interests rather than seeking truth.

But while the Sophists taught rhetoric as an instrument which could be used to pursue any ends, Protagoras recognised virtue as a necessary component of the art of politics. According to Kerferd, despite Plato's profoundly anti-democratic sentiments (1981: 146-47), we discover in his *Protagoras* the first theoretical defence of participatory democracy.[9] In what is known as his Great Speech, Protagoras maintains that in order for humans to live together in communities, Zeus sent Hermes to endow each with the gifts of 'justice and respect for their fellows' (*Protagoras*: 322c-d). Thus the Athenians listened to every man's disclosures, 'for they think that everyone must share in this kind of virtue; otherwise the state could not exist' (323a). Nevertheless, as is revealed by the use of punishment as a form of instruction of right and wrong, virtue is not regarded as 'innate or automatic', but as requiring teaching and effort (323c-24c). Natural ability in the arts is not distributed on a hereditary basis. Nor is virtue found in equal quantities in all people. As with playing the flute, some people excel more than others in the political virtues (327-28b). It is thus necessary for a community to deliberate upon the relative merits of different views and perceptions disclosed in the political arena. But while these disclosures might reveal that not all men's advice is equally good, 'every citizen had something that was at least potentially of value to contribute to debates on moral and political questions' (Kerferd, 1981: 147).

Man was the centre of attention in the democratic arena. That he also came to be seen as the locus of truth is evident in Protagoras' famous saying, 'man is the measure of all things – alike of the being of things that are and of the not-being of things that are not' (*Theaetetus*: 152a). To find truth, such that it exists, man no longer needed to supplicate to the gods for its revelation nor seek Plato's objective reality, but look within his 'self', that is, to his own perceptions. As Plato goes on to explain Protragoras's position, 'any given thing "is to me such as it appears to me, and is to you such as it appears to you", you and I being men' (*Theaetetus*: 152a). Thus, when the same wind is blowing, if it feels cold to you and hot to others, then it *is* cold for you and hot for others. 'They *are* to each man such as he *perceives* them' (*Theaetetus*: 152c). In other words, the wind is both warm and cold as men perceive different properties at different times depending on their conditions.[10]

It follows that when we speak, even when disclosing a 'truth' about the objective world, we reveal our selves, that is, our perceptions and views as well as our capacity for expression and understanding. Speech is an act of self-disclosure. According to Arendt:

In acting and speaking, men show who they are, reveal actively their unique personal identities and thus make their appearance in the human world, while their physical identities appear without any activity of their own in the unique shape of the body and sound of the voice. The disclosure of 'who' we are in contradistinction to 'what' somebody is – his qualities, gifts, talents, and shortcomings, which he may display and hide – is implicit in everything somebody says and does (1958: 179).

Everything we say is a part of who we are. Our speech, thoughts and feelings are all intertwined. We might not know who we reveal when we speak, but we inevitably risk this disclosure in the act of speech. For Arendt, the revelation of who we are is most apparent in 'human togetherness', when people are *with* others, rather than in competition (1958: 180). Thus, when we feel secure in the knowledge that we are accepted, as we do in the company of close friends, we disclose far more of ourselves. We let down our guard and lay aside our public mask. Such intimate self-disclosure might be inappropriate, indeed, ineffective and unpersuasive in the political sphere. Nevertheless, genuine discussion even in the political sphere, where the objective is to understand each others' views and arrive at a consensus, demands the authentic disclosure of one's views, concerns and problems. By contrast, according to Arendt, when people are combatively pitted for or against each other, speech becomes 'mere talk', a means to an end (1958: 180). It is merely a presentation of 'what we are' as a combatant and competitor with our public persona privileged over the more profound disclosure of 'who we are'. Even in such moments of display our masks reveal important parts of who we are. In a competitive environment, we seek to conceal much of ourselves and, in particular, our vulnerabilities, whilst we publicise those abilities and qualities which will enhance our chances of victory. But as competitors in a political arena, our efforts may meet with either success or failure.

Despite Arendt's view that the political arena of Athens provided the opportunity for male Athenians to disclose who they were to their fellow citizens (1958: 197-98), the spectacle of speech was always in danger of becoming 'mere talk'. To be sure, citizens came together in the Assembly for the common purpose of self-government over their city-state and empire. Although Sophists boasted of their ability to take any side of an argument in their displays and argue it with equal success, in the Assembly citizens disclosed their own perceptions of what they considered to be in the interests of the common good, or at least their own. It is important to recall that the arena is, by definition, a place of competition. The rules of the game determined that speakers in the Assembly were always for or against others. The need for a spectacle to dazzle the audience to gain and keep its attention meant that the disclosure of 'what someone was', that is, his abilities and talents as an orator, as described above in the case of Pericles,[11] were privileged over the more profound disclosure of 'who he was'. On display was a public persona: 'Here I am, I am a general, be amazed, moved and persuaded by my eloquence.'

Ultimately, the arena's rules of engagement stifled the full revelatory quality of its main spectacle, speech. As Socrates fatally discovered, the objective of political speech in Athens was confined to publicising only those parts of one's self which would assist in the task of persuasion. Certain 'formalities' had to be observed. Rather than a site for the authentic disclosure of one's self to one's fellow citizens, the partisan competitiveness of the arena and the potentially high cost of failure through ostracism or the death penalty demanded a performance rather than self-enactment. Disclosure, such as it became, was increasingly confined to publicity for one's public mask. As the emphasis shifted from the Athenian ideal of speech, in which greatness and public honour were achieved in the action of speech independent of the outcome (Arendt, 1958: 205), to the politicians' strategic concern with victory and defeat, Athenian democracy began to crumble. By the close of the fifth century BC the 'golden era' was at an end. All that now remains of the first political arena is a mere ruin of the podium ravaged by the ages.

The spectacle of the Colosseum

The arena, as a site of combat, has never been more vividly displayed than in the Colosseum of Rome. Dazzling exhibitions of violence and bloodshed were the main attraction for the 50,000 spectators who delighted in the kill. In celebration of its grand opening in 80 AD, the Emperor Titus staged one of the most bloodthirsty exhibitions of all time with a hundred days of mass slaughter both of men and animals. The Emperor entered the arena to the spectacle of a packed audience which rose to greet him with waving handkerchiefs, deafening applause and shouts for a long life and reign. He returned their greetings from the podium and ordered the show to begin (Pearson, 1973: 7-12). It was a spectacular public display of power and solidarity which also gave the Emperor, in the wake of the Republic, a semblance of popular support through mass entertainment. From the imperial box he appeared like a generous god sharing the spoils of the empire with his public and simultaneously, in his role as spectator, as one with his subjects. In ancient Rome, political publicity was developed to its most extravagant level.

The idea that 'the arena is only one step above the jungle, where there can be only one victor and no survivor' (Haggard, 1984), was dramatically enacted in the Colosseum. The entertainment began with the spectacle of exotic animals from the farthest reaches of the empire. Lions, bears, leopards, antelopes, hyenas, cranes and gazelles were let loose only to be hunted down and killed. The *bestiarii*, specially trained hunters wearing only a linen tunic and belt, and armed with a sharp, long-bladed spear, often became the prey. The scene was elaborately staged with trees and boulders around which the *bestiarri* would hunt and be hunted. As the orchestra played, the unfortunate animals were speared and the men mauled, much to the sadistic enjoyment of the audience (Pearson, 1973: 13, 117). Here, as Plass (1997: 42) writes, was a display of 'imperial authority over nature itself'. Animals wounded but still alive at the end of the event were killed by the slaves who cleared the arena, then spread and raked fresh sand to absorb the blood which would be spilled anew in the ensuing spectacle.[12]

To the fanfare of horns and trumpets, the gladiators, dressed in glistening armour, magnificent plumes and cloaks, marched proudly into the arena. As the crowd grew silent, these men highly trained in the art of combat lined up beneath the podium for their official greeting to the Emperor: 'We who are about to die salute you!' All eyes were upon them as the Emperor sanctioned the arena as a legitimate site for lethal sport with the traditional checking of the blades' sharpness. As the Roman war trumpets blared, the contest commenced (Pearson, 1973: 15-16). In this electric atmosphere where life and death were literally determined, spectators cheered their favourite teams and star performers,[13] and jeered at the opposition with intense enthusiasm and zest. The spectators, exhibiting disappointment at their team's 'loss' or excitement at its 'victory', were intimately involved with the action. In the security afforded them by the arena's protective wall between the field of combat and their seats, the audience experienced vicariously the highs and lows of battle.

In a militaristic society during peace-time, Pearson contends, these death-games effectively indulged the Romans' 'war-like instincts' and offered the spectators a certain 'involvement in Rome's warlike past' (1973: 148). This affinity with the past was most evident in their spectacular re-enactments of battles. As the final event on the Colosseum's inaugural day, for example, the main arena was flooded for the gladiatorial display of 'the classic bloody naval battle between Corinth and Corfu' (Pearson, 1973: 21-22). But the Colosseum was far more than a site of re-presentation. Within the confines of its structure, cut off from everyday activities, the spectacle of the arena had a dynamic and an ethos of its own. The contests between the gladiators were unmistakably real, as was the blood which spilled from their wounds. Rules were observed. When it came to the kill, convention demanded that the victor dispose of the vanquished quickly and efficiently, and that the vanquished die with dignity and 'no fuss'. Any genuine disclosure of fear in a desperate plea for mercy was highly distasteful to the spectators (Pearson, 1973: 107-08) and a betrayal of cowardice. Even in this final moment of truth, the arena's rules of engagement bound these men to maintain their gladiatorial persona. For the gladiators, dying was an art just as oratory had been for Athenian politicians. It was essential that the mask of glory be retained to the end. Neither the gladiators nor the audience wanted to know the dying man's fears or hopes, sorrows or joys, his ultimate self-disclosures.

It was no coincidence that the Colosseum was built shortly after the democratic system was changed to an imperial one. As the people lost their right to vote, the arena became a surrogate for the *popolo's* sense of power over life, death, and the destiny of their city. Reduced to passive onlookers of the political realm, the people were nonetheless active participants in the fate of the gladiators:

> The fallen fighter, if he was in a state to move, laid down his shield, and raised one finger of his left hand to plea for mercy. The decision whether his life should be spared rested with the provider of the games; but he generally found it politic to take account of the spectators' loudly expressed views. Thumbs up, and a waving of the handkerchiefs, meant that the man should be spared, thumbs down that he should not (Grant, 1967: 74-75).

Just as we saw how the performance of orators in the Assembly persuaded the Athenian citizens to vote either for or against matters of life and death, the quality of the gladiators' performance in the arena persuaded the Romans either to grant, or take, the life of defeated contestants. With thumbs down, the effect of the spectators' decision was dramatically immediate and witnessed with great fascination. Claudius, for one, revelled in watching the gladiators' faces as they died (Plass, 1997: 20). Commentators have suggested that, for the Romans morally and psychologically, 'seeing a man killed [in the arena] is much *like* killing him' (my emphasis, Athenagoras, *Embassy*: 35 cited in Plass, 1997: 19). That would seem to be an understatement. Far from being passive onlookers of action performed by others, in the gladiatorial contests the arena's spectators ordered the kill.

In the Periclean Age, the Athenian Assembly was restricted to male citizens born of Athenian parentage on both sides. Only a third of the population were eligible to attend the site of 'the people' (Thornley, 1996: 77). Admission to the Colosseum was far less exclusionary. Here, bathed in blood, was the greatest of the truly popular arenas established throughout the Roman Empire. Though slaves and criminals generally took the part of the performers, and despite the hazardous nature of their role, it would be mistaken to see them entirely as outsiders, mere unfortunates and political scapegoats. Both hated and celebrated, the gladiators held an ambiguous place in Roman society. Outcasts from society, in the arena they were the main attraction: 'For this brief moment this rejected man could feel himself part of the splendour of the Empire, and it is hard to think of any thrill to equal that of victory – the sheer relief, the mass applause, the palm presented by the Emperor' (Pearson, 1973: 106). Fame, fortune and freedom were there to be won. Such was the lure of fame that champions often refused to retire when offered their freedom. Despite the gladiators' low social status, free men also began to seek fame in the arena and use this means to escape from debt. Until the door was closed to them in 200 AD by Emperor Septimius Severus, women, too, fought as volunteers in the arena (Grant, 1967: 30-35).

The spectacle was to be enjoyed by all ranks and classes with everyone having a place, according to status, in the segregated seating arrangements. Unlike the Athenian Assembly, women were a part of the public experience and spectacle of the Colosseum. The seats were made of marble and the cushions of silk. The Colosseum's luxurious decor won for it the reputation as 'the earliest "People's Palace" in the world' (Pearson, 1973: 83). With this 'openness', however, came restrictions. A balcony above was reserved for the senators, the first row for the Emperor's knights, and the imperial box for the Emperor, his family, guests, the vestal virgins and priests. The rest of the population were sorted by class as the tiers of seats ascended toward the sky, three-hundred feet above the Emperor's podium. Order was further maintained through the construction of special balconies for guards and the stairways designed for ready control in case of riot. As Pearson indicates, one of the greatest testaments of the architect's skill is the lack of a single record of the crowd becoming uncontrollable (1973: 81-82). In an atmosphere where the orgy of blood and violence brought the spectators to near hysteria, the Colosseum's design was truly a marvel of social engineering and crowd control.

It was as if all the genius, excess, might, cruelty and contradictions of the Roman Empire were embodied in the Colosseum. As grandiose architecture, it was another of the empire's triumphs. Its imposing size, the use of stone in place of the wood of earlier amphitheatres, its facade of marble, and its elaborate decoration all contributed to the awe it generated. Outside the arena the people had lost all political power, whereas inside the spectators were crucial participants in the life and death action. Although staged as a dramatic re-presentation of past glories, behind its theatrical disguise was disclosed the reality of lethal combat to a packed and enthusiastic audience. The rules of engagement in this life and death game required that gladiators retain their public persona, hiding their inner identities behind the mask of courage, pride and honour even in their final act of dying. Far from a site of authentic self-disclosure, the Roman Colosseum, with its spectacular displays of bloodlust, was a living arena to glorify ancient Roman values, publicise the Emperor's wealth, generosity and absolute power, and stupefy his subjects in a mutual deed of carnage. As the empire collapsed, the Colosseum, too, was closed as a site of combat.

The ritual of representative democracy

In western democracies today, arenas of sport and mass entertainment overshadow the 'political arena'. In place of the participatory democracy of the Athenian Assembly, modern democratic 'arenas' are sites of 'popular representation'. And instead of the blood-soaked sand from whence the word arena derives, there are luxurious sound-deafening wall-to-wall carpets.

Derived from the Latin *representare*, which means 'to make present or manifest or to present again', the word 'represent' first appeared in English around the late fourteenth century when, according to the *Oxford English Dictionary*, it meant '"to bring oneself or another into the presence of someone", "to symbolize or embody concretely", "to bring before the mind"', whilst '"representative" meant "serving to represent, figure, portray or symbolize"' (Pitkin, 1967: 243). In the fifteenth century the term 'represent' was 'applied to inanimate objects which "stand in the place of or correspond to" something or someone' and 'the noun "representation" first appeared with the meaning of "image, likeness, or picture"' (Pitkin, 1967: 243). By the seventeenth century the meanings of these words had developed from their original religious and artistic applications 'to refer to any substituted presence, including people standing for other people' (Pitkin, 1967: 247-48). They were also applied to Parliament as a whole and especially to the Commons when in 1641 they referred to themselves, in contrast to the Lords, 'as "the Representative Body of the whole Kingdom"'. At the same time, the term 'representative' evolved as a noun to denote a member of Parliament. Thus it began to take on the meaning 'from the earlier "standing for" by way of substitution and substituted presence, to something like "acting for"' (Pitkin, 1967: 248).

The substantive concept of 'acting for' means that the role of the representative in the British Commons and United States Congress is not just to re-present the views or wishes of their constituents in a descriptive sense of 'standing in for'. In the first place, their constituents' desires will always be at odds with each other. Remote from the halls of government, they may also have no view at all or be poorly informed on certain issues. As Pitkin further indicates, a number of different demands and obligations are visited upon modern representatives, some of which are to their party, and others to their colleagues, various interest groups and the nation as a whole (1967: 214-15, 219-20).

The notion of 'acting for' entails the idea that politicians *act*, not just consult and mirror the views of others. Indeed, it may be in the public interest, at times, to act contrary to the immediate wishes of the electorate. At the same time, representatives are obligated to consult with their constituency, be responsive to their views, and act in their interests. Otherwise they are in jeopardy of failing 'to act *for*' those they formally represent (Pitkin, 1967: 210-11, 224). The balance between the extremes of 'standing in for' and 'acting for' approximates the notion of trusteeship whereby representatives are regarded as authorised and entrusted, through the process of regular elections, to make judgements on their constituents' behalf and in the public interest. If they fail to do so responsively and effectively, they can be held accountable at election time (McKay, 1989: 128).

The representative 'arena' is a site of self-presentation. The ability of representatives to make their *own* judgements in the interest of others is on show to the public. This self-exhibitionism is more manifest in the Congress where party lines are not as rigidly adhered to as in the Commons. British MPs who fail to conform to their party's position by crossing the floor face the possibility of severe party discipline through expulsion, which would invariably entail loss at the next election. Party whips have not carried out this penalty since the early 1940s. Far more likely would be the refusal of their party, either at the constituent or central level, to accept their re-selection since party members normally want to ensure their representatives adhere to party policy (Madgwick, 1984: 177). In this respect British MPs 'stand in for' their party to a far greater extent than members of Congress, who have more independence to act for themselves and in so doing disclose more of themselves in the 'arena'.

Nevertheless, in both cases, politicians' egos are disclosed publicly through their speech. When they speak in the Commons or Congress, whether in the form of questions, answers or a monologue, they act as they see fit in the interests of others and themselves, whether or not they follow a party line. If they act according to party lines, it might mean on a particular issue they present a view with which they are not in entire agreement at a personal level, but their decision to support their party is nonetheless what they consider to be in the ultimate interests of both their constituents and themselves. In accord with the notion of 'acting for', representatives act on the assumption that they know what is best for the good of the people and better than those who have not been elected.

A case in point was the Clinton impeachment trial which the members of Congress decided to conduct according to their own judgement in relation to the House prosecutors' findings in the case. And yet their judgement of what was in the interests of American democracy, according to all national opinion polls, went against the overwhelming sentiment of the public. Unlike the Athenian Assembly in which all male citizens acted for the state, the public must now turn to their representatives to have what is 'good' disclosed to them.

Like the public relations model of political campaigning, which was perfected by Ronald Reagan and Margaret Thatcher in the 1980s and designed to limit debate,[14] the publicity and self-advertisement characteristic of modern representative forums have largely reduced the competitiveness and action of the arena to a theatrical performance. The theatre of speech is most clearly displayed in the Prime Minister's Question Time which is held in the Commons twice a week for a mere fifteen to twenty minutes. The scene unfolds before an overflowing House as the chamber was designed deliberately after its devastation in World War I with insufficient seats for the six-hundred and fifty MPs. For Winston Churchill, the theatre of debate with its 'sense of crowd and urgency' was far more important than the Commons' representative role (Coghill and Babbage, 1991: 17). With standing room only, this is the time the Prime Minister is meant to be held accountable, as Head of the Government, for policy and administration.

The Prime Minister is well prepared to meet any challenge which might arise. Normally, questions must be submitted in writing with not less than forty-eight hours notice. Fewer than one in ten questions receives an oral answer; the rest are replied to in writing. Of those which reach the chamber, supplementary questions may be asked once the Prime Minister has presented his or her initial reply. However, with the weight of carefully prepared research, the brevity of question time, and the capacity of the Prime Minister to choose which questions to answer and thereby disclose only what he or she deems appropriate, rarely, if ever, is the Opposition able to expose weaknesses in the Prime Minister's case through this process. Few who have witnessed the staging of this event could disagree with Wyatt's view that as an instrument of democracy it is both 'useless' and a 'charade' (Madgwick, 1984: 223). It is nonetheless ritually performed every Tuesday and Thursday as the Prime Minister's commanding position is publicised to the audience. An uproar would surely ensue if a Prime Minister proposed to abolish this 'charade'.

The facade of combat has been further formalised in the spatial arrangement of the Commons with the government and opposition situated on opposing sides of the House. In the discussions over the rebuilding of the Commons, Churchill argued vehemently for the retention of this arrangement because it best served to delineate the two sides, thus ensuring that crossing the floor would remain an overt act requiring considerable reflection. Whilst he regarded a small chamber as most conducive to 'the conversational style' of the Commons, critics have argued that it 'encourages confrontation and adversarial politics' (Coghill and Babbage, 1991: 17). Indeed, allusions to the combative nature of the arena were retained when the Commons was refurbished with the two sides 'kept apart' by the length of two swords and the bloodline demarcating the boundary which MPs are not meant to cross. But whilst parliamentary debate is often likened to a gladiatorial contest, the similarity between modern politicians and gladiators is confined to their ambiguous position in society as both celebrated and despised. Although debates can be rowdy and aggressive, such that they privilege those who are assertive, confident, loud and egotistical,[15] the game remains a battle only in a ritualistic sense.

Rules of engagement which are designed to bind, discipline and constrain the action and disclosures within the enclosure of parliamentary procedures are enforced by the Speaker. Following a debate, the Speaker decides whether a vote on the motion before them is necessary by calling out to the two sides: 'As many as are of the opinion say 'Aye', the contrary 'No'. Depending on which side sounds more numerous the Speaker announces: 'I think the Ayes (or the Noes) have it'. If the other side protests, the Speaker calls a formal vote, or a division, with the order 'to clear the Lobby' and the division bell is rung throughout the Parliament to inform members to hurry toward the Division Lobbies. After the clerks for both the Aye and No Lobby have registered the members' names for *Hansard*, the doors are opened for the members to enter for the count. It is the role of the last member through to shout 'All out' and the Lobby doors are locked eight minutes after the Speaker first put the question. With the result recorded, the tellers enter the chamber and the senior teller on the victorious side reveals the outcome (Stones, 1990: 5-8). Yet, even before any politician speaks in the debate preceding this elaborately staged ritual, everyone already knows who will be the winner, as the government has the majority of seats and, hence, votes.

The looser party allegiance in Congress, by contrast, means winners and losers are still created on the basis of votes in the House and Senate. Party whips exist but, unlike party whips in the British system, they have few sanctions with which to oblige members to conform to a party position, which in any case is often non-existent. Rather, according to McKay, the job of congressional party whips 'is to persuade, negotiate, bargain and cajole members into broad agreement on particular items of legislation' (1989: 151). This political manoeuvring takes place, however, outside the chambers of the House and Senate. Similarly, it is in the committees that legislation is framed, amended and rejected. Here members' power is truly exercised, albeit with the proviso that there is a clear hierarchy of prestige and influence amongst the different committees as well as the subcommittees. Nor is committee membership determined on the floor, but in party committees which are selected by party caucuses. Lobbyists, the 'representatives' of organised interest groups, constitute one of the most influential forces of persuasion upon congressional committees and individual members. Although reforms have meant members are now more able to attach riders and amendments to bills on the floor, it is still largely the case that bills are in their final stage when they reach this point (MacKay, 1989: 148, 153-54). Debate on the floor is largely irrelevant to the success or otherwise of a bill. Rather than oratory as a force of persuasion, the action of the House and Senate in Congress is limited to the floor vote.

The arena, once a place where life and death were actually determined, survives in these modern democracies as a stage for performance, but this performance is largely a ceremonial ritual. Unlike the Athenian Assembly in which words were not only a force of publicity but crucially a force of persuasion, speech in these modern forums has been reduced to self-presentation and publicity. The true contests and content of political debates with the need to persuade others for victory occur outside the main 'arenas' and often secretly behind closed doors or away from the public forum in Cabinet, members' offices, party caucuses or favourite restaurants. This does not mean that heated debates on important matters do not occur on the floor as they did in the Athenian Assembly. Members of Parliament and the Congress do, at times, exhibit passion, wit and earnestness. Although Question Time in the Commons might be a 'charade', the atmosphere when the House is packed can be enthralling. On occasion it can be good, or at least popular, theatre. Tickets for Question Time are always in demand. But the action of politics lies largely outside these public forums in the shadows of the 'arena'. For much of the time, the contest is a 're-presentation' in the artistic and theatrical sense of an act of portrayal. The battles are won and lost elsewhere.

In this context, the public is reduced to passivity. There is none of the cheering and jeering by the mass of spectators as in the Colosseum or modern sporting arenas. Rules of procedure demand that silence be maintained in the public galleries. To speak out would mean expulsion. On the first day of the Clinton impeachment trial, hundreds of people were reported to have lined up in the freezing rain for entrance to the public gallery of the Senate chamber. With only fifty seats in the gallery, the proceedings began to take on the character of a 'peep show' as the public were rotated every fifteen minutes to enable as many silent witnesses as possible to catch a glimpse.

In the performance of representative democracy, far from being spectators who take part in the arena's action, the public have been reduced to voyeurs. To be sure, the public dimension of the Congress and Commons is considerably enhanced through the media. Whilst sitting at home, you still have a sense of being an onlooker and a part of a wider television audience. But, despite the comfort of sitting in your lounge chair while watching your favourite sport, this mediated experience is not identical to the direct experience in which, as a spectator, you become a part of the action and spectacle. You may urge your team on, but they will not hear you when you are at home. Excitement in the lounge room in front of the television is thus accompanied by a sense of distance and alienation from the 'real' crowd. The spectator in an arena is not just a passive witness. The spectators are themselves a massive spectacle. The highly charged atmosphere of a major football match and the players' performance would surely be different without their presence in the stands. By contrast, in the modern 'political arena', despite the facade of public accountability, the removal of the silent witnesses from the public galleries would have no substantial effect upon the ritual of parliamentary and congressional proceedings.

In a sense, representatives themselves 'stand in' as active spectators. Whereas the public have a dignified silence imposed upon them, in the Commons the MPs hurrah and cheer their own side and heckle and taunt their opponents. It is a rowdy scene with the Speaker consistently calling them to order. Although the Speaker always has the power to dismiss the unruly politician, a high level of what would be considered 'misbehaviour' in many public settings is tolerated in the ethos of the chamber. It seems clear that MPs' performances are intended less for the public's benefit than for their colleague-spectators. Politicians who can rise above the taunting and remain undaunted by the aggressive atmosphere exhibit important skills and leadership potential to their fellow party members. Similarly, in Congress those who take the rostrum publicise their abilities to their colleagues who might well be sufficiently impressed to assist them to attain an important committee position. A far more abstract connection exists between members' performances on the floor and the responses of the public outside these enclosures, many of whom simply take no notice.

This failure to notice is the norm for members of Congress and the Commons. Whilst broad comedy or mock tragedy occur on occasion, dull performances and mumbled speeches are common. Apart from the main events such as Question Time, which are now routine exercises in media-driven grandstanding, or the rare occasions when important or sensational issues are on the agenda, the chambers are sparsely attended. Members are known to fall asleep, fidget and read newspapers as speakers deliver long-winded and tedious monologues. As the Democrat, Max Cleland, was quoted as saying concerning the inaugural day of the Clinton impeachment trial: 'Sitting there and not saying anything for five or six hours, that's an unnatural act for a US senator' (*The Weekend Australian*, 1999: 12). Even on this historic day, with the seemingly unending speeches delivered in monotone drones, some senators nodded off, whilst others began to whisper or pass notes like school children. The 'arena' can only remain animated as long as the spectators are also participants. In the silence imposed upon the one-hundred senators on this day, their attention to and their identification with the performance quickly waned. For the general public in the gallery above, enforced silence is a strict rule of non-engagement. In this respect, in contrast to the spectacle of the arena, the forums of representative democracy take on the character of museums in which the public passively view strange artefacts with which they have little, if any, identification. Enthusiasts exist, but they are a rare breed.

Conclusion

Contrary to common depictions of the spectator as a passive onlooker, this chapter has argued that spectator participation is an essential feature of the arena's spectacle. The symbiotic relationship between the performer and spectator was most clearly illustrated in the Athenian Assembly as individual members of the audience could potentially take the podium to speak and thereby have all eyes upon him. The spectacle took the form of persuasive speech. Yet the competitiveness inherent in the concept of the arena meant that, rather than a form of authentic self-disclosure, speech in the Assembly was increasingly reduced to 'mere talk' in which publicity and the desire to win through persuasion were the main game.

In contrast to the active political citizenship of Athenian males, spectators in the Colosseum have often been described as passive onlookers of a spectacle enacted by others. However, while it is true that the Roman populace became mere witnesses, at best, of imperial political activity, within the arena they held the power to decide the fate of the performers. The dazzling blood spectacles staged in the Colosseum, like modern sporting events, reveal how spectators in the arena are themselves a massive spectacle, intimately tied to the action, experiencing the highs and lows of the battle for their teams' victory, which they disclose through the speech acts of cheering and jeering. Publicity was taken to its extreme in the Roman arena where extravagant displays were designed to disclose the wealth, generosity and might of the Emperor by satisfying the bloodlust of the spectators.

By contrast, in modern representative forums, the public are reduced to silence as they passively witness the action of their representatives who 'act for' them both as speakers and active spectators. As sites of ceremonial ritual, publicity and self-presentation, rather than active debate, persuasion and contest, the Commons and Congress have more in common with the theatre than the win and lose, live or die action of the arena. The issue here is not that Cabinet, committees or party meetings may not be more appropriate sites for debate, but that the main 'arenas' are no longer the place in which the real action of the political decision-making process is disclosed to the public. With the public reduced to voyeurs of elaborately staged parliamentary and congressional rituals, serving almost exclusively as vehicles of self-publicity, the Commons and Congress can only be called 'arenas' in a symbolic sense. In essence, they are museums.

The public spectacle of actual competition, at least in these representative democracies, is today the exclusive domain of modern sporting arenas. Here, every weekend, we find intensely loyal, colourful and enthusiastic spectators participating in the spectacle of the arena on a scale unknown to parliamentary and congressional proceedings, except perhaps in politicians' dreams.

Notes

[1] The term 'public' is employed here to denote the overtness of that which is witnessed. It is not a general definition of the term and is in no way intended to challenge the feminist insight that the private sphere of the family is publicly defined and regulated by the state.

[2] Murray Edelman (1988) was among the first to use the term 'spectacle' extensively as a metaphor for the modern democratic system. However, our understandings of this term differ significantly. Whilst I agree with Edelman that in modern representative democracies the public have been reduced to passive onlookers rather than participants, I disagree that this is because they are spectators of a spectacle (1988: 35). On the contrary, I argue that spectators are a part of, and participants in, the spectacle of an arena as is evident in most modern sporting stadiums. When the game, however, lacks the competitive spirit expected in the arena and is replaced by calculated 'safe-play' sporting commentators quite rightly point out that there is no spectacle and hence the audience exhibits general apathy and passivity toward the game. In contrast to Edelman, it is argued here that the modern political game, at least, as it is

performed in the chambers of Parliament and Congress is no longer a spectacle. Rather than spectators of a spectacle, the public have been reduced to voyeurs of ritualised performance.

[3] The term 'performative', derived from the word 'perform', is used in J.L. Austin's (1975: 6) sense and 'indicates that the issuing of the utterance is the performing of an action' in contrast to a sentence or utterance which is descriptive of an action.

[4] As British football supporters will know, on the recommendation of Justice Taylor's Report into the game, the wire barriers preventing pitch invasions have been removed from British football stadiums. Nevertheless, the horrific image at Hillsborough Stadium of ninety-six Liverpool football fans being crushed to death against these cages when the turnstiles failed to count accurately the number of spectators entering the enclosure in 1989 remains a vivid one for many and, in particular, for people in Liverpool and Sheffield.

[5] Both Hans-Georg Gadamer and Hannah Arendt indicate that due to the Latin translation of Artistole's definition as *animal rationale*, 'rational animal', such that *logos* was interpreted as reason and thought, Aristotle's definition has been misunderstood as distinguishing human beings by their capacity for reason. The primary meaning of the Greek word *logos*, however, is language and speech (Gadamer, 1976: 59; Arendt, 1958: 27).

[6] As distinct from Thucydides, the son of Melesias, who was Pericles' political opponent.

[7] Ostracism entailed ten years' banishment, although those ostracised retained their financial status and citizenship. Each year the Assembly voted whether or not to hold an ostracism. If the vote was in the affirmative, citizens lined up on a set day and cast their vote in a special enclosure within the *Agora,* or Council chambers. 6,000 votes were required for a quorum and the person whose name was inscribed on the largest number of potsherds had ten days to leave Attica (Thornley, 1996: 43; Starr, 1990: 16).

[8] Only Gorgias specialised exclusively in the art of oratory. Other Sophists also taught astronomy, arithmetic, geometry or music, whilst Protagoras taught the art of politics (*Protagoras*: 318e).

[9] By contrast, Coby asserts that '[a]s an art of political virtue, sophistry is manifestly undemocratic' (1987: 50). The idea that virtue needs to be learnt suggests, to him, that those who excel in this art ought to have greater input than those with less expertise, thus creating an intellectual oligarchy. However, Coby fails to recognise that, as Pericles indicated in his famous Funeral Oration, whilst Athenian democracy was egalitarian in its assumptions, it was also designed to reward those who excelled.

[10] For a fuller discussion of various possible interpretations of Protagoras' famous saying see Cornford's commentary (Plato, 1957: 32-36).

[11] According to Plutarch's historical judgement, it would appear that to the best of his ability Pericles would keep any self-disclosure unsuited to his aim of achieving victory in the Assembly hidden. For example, Plutarch reports that 'even Pericles was extremely cautious in his use of words, so much so that

whenever he rose to speak, he uttered a prayer that no word might escape his lips which was unsuited to the matter' (1960: *Pericles*, 8). Nor did he speak on every matter, but only when necessary and when he would achieve maximum effect. Plutarch further informs us that during his days as a politician Pericles avoided familiar intercourse with either the people or his friends because 'in familiar relationships it is hard to keep an imposing exterior which is assumed for appearances sake' (1960: *Pericles*, 7).

[12] According to the *Oxford English Dictionary* the word 'arena' is derived from the Latin *harena* and was originally used to denote '[t]he central part of an amphitheatre, in which combats or spectacular displays take place, and which was originally strewn with sand to absorb the blood of the wounded and slain. Used also, by extension, of the whole amphitheatre.'

[13] In the Colosseum the two main opponents were the 'lights' who had small circular Grecian style shields and lighter armour thus relying on their speed and agility against the 'heavies' who relied on their strength and heavier armour. There were also the *retiarri*, or net-fighters who had virtually no armour and the shortest life-span (Pearson, 1973: 15).

[14] For a fuller discussion of the public relations model used by Reagan in the 1984 Presidency election see Johnstone (1995: 99-103). Thatcher's leadership of the Conservative Party during the 1980s was also marked by a greater reliance on public relations and advertising agencies, in particular Satchi and Satchi. Debate was eliminated from the main forum of party conferences, which were transformed into public relations events to publicise the party's programme through a show of order, unity and 'slickness'. The British Labour Party later followed suit in an attempt to change the public's perception of a party riddled with factionalism.

[15] It is sometimes thought that the aggressive nature of parliamentary debates also privileges men over women who prefer more cooperative and collaborative working styles. There is no doubt that parliaments throughout the Commonwealth are largely forums for men while female representatives remain a minority. The under representation of women also gives these forums what many would regard as a definite 'male' atmosphere. But it need not follow that the adversarial nature of the debates would change with increased female participation. For example, Senator Norma Cox Astwood (Bermuda) argues that those women who can overcome the financial, educational and party organisational impediments to their election 'are usually sufficiently assertive to compete successfully in the political arena. Politics will not attract the meek and submissive of either gender' (1990: 156). Pippa Norris' study into hours worked by British MPs on parliamentary matters further reveals that rather than avoiding the debating chamber, female MPs spend marginally more time per week than their male colleagues in parliamentary debates (1996: 101).

References

Arendt, H. (1958), *The Human Condition*, University of Chicago Press, Chicago and London.

Aristophanes (1978), *The Knights*, A.H. Sommerstein, trans. in *The Birds and Other Plays*, Penguin, Harmondsworth.

Astwood, N.C. (1990), 'Women in Politics: A Challenge to Tradition', *The Parliamentarian*, vol. LXXI, no. 3, pp. 153-56.

Austin, L.J. (1975), *How To Do Things With Words*, 2nd ed., Oxford University Press, Oxford and New York.

Coby, P. (1987), *Socrates and the Sophistic Enlightenment: A Commentary on Plato's Protagoras*, Lewisburg Bucknell University Press, London and Toronto.

Coghill, K. and Babbage, D. (1991), 'Seating in Legislatures', *Legislative Studies*, vol. 5, no. 2, pp. 15-22.

Edelman, M. (1988), *Constructing the Political Spectacle*, University of Chicago Press, Chicago and London.

Fornara, C.W. and Samons, L.J. (1991), *Athens from Cleisthenes to Pericles*, University of California Press, Berkeley.

Gadamer, H.G. (1976), *Philosophical Hermeneutics*, D.E. Linge trans., University of California Press, Berkeley.

Grant, M. (1967), *Gladiators*, Weidenfeld and Nicolson, London.

Guthrie, W.C. (1971), *The Sophists*, Cambridge University Press, Cambridge.

Haggard, W. (1984), *The Arena*, Severn House, London.

Johnstone, C.L. (1995), 'Reagan, Rhetoric, and the Public Philosophy: Ethics and Politics in the 1984 Campaign', *The Southern Communication Journal*, vol. 60, no. 2, pp. 93-108.

Kerferd, G.B. (1981), *The Sophistic Movement*, Cambridge University Press, Cambridge.

Madgwick, P.J. (1984), *Introduction to British Politics*, 3rd ed., Stanley Thornes, Cheltenham.

McKay, D. (1989), *American Politics and Society*, 2nd ed., Basil Blackwell, Oxford.

Norris, P. (1996), 'Women Politicians: Transforming Westminster?', *Parliamentary Affairs: A Journal of Comparative Politics*, vol. 49, no. 1, pp. 89-102.

Pearson, J. (1973), *Arena: The Story of the Colosseum*, Thames and Hudson, London.

Pitkin, H. (1967), *The Concept of Representation*, University of California Press, Berkeley and Los Angeles.

Plass, P. (1995), *The Game of Death in Ancient Rome: Arena Sport and Political Suicide*, University of Wisconsin Press, Wisconsin.

Plato (1961), *The Collected Dialogues of Plato*, E. Hamilton and H. Cairns (eds), Princeton University Press, Princeton, New Jersey.

_____ (1957), *Theaetetus*, F.M. Cornford ed. and trans., Bobb-Merrill, Indianapolis.

Plutarch (1960), *The Rise and Fall of Athens: Nine Greek Lives*, I. Scott-Kilvert trans., Penguin, Harmondsworth.

Raaflaub K.A. (1990), 'Perceptions of Democracy in Fifth-Century Athens' in W.R. Connor *et al.*, *Aspects of Athenian Democracy*, Museum Tusculanum Press, Copenhagen, pp. 7-32.

Starr, C.G. (1990), *The Birth of Athenian Democracy*, Oxford University Press, Oxford.

Stones, E. (1990), *Debates: How Parliament Discusses Things*, The Parliamentary Education Unit, London.

Thornley, J. (1996), *Athenian Democracy*, Routledge, London and New York.

Thucydides (1960), *The History of the Peloponnesian War*, R. Livingstone trans., Oxford University Press, New York.

(1999), *The Weekend Australian*, January 16-17, p. 12.

2 Language and Disclosure: Habermas and the Struggle for Reason

ANGELA CLARE

Introduction

Some of the most keenly contested debates over Habermas's theory of communicative action turn on the idea of language as *disclosure*. These debates begin with the shared assumption that language constitutes the world we live in by disclosing meaning to us. The way the world is revealed or interpreted in language shapes how things look and sound, what we see, hear and feel about them.

Language not only forms our understanding of the world by providing us with interpretations of it, but gives us the means to interpret new experiences, even allowing us to recognise that certain experiences *cannot* be captured in language. If our knowledge is so intimately attached to the world-disclosing power of language, then clearly there is much at stake in precisely how we understand the concept of disclosure. How the world is disclosed shapes the judgements we can make about it, determining what we see as good, bad, desirable or offensive. Our notions of beauty or disgust; of people as outgoing, insecure, friendly or alienated; of phrases such as 'a real little boy', or 'just like a girl', all depend on a semantic world that is continually disclosed to us in language. This view does not imply that language creates a world that would not exist outside of our linguistic horizons, but rather holds that language provides a framework wherein our experience can be understood, its meaning evaluated and, if need be, transformed to suit different circumstances.

This discussion examines some key points of contention surrounding the theme of disclosure in the work of Jürgen Habermas and several of his critics (Taylor, 1991; Larmore, 1996; Rorty, 1996; Bernstein, 1995). In a nutshell, the debate turns on whether language as disclosure or language as rational action is the more appropriate basis for knowledge. Habermas highlights the universal structures of communication, the critical accomplishments they make possible and the cognitive distance between the aesthetically-disclosed world and rationality of communicative action. The opposing view rejects the possibility that knowledge can be detached from its disclosed world in this fashion. It holds that language and knowledge are not universal but historically specific: we do not need to look beyond the world-disclosing function of language to explain our moral values, scientific achievements, or the possibility of transformation and critique. For Habermas, however, this blurs the distinction between aesthetics and knowledge, reducing truth and rightness to contingent artefacts of human endeavours.

In the present climate of post-modernism and its fluid, heterogeneous and largely aesthetic model of knowledge,[1] it is easy to dismiss Habermas's work as too rigid, rationalist and idealistic. In contrast, I want to present a reading of Habermas's work that reveals its theoretical sophistication as well as its moral relevance. It is sobering to remember, for instance, that Habermas's commitment to a universalist ethics is informed by the conviction that Nazi death camps represented the culmination of a series of European backlashes against the universalist principles of modern, rationalised Europe (1994: 71).[2] In Germany's case, the universalism was inherent not only in the encroachment of global capitalism but in the (failed) attempt to secularise and democratise the state.

Habermas's project is to protect society from just such violent political excesses. Morality must have – and does have, he insists – a more secure basis than the aesthetically-disclosed world and the particular political forms it may take, whether that be a militaristic and anti-Semitic German nationalism, ethnic tribalism, apartheid, or patriarchal and autocratic social systems. Knowledge and morality must meet certain criteria *external* to a given society's world-view in order to be true or right. Precisely because disclosure is intimately linked with the emotional and localised expression of kinship, race or nation – whether in ethical and religious solidarities, art traditions or murderously oppressive régimes – Habermas rejects the possibility that disclosure could ever be a solid, open ground for human knowledge. Knowledge need not be abandoned to a disempowering relativity. It can instead be used to reveal the universal aspects of communication that allow us to justify our claims to knowledge by appeal to public arenas beyond our own, based on the ideal of free and open discussion (1996b: 21).

It is important to acknowledge, however, that Habermas as well as his critics see the world-disclosing function of language as the key to our understanding of the world. The meaning of our experience is only accessible through hermeneutic or interpretative efforts, not through any purported neutral, scientific analysis (1994: 64). Habermas indeed goes a long way with his hermeneutic critics before points of difference emerge. He agrees with the way Charles Taylor's 'expressivist' position demonstrates:

> ...how every language opens up a grammatically pre-structured space, how it permits what is-in-the-world to appear there in a certain manner and, at the same time, enables interpersonal relations to be regulated legitimately as well as making possible the spontaneous self-presentation of creative-expressive subjects. 'World disclosure' means for Taylor, as for Humboldt, that language is the constitutive organ not only of thought, but also of both social practice and experience, of the formation of ego and group identities (1991: 221).

Given its hermeneutic underpinnings as well as its advocacy of free and open communication, it is something of a surprise that Habermas's theory of communicative action sets itself in *opposition* to the world-disclosing function of language. This arises out of what he sees as a basic division in the function of language itself, namely, a distinction between problem-solving versus world-disclosing functions. Language as problem-solving refers to the linguistic coordination of action: how we are to go about solving the problems that confront us as individuals and as members of a community. It is in this functional sense that language is intrinsically oriented towards understanding, agreement and reciprocity (1984: 397). To solve problems we must strive to understand each other, to listen to others and to reach agreement. Accordingly, language – or as Habermas puts it, speech acts – implicitly involves claims to validity: suggestions, as it were, that seek to gain the approval of others.

Language as world-disclosing is, on the other hand, only indirectly related to how we solve problems in the world. It is associated instead with creativity, discovery, aesthetics, the ends-generating functions of ethics and religion and existential questions of self-identification (1991: 249).[3] As a deontological or rights-based moral theory, communicative action concerns itself with the way in which we solve the conflicts at hand, not the meaning or content of those conflicts. It refuses to prescribe in other words an end goal, or *telos*, of human good towards which we should strive. Disclosure, however, is equated with just such substantive goals which are revealed to us in our given, everyday 'lifeworld' knowledge: the realm of ethical, value-laden life into which we are born, and in which we develop our identities and form our individual and collective personalities.

Under modern processes of rationalisation, according to Habermas, the status of disclosed knowledge begins to crumble, and this is not a necessarily bad thing. Lifeworld conflicts increase as the result of the breakdown of traditional forms of authority, the concomitant rise in individualism and proliferation of life choices. In these circumstances, once an element in the lifeworld becomes a source of conflict, there is no other authority to which we might turn save rational discourse. In the process of discursive testing, our unproblematised lifeworld knowledge changes its character: it is no longer sufficient as a meaning-creating and validating mode of discourse. It is forced to respond to rational evaluation, changing from the *subject* of discourse – that is, its constitutive background condition – to its *object*: Is *this* the best way to deal with the problem?

Unsurprisingly, Habermas's distinction between disclosure and rational action is not a straightforward matter. As a distinct yet apparently all-pervasive category of language, disclosure assumes a mantle of intrigue: why exactly is it incompatible with, perhaps even threatening to, rational communication? It is noteworthy that Habermas does not dismiss the affective, expressive and aesthetic world as unimportant; he readily admits its role in constituting self, community and everything we hold of value within it, including the integration and expansion of knowledge spheres. Yet disclosure is at times dismissed as superfluous, even subversive of, rational action in a modern, 'post-conventional'[4] society. The question is whether this tension in Habermas's thinking represents merely a symptom of an illusory universalist and scientistic paradigm, as some critics have suggested, or a brave attempt to rescue reason from a narrow understanding which relegates morality to the relativities of taste, culture and historical contingency.

This question and others that arise in the course of discussion open up broad avenues of philosophical inquiry which in this context can only be touched upon.[5] Rather than attempt the fruitless exercise of reconciling the tension between reason and disclosure in Habermas's thought, I will offer instead a reading of communicative action that highlights the strengths of the dialectical relation between them, a reading for which Habermas, perhaps despite himself, provides ample grounds. Far from excluding disclosure, I argue for an understanding of communicative action as an enactment of rational principles, a *dialectical* process both in the sense of a critical approach to argumentation, and in the sense of the action and counter-action of opposing forces.

Communicative action and disclosure

It is useful to read Habermas's theory as an attempt to sustain the moral force of pre-modern society in the context of modernity's reflexive, communicative rationality and its disenchanted world. The process of rationalisation that has occurred in Western industrial societies, conventionally seen by critical theorists as irredeemably negative, is here far more constructively figured. Against Weber and the early Frankfurt School, historical modernity has not simply moved unremittingly towards the domination of instrumental rationality. Modernity has instead been accompanied by the potential for the development of an independent, normative, communicative form of rationalisation in the lifeworld, a strengthening of knowledge which carries with it the possibility of overcoming modernity's repressive effects. Thus while the modern rationalisation of knowledge into distinct spheres – scientific, aesthetic, legal and normative – has permitted the technological and bureaucratic domination of life, it has also expanded our cognitive power to recognise and control these forms of domination. This notion of dual development frames Habermas's critique of capitalist systems and advanced industrial societies. The advance of technological and economic systems is at least potentially countered by normative advances in democratic processes of will-formation: it is this simultaneous development that is missed by modernity's more pessimistic critics.

However, if there is no way to escape our context of world interpretation and the standards of evaluation they permit, what criteria can we now draw upon to evaluate different ways of knowing? Can universal standards of validity ever be found within secular, pluralist societies where foundational principles of knowledge have been abandoned? We have an alternative, Habermas insists, to the desolate choice between relativism or scientistic positivism: 'If there is any such standard at all, it must be inherent in historical life' (1996b: 11). It is possible to derive such a standard, Habermas argues, because meaning and validity in modernity are increasingly determined not by world-disclosing language but by rational processes of communication. As life forms, values and beliefs have been increasingly freed from pre-determined social roles and economic structures, 'cultural traditions and processes of socialization came under the pressure of reflection, so that actors themselves gradually made them into topics of discussion' (1996a: 95). In modernity a belief is no longer meaningful or legitimate simply because it lies in our cultural tradition, but because we can provide good reasons to support it. In the transition from pre-modern to modern, from community to society, morality, too, is rationalised. Whereas pre-modern morality is grounded in an absolute dependency on God, Habermas locates the binding force of modern morality not in the sacred, nor even in the humanist recognition of a social good, but in the structures of argumentation and validity claims immanent in speech acts.

Societies undergoing such structural change evolve learning processes that derive from dialogic interaction, gradually achieving a 'post-conventional' level of morality: that is, participants are increasingly able to stand back from their lifeworld, call into question the validity of their beliefs and assumptions, and test those beliefs through open and unforced discussion. By bracketing our own particular interests as just one set among many and imaginatively conceiving different subject positions on the evidence of other's arguments, we are able to develop rational resolutions to conflict which go beyond limited historical contexts to claim universal validity (1984: 8). Social integration shifts from a belief-based to a consent and will-based account, a focus on the fact *that* values are shared, not *what* is shared (Bernstein, 1995: 97). Communicative action therefore involves a distancing from the immediate contexts of action for our day to day immersion in private interests. Subjective questions – What is the best thing for me to do? How can I solve this problem? – are replaced by the adoption of a generalised hypothetical stance to practical issues: What is the best thing for us (as an inclusive society that potentially extends beyond this time and space) to do?[6]

Precisely because, for Habermas, modern societies are characterised by the absence of a common ethos, it no longer becomes possible to assume that any one view of the good life is universally applicable. In consequence, moral theory cannot specify the empirical conditions under which norms can be put into practice. This is up to social practice itself. Restricted to universals, moral theory must now proceed on a procedural level. Agreement can only be reached on *how* everyone is to agree or disagree, not on *what* is agreed or disagreed, if it is not to violate the freedoms of individuals. A postconventional morality cannot, in other words, pronounce on the merit of a whole social life or world-view, its meaning, cultural forms, or values. Nor can it prescribe an individual's personal values, because these ethical forms are particular and context-dependent.

We can no longer accept Rousseau's solution, therefore, which made freedom contingent on the shared ethos of a small community 'who already agree in advance on their value orientations', and where the more numerous and diverse the people, the greater the coercive force government must exercise (1996a: 102). The distinction between form and content, and therefore between rational action and disclosure, becomes increasingly important as levels of social diversity rise. This is so because all lifeworlds in modernity have to reproduce themselves through the agency of actions oriented toward achieving understanding. Lifeworlds can no longer rely on the authority of tradition, 'so the general character of communicative rationality stands out within the multiplicity of concrete forms of life' (1991: 220). When we adhere to these distinctions, knowledge can be evaluated according to its appropriate, distinctive logics or criteria, unleashing its rational and emancipatory potential.[7]

World-disclosure

Where does disclosure fit into this model? We have seen that Habermas divides language into world-disclosing and problem-solving functions. Within the category of problem-solving language there are three further sub-divisions: 1) the presentation of factual matters (resulting in the production of objective knowledge and truth claims); 2) the creation of interpersonal relations (moral discourse and claims to rightness); 3) the expression of subjective experience or expressive self-presentation (claims to subjective truthfulness) (1991: 227). The distinction between these modes of language, or spheres of knowledge, can best be understood through the mechanism of validity claims. In all these categories, including the constitutive, world-disclosing function, speech acts raise validity claims aimed at intersubjective recognition and can be rationally evaluated. They are differentiated according to the way in which they can be justified when they are problematic; the kind of reasons, that is – factual, moral, ethical-existential or aesthetic – drawn upon to justify the claim.

The distinction between problem-solving and world-disclosing claims rests on the criteria of *universalisability*. Whereas the truth of objective facts, the rightness of norms and the truthfulness of subjective-expressive claims refer to processes of justification that occur *within* a disclosed world-view, world-disclosing language refers to the aesthetic and ethical perspectives that make up that world-view. Its claims are primarily concerned with aesthetic harmony and evaluative cogency, slanted towards the validity of 'assuming world-shaping modes of perception' (1991: 227). So whereas the structure of action-coordinating claims can be abstracted from everyday discourse to extend across spatio-temporal boundaries, the aesthetic nature of disclosure means that it cannot raise claims that go beyond the world-view they are presenting.

Aesthetic and ethical claims typically pertain to questions of particular interest, matters primarily concerned with the self and its desires, goals and achievements, questions of who we are and who we want to be, of what kind of life we want to lead. 'Black is beautiful', 'God is love' or 'all men are bastards', for instance, possess a particularity coextensive with a community, group or individual's whole 'way of seeing'. Such claims assert matters of preference and value, rather than general rightness or truth. Therefore they do not hold the same cognitive status as scientific or moral-practical knowledge.[8] By definition – indeed, even to be comprehensible – they presuppose prior ethical or aesthetic agreement. They cannot be adequately understood on a cognitive level, but must be lived or experienced in their respective contexts of meaning.

World-disclosing language remains bound by its context, therefore, in that it lacks a universal structure which can be abstracted from it. Whereas normative and objective claims can in principle be generalised beyond their social contexts, there is no hope for consensus on world-disclosing claims. They are interpretations. They 'can be deep or shallow, but not true or false' (1996b: 11).[9] There is no ethical, religious or aesthetic world-view that is any 'closer to God' than the next, for there is no external criteria by which they can be evaluated. This is not to say that ethical, existential or aesthetic questions may not assume primacy in our everyday life over generalised, moral matters; the former are, Habermas acknowledges, 'usually of far more pressing concern for us' (1993: 151). Nevertheless, world-disclosing interpretative claims 'point in a different direction from moral questions: the regulation of interpersonal conflicts of action resulting from opposed interests is not yet an issue' (1993: 6).

The particular-universal distinction between ethics and morality has been widely criticised in Habermas's work, and goes to the heart of the debate over language as world-disclosing or as action coordinating. Surely what is collectively good and personally desirable cannot be separated from what we see as right or just?[10] In a sense Habermas agrees with the gist of this objection. Thus the justification of a norm – its universal validity – must be accompanied by its application in actual contexts, a process which *includes* aesthetic and ethical discourse.[11] Similarly, each validity sphere can be said to disclose a world-view in its own way. But the importance for Habermas's project of this often problematic distinction between form and content – between knowledge and aesthetics – cannot be overstated. The aim of this discussion is to show why Habermas cannot accept the hermeneutic assumption that knowledge is interpretation, and therefore ultimately aesthetic.

Knowledge beyond disclosure

In modern society, Habermas argues, knowledge goes *beyond* disclosure in its ability to tap into the rational structures inherent in all forms of lifeworld communication, but it does not reject disclosure. Disclosure occurs both through aesthetic and ethical discourse and in the theoretical or hypothetical discourse of communicative action. In both processes we reveal our identities, values and interests. Habermas, in fact, admits that the world-constitutive and world-creative role of disclosure supplies the necessary conditions for communicative action. We learn what the world is, what experience means, through the disclosing function of language. Disclosure makes known to us the intimacy of sensuous, mimetic experience with others and the natural world, the production or reception of a work of art, the creative results of imagination and discovery, non-verbal expression as well as forms of linguistic disclosure not directly aimed at exchanging functional information or securing shared meanings: gossip, anecdotes, irony, verbal 'display', seduction, the interpretation of perspectives, the affirmation of self-identity, self-reassurance through others, the forming of affective bonds. These may all *indirectly* involve objective, normative or subjective claims, but they are *primarily* disclosing in that their principal aim is to reveal a certain way of looking at the world.

In shifting the discourse of disclosure to a dialogic, self-reflective, problem-solving setting, we also reveal the possibility of a validity that goes beyond our personal preferences.[12] Unlike Locke's account of England after a civil war, or Rousseau's anticipation of revolution, this does not involve a process of disclosing a pre-existing general will, or discovering a supervening common good. It is rather a continuous process of rational will-*formation*, of constructing and testing intersubjectively the norms that will govern social life.

The advantage of Habermas's focus on normative consensus rather than purely abstract universals,[13] or on any single account of justice or ethics, is that we – modern theorists of morality – can combine the best from Kant's moral universalism and Aristotle's ethical particularism to inform principles of action, procedure and structure in a rational account of the good life (Outhwaite, 1994: 55). The question is whether this approach represents a subversion of community values and concomitant loss of moral understanding, a loss that coincides with the shift to procedural rationalism, or whether it represents a new mode of moral action that represents the growing autonomy of social structures.

In light of Habermas's aim to recuperate a rational space for modern morality distinct from the objectifying criteria of the natural sciences – in other words, to demonstrate that not only the objective world but moral action is capable of consensus – the functionalism of his schema does appear paradoxical. Is Habermas not subjecting morality precisely to the objectifying methods of the natural sciences from which he wants to save it? How can the world-disclosing, cultural, affective, metaphoric and playful modes of language be distinguished from communicative reason?

What of the cognitive elements of aesthetics, or the role of creation and discovery, the generation of new modes of knowledge in all three categories that may emerge from intuitive, context-specific knowledge? (Outhwaite, 1994: 31) What of art and its struggle against the all-pervasive claims of propositional rationality? Of love and mimetic affinity?

We might be forgiven for thinking that the primary role of language, according to Habermas, is to redeem its own use value; the rest is entertainment. The discussion below will elaborate on these criticisms of Habermas's treatment of disclosure. It will be followed by an attempt to determine how his theory of communication can be defended from them.

Knowledge as reason or disclosure?

That intersubjective speech acts are necessary for there to be a disclosed world, and vice versa, is not in question here. Rather, the point of contention between rational action versus disclosure turns on the relation between disclosure and knowledge. Are structures of thought shaped by cognitive validity claims, or is the 'world' made and re-made through disclosure? Does our social and phenomenal world pre-exist speech acts, or does it emerge through dialogue? If disclosure is equated with a linguistically constituted world of meaning – that is, if disclosure opens up or unveils what has not previously been accessible to us through the revelation of private truths and new kinds of experience, creation or discovery – how can it be excluded from rational and moral discourse?

Communicative action emphasises the intersubjective coordination necessary for social life: the idea that we understand and create the world by coming to agreement about various aspects of it. The converse view of language as world-disclosure emphasises the notion that meaning is not *agreed upon* but *revealed* to us. In this latter view, Habermas dismisses the world-articulating and world-disclosing dimensions of everyday language too lightly in favour of a world-view that over-burdens our capacity to move reflexively between a series of cognitive distinctions. Both philosophically and in terms of everyday human interaction it would be costly to sustain the distinctions Habermas draws between the moral and the ethical, disclosure and problem-solving, particular and universal. The meaning-constituting function of disclosure is a fundamental and ineradicable feature of language, and far from being distinct from problem-solving functions, is coextensive with *all* modes of language. As self-interpreting beings we are incapable of transcending our own subjectivity, yet the strong idealisations involved in understanding speech acts as validity claims presuppose just such transcendence. In order to find reasons and justifications open to everyone in heeding validity claims, Bernstein points out, 'I would have to discount my subjectivity, the quite particular alignment between me and the world that is staked in the interpretative claim' (Bernstein, 1995: 220). But this is impossible. After all, if a moral principle is to be justified it must be appropriately applied to a given situation, and this brings into play the particular ethical and aesthetic world-views of those involved.

If language is understood as interpretation, however, no such difficulty arises. Moral discourse becomes inseparable from disclosure because it is intimately connected to aesthetic and ethical claims, and ungeneralisable world-views. The *universality* of truth and rightness is both illusory and redundant, for normative agreement requires the consideration of subjective accounts of experience and ethical perspectives. Habermas's distinction between justification and application indeed implicitly concedes the irrelevance of universal principles, for justification here *depends on* the contextual application of norms: a norm is only just if it meets the approval of *these* people in *this* context.

Advocates of the disclosure model go on to argue that if communicative reason cannot coherently call up the criteria necessary to evaluate substantive world-views and aesthetic or cultural forms, then the implication is that it is not a universally applicable theory but falls itself within a particular world-view. Habermas's view of reason, then, is a cultural product of Western industrialised society, the disclosure of a *particular* way of life. Rather than subscribe to Enlightenment rationality, we may believe the predominant force in human affairs to be such non-cognitive powers as spirit ancestors, the Divine, sexuality (Freud), will to power (Nietzsche, Foucault) or social solidarity (Durkheim). Others, such as post-modernists, might hold that language and knowledge are not reducible to *any* hierarchy of purpose.

Habermas's description of rationalisation is, in short, historically questionable. He has overstated the processes of secularisation leading to modernity, and is mistaken to think that this era has heralded the breakdown of social integration and belief based on convention. On the contrary, it is far from obvious today that the cognitive processes involved in communicative action have already replaced tradition as the binding force of postconventional morality. Contemporary moral debate is frequently characterised by disagreement over the role of metaphysics and religion in framing our moral judgements. Thus Habermas's universal project is grounded on what is itself contested. 'Good' reasons continue to stop short of secular, rational knowledge: the failure in Northern Ireland and Israel to secure consensus after years of effort and the irrational xenophobia of right-wing political movements around the world are three among numerous examples that can be called to mind. In sum, Habermas's conception of modernity is not sufficiently broad: modern experience is characterised by the expectation that 'metaphysics and postmetaphysics will remain an enduring object of reasonable disagreement' (Larmore, 1996: 216).

The grounding of knowledge

In upholding faith in reason alone as the ground of morality in modernity, Habermas also upholds the citizen-man distinction that, from Rousseau and Marx, has been repeatedly attacked as socially and individually destructive.[14] The rational *citoyen* capable of participating in an impartial fashion in public life remains forever cut off from the private *homme* of self-interested desires and non-rational motivations. Habermas's theory becomes not the solution but part of the problem of contemporary social disintegration and alienation, for the 'deficit of affect can never be recuperated in logical or transcendental argument' (Bernstein, 1995: 94).

From this viewpoint, it is difficult to avoid the conclusion that communicative action radically undermines the narrative content of meaning and self: if our identity is based in a lifeworld perceived as conventional and therefore contingent, continually scrutinised by rational reappraisal, it becomes eroded and increasingly meaningless, with fewer and fewer solid grounds for identity. What opposes this disintegration of self is precisely what Habermas excludes from his theory of communicative action: the unifying affect of aesthetic disclosure (Larmore, 1996: 216). The disclosed, coherent world of community and self has its own metaphysical aspect of validity that defies cognitive evaluation. Reason can only regulate actions, not feelings, which can only be engaged, directed and transformed by the exemplary work of aesthetic disclosure. Communicative action's conceptual framework *orders* the world, but cannot disclose it. It appears, in consequence, that when all traces of the pre-modern, enchanted world are expunged the 'postconventional subject' will truly come into its own. If this is the ultimate project of the enlightenment, it would seem that the quest for pure reflexivity is a slow march for freedom at the expense of happiness.

Knowledge is founded not on rational agreement, but on the disclosure of the world through language and experience. Similarly, the motivation for moral conduct is not to be found in the structures of rational, post-conventional discourse but in cultural values that are inculcated on a personal and subjective level. Habermas does not sufficiently take into account that we have an existential and psychological interest in the grounding of our identity in each other's esteem, not just a practical interest in cooperation. Culture is the source of social values, affective feelings and morality; to attempt to derive these – much less to purge and renew them – from ahistorical, universal principles is to deny the very wellspring from which they arise (Taylor, 1989: 51-52). Thus art and aesthetic experience remain central to the contemporary moral project: 'The great epiphanic work actually can put us in contact with the sources it taps' (Taylor, 1989: 74).

This view need not entrap knowledge into a closed, pre-existing horizon of meaning, however, precisely because disclosure not only involves the revelation of what already exists in the social and natural world, but also encompasses contexts of creation, discovery and innovation. The disclosure of discovery and creation occurs *outside* of rational dialogue, and is even rejected by it: take, for instance, the length of time required for radical scientific theories to become commonly accepted knowledge. Communicative action's emphasis on consensus risks *blocking* the knowledge that arises from creativity, intuition and mimetic affinity by gleaning only what everyone can collectively believe. Truth is best understood not as consensus but as *disclosure*: something is true, or right, not because it can secure some hypothetical universal agreement, but because it has disclosed something true or right about the world in which we live. Thus Habermas's equation of meaning with validity in a post-conventional society – the idea that meaning depends not on convention or correspondence with the actual world but on intersubjective processes of justification – obscures the fact that meaning and truth may be crushed by the weight of this intersubjective imperative.

Clearly the need to transcend what is given in language as well as its social context is crucial to the dichotomy Habermas establishes between problem-solving and world-disclosing language. But the need to escape the potentially stultifying and repressive effects of conventional thinking is shared by those who advocate a more expressivist, interpretative approach to knowledge. What makes an intersubjectively validated claim different from a conglomeration of pre-existing individual wills, or the end-result of one particular, albeit collective, viewpoint? Can communicative action create *new* meanings and truths, or does it simply disclose existing personal interests?

The dialectic of disclosure and communicative action

The foregoing critiques make a number of important points concerning the aesthetically-disclosed basis of knowledge, points that Habermas would often do well to address in a more satisfactory manner. They fail, however, to do justice to the central achievements of the theory of communicative action and the task it sets philosophy to sift through the complexity of human communication to reveal its universal normative principles. They also overstate the case: Habermas does not shift the total burden of modern morality onto an abstract, formal reason. Instead he formulates a reciprocal relation between the cultural, aesthetic lifeworld and communicative action, granting the disclosed realm its own distinctive role in the process of knowledge formation. If the theory of communicative action is seen not as an *alternative* to communitarian, hermeneutic and phenomenological models of knowledge but as *complementary* to them, the opposition between disclosure from rational action becomes defensible.

Consider one of the most challenging points to which Habermas must respond: whether knowledge and morality are given to us through cultural forms or whether they emerge in intersubjective dialogue by virtue of the universal structures of communication. Richard Rorty (1996) has argued that world disclosure *does* initiate change, inadvertently providing us with solutions that do not occur to us through systematic argument, the force of better reasons, or cognitive learning processes. Rorty recalls a well known case involving the Supreme Court in Canada. In the 1920s, the court was required to pass judgement on women's claims to be admitted into the Senate on the grounds that, according to the constitutional wording, it was open to all 'persons'. Women argued that since they were also persons, they should not be excluded from the Senate. The judges concluded, however, that it could not have been the intention of those who initially drew up the constitution to include women, and therefore rejected the case. Rorty's point is that despite the women's airtight logical argument, the legal system simply failed to possess the moral imagination necessary to interpret the law differently. Change occurs not through rational argument, but through a series of often unintentional events – even moral and national debacles – that stretch our moral imagination and aesthetic interpretations. We just 'muddle through', and at the end we are living in 'a newly disclosed world' (Rorty, 1996: 87). On this view, we learn to become more self-critical subjects and increase the transparency of our lifeworld and processes of identity formation thanks to transformations in the structures of *cultural* modes of thought, modes which are not universally applicable.

Habermas does not try to hide the fact that 'a universalistic morality is dependent on supplementation by structurally analogous forms of life' (1991: 221). Lifeworlds themselves undergo a process of rationalisation. Under the manifold influences of communication their formal structures increasingly correspond to one another. A Habermasian response therefore draws attention to women's ability eventually to win their case precisely because of the universal categories of knowledge and learning processes modernity has opened up. The law may well depend on social changes within the lifeworld, but these changes are themselves the result of processes of rationalisation. The reasons drawn upon to resist women's claims to suffrage in the 1920s quickly lost plausibility not only because they did not match with the reality of men's and women's lives at that time. While many judges and legislators may have continued to doubt women's capacity to be effective citizens, there were no convincing formal or legal reasons to deny women the political citizenship that had been universally extended to men by the late nineteenth century. If lawyers, for example, elaborate the concept of 'person' as a legal fiction, an entity devoid of substantive identity, it may eventually be understood that, as a fiction, it might just as well include women as well as men.

The landmark 1973 decision to legalise abortion in the United States is based on a similar distinction between formal rights and substantive ethics. Supreme Court Judge Harry Blackmun, who handed down the decision, has been quoted as saying 'I am not for abortion. I hope my family never has to make such a decision.' Yet despite his conservative political views he nonetheless concluded that a woman's 'fundamental' right of personal privacy was 'broad enough to encompass a woman's decision whether or not to terminate her pregnancy'.[15] With this emphasis on the universal, rights-based structures of moral discourse, it is unsurprising that Habermas sees in legal systems the institutional vanguard of communicative rationality.[16]

The learning processes that unfold within cultures occur on an everyday level of interaction, propelled by a reciprocal relation between the disclosed world and communicative reason. As structural changes occur in everyday belief patterns – what Habermas might call the differentiation of validity spheres – the lifeworld's orientation towards understanding evolves towards increasingly reflexive, democratic processes of will formation. In this process culturally specific aesthetic and ethical values can be cognitively assessed by formal, or universalisable, structures of communication. The motivational conditions of morality – solidarity, care, trust, and responsibility – continue to depend on a disclosed lifeworld that precedes rational dialogue. As Habermas concedes, the motivation to act rationally depends on *affective* as well as cognitive conditions. There is no direct motivating force, or at best a weak one, to be found within rational argumentation itself (1993: 33-35). Thus, although moral duty is now grounded in rational processes, the source of moral feeling is still disclosed in lifeworld interactions:

We learn what moral, and in particular, immoral, action involves prior to all philosophizing; it impresses itself upon us no less insistently in feelings of sympathy with the violated integrity of others than in the experience of violation or fear of violation of our own integrity (1993: 76).

If we consider the transformations in women's social status over the last thirty years or so, legal historians can surely argue that formalised 'learning processes' such as legislation, commission reports and litigation have been at least as characteristic of the women's movement as 'muddling through'. The world-disclosing effects of feminist art and literature – for instance ground-breaking works such as *The Feminine Mystique* or *The Women's Room* – blend into both legal and everyday discourse. The way formal public debate on women's issues informs and is informed by many avenues of popular representation demonstrates that no single discourse has priority over another. Rather, there are mutual and reciprocal interrelationships.

Habermas stresses, however, that only within a rationally structured world-view could such change occur. Despite any aesthetic reluctance, legislators and judges have been obliged to accept the principle of equality of men and women by force of reason. The very fact that we are able to effect such change, Habermas points out, is only possible within a cognitive framework that allows the foundations of our beliefs to become a 'theme' or 'problem' for general debate in the first place. Rorty's advocacy of free and open dialogue is itself an expression of a universalist morality. It goes beyond the limited horizons of disclosure to posit an inclusive community of human beings (1996b: 23). If *everything* can be included within the disclosed world, as Rorty argues, then no distinctions can be drawn between objectivity or subjectivity, discovery or invention. There can be no distinction between making and finding, reality and appearance. Despite his pragmatic acceptance of this kind of relativism, Rorty's claims implicitly depend upon our ability to distinguish between what works and why, between truth and fiction, manipulation and tolerance. Such claims depend on *cognitive* validity and not merely aesthetic choices.

The motivational and aesthetic dimensions of action and thought are not therefore suppressed in communicative action, but are instead filtered through cognitive processes of argumentation. Morally and ethically antagonistic elements of modern cultures are rejected by lifeworlds increasingly structured according to rational principles. Such a recognition offers a striking antidote to the post-modern aestheticisation of everyday life. Communicative action becomes a means of protecting the public arena from the unreflexive spectacle and the reduction of knowledge to art. It may help to build a more sedate, but more just, political sphere.

Habermas therefore deems disclosure an insufficient basis for post-conventional knowledge. It is a position characterised by his refusal to collapse the distinctions between objective, normative and subjective and aesthetic validity. But there remains a persistent suspicion that Habermas's notion of disclosure, no matter how much he insists on its interaction with communicative action, simply fades into a pre-reflexive, background understanding, leaving its action-coordinating counterparts to the formation and evaluation of knowledge. Habermas's depiction of world-disclosing knowledge certainly implies a moment of passivity or receptiveness toward what is disclosed to us through language, discovery, or creation. After all, discourses of disclosure remain 'contingent on the *prior* telos of a consciously pursued way of life' (1993: 12); they have not yet moved to thematise the world-view on which they depend, but remain on the level of aesthetics. The principles of justice are intersubjectively *constructed* rather than discovered (1993: 28); they depend on the work of intersubjective testing, and not simply on creation, discovery or revelation.

Yet how can this pre-reflexive status of disclosure be reconciled with the fact that it *also* includes new experiences, discovery, innovative and creative ends-generating functions which 'reveal anew an apparently familiar reality' (Cooke, 1995: 75)? Habermas himself admits that disclosure generates knowledge that escapes the totality of pre-existing lifeworld resources:

> Experiences confute expectations, go against the customary forms of perception, trigger surprises, make us conscious of new things. Experiences are always *new* experiences and represent a counterbalance to what we are familiar with and take for granted (1994: 65).

The crucial missing dimension here is the *cognitive* function of communicative action. Although disclosure may involve the production and communication of meaning, it is not a cognitively reflective, intersubjective process in the same way as communicative action, which demands a more critical, dialogic role for participants. Certainly there are plenty of examples of scientific discovery as well as artistic creation where new knowledge, or new ways of seeing, are disclosed to the scientist or artist. But although they may trigger new ways of seeing, world-disclosing experiences remain passive from a cognitive viewpoint in that they occur *to* the subject. Such experiences may be immensely meaningful for those involved, but in order to be accepted as moral guides, or new modes of knowledge, they need to be justified through open, rational discourse. The validity of new ways of seeing – according to a theory of action – is only revealed retrospectively, through intersubjective processes of *validation*.

Thus on the one hand Habermas acknowledges our inability to escape the disclosed semantic world; indeed, a prior disclosed world is a necessary condition for communicative action. On the other hand, the action-coordinating function of language cannot be permitted to be overshadowed by world-disclosing language, which tends in consequence to be depicted as a passive, conventional sphere requiring discursive testing. Objecting to Taylor's prioritisation of disclosure, Habermas argues that in modernity:

> the modes of action constituted by a linguistic view of the world operate in the light of a communicative rationality that imposes an orientation toward validity claims on the participants and in this way triggers off learning processes that may have a retroactive effect on the previous understanding of the world. Taylor is wrong to allow this problem-solving capacity of language to disappear behind its capacity for world-disclosure (1991: 222).

Here Habermas is objecting to what he sees as the 'totalisation' of the world-disclosing function of language – totalising in the sense that nothing is seen to lie *outside* of a disclosed world-view. What separates discovery, creation, art and aesthetic evaluation from communicative action is not that they are not validity claims, for they are. Rather, it is the fact that they rely too heavily on a *mono*subjective, and not an intersubjective, understanding of action. On Taylor's view, either the individual is the 'agent' who discloses knowledge through discovery, creativity or intuition, or it is language understood as a totality, a kind of meta-subject or system acting out its functions through speech acts. In either case, Habermas feels that there is insufficient recognition of the cognitive achievements made possible by *structural* changes in knowledge. Instead they tend to be understood as discreet, particular events.

Because Taylor sees language as a whole, he also neglects the moments of difference in language, its breaks in meaning. Precisely because it is *symbolic* action, language carries with it a potential distance from the world. Habermas's dialogic model of knowledge rejects both the unified, Cartesian subject, from whose singular ego knowledge derives, and the pre-modern, collective self, uncritically immersed in its lifeworld. His self is a *diffracted* one: modern selves no longer develop only as subjects within specific collective totalities, they also develop as unique individuals and subjects in general (1991: 220). Following Humboldt, subjectivity can only be understood through relations with other subjects. The knowledge produced by these relations is itself split, revealing at once the force of language as a given system or world-view, and the inevitable proliferation of meaning with the emergence of individualism:

> all understanding is simultaneously a non-comprehension, all agreement in ideas and emotions is at the same time a divergence. In the manner in which language is modified by each individual, there is revealed, in contrast to its previously expounded potency, a power of man over it (Habermas 1991: 216).

Habermas's point is that under modern conditions we cannot help but adopt an increasingly critical attitude to our background of lifeworld knowledge. This attitude is not the *same* as disclosure: what is disclosed no longer produces knowledge, but is now made the object of our reflection. The equation of knowledge with disclosure side-steps the further, crucial stage of cognitive testing through rational processes of argumentation. This leaves knowledge dependent on the vagaries of subjective experience, be that individual or the experience of a pre-reflexive collectivity: 'The assimilation of all meaningful objects to manifestations of something subjective poisons the cognitive status of...philosophy' (1996b: 12). Thus, in modernity, the function of world-disclosing language as the constituent of meaning is overtaken by the reflective work of participants in dialogue. The reproduction of lifeworlds is no longer merely channelled through the medium of action oriented towards reaching understanding, but 'is a burden placed on the interpretative achievements of the actors themselves' (1991: 221).

Yet, ironically, communicative action only develops hand in hand with disclosure. The proliferation of individualism in modernity has brought with it more disclosure than ever before, but this increased reflection into life histories and diverse forms of life has accompanied and strengthened the processes of rational justification. Thus Habermas argues that the *surprising* and the *familiar* are complementary phenomena; new experiences can only be understood when they are supported by a lifeworld consensus. This, in turn, creates a divergence between world-disclosing and problem-solving language, or between anathematised and thematised knowledge: 'The problematizing force of critical experiences separates the lifeworld's background from the foreground' (1994: 73). At the same time, experiences themselves are differentiated according to how we deal practically with the world through 'our instrumental coping with things and events' (1994: 73). As world-disclosing experiences proliferate, they are increasingly distinguished from the objective world and the normative realm of interpersonal relationships. The experiences of our inner nature, our body, needs and feelings are only *indirectly* linked to this cognitive, practical world. Experiences are increasingly aligned not with knowledge as such but with aesthetic, affective and creative spheres of human action:

> Aesthetic experiences are not linked to particular practices; they are not related to cognitive-instrumental skills and moral beliefs that grow out of innerworldly learning processes; they are bound up with the world-constituting, world-disclosing function of language (1994: 74).

Precisely because the proliferation of disclosure is tied to the breakdown of homogeneous social world-views, its status as generalisable knowledge has inevitably been devalued. It is not merely in theory that this change has been effected: under the practical conditions of modernity, the demand for justification can be met only by moral discourse (1996: 97). No longer content with the revelatory functions of language, we demand that disclosure 'succeed' within the practical world in terms of its problem-solving capacities. Habermas, therefore, emphasises the critical and evaluative dimension involved in everyday language: the 'world-disclosing force of an interpreting language has to *prove itself* within the world' (1991: 221). Everyday communicative action develops and thematises what is given *through* disclosure and subjects it to incessant testing; world-views thus change in the wake of 'inner-worldly' processes of learning (1991: 24). This is not an either/or question:

> I would propose, instead, that the interaction between world disclosure and innerworldly learning processes works in a symmetrical way. Linguistic knowledge and world-disclosure interpenetrate. They feedback to each other, each enabling the acquisition of the other (1996b: 24).

Habermas indeed believes that as ethics, values and world-views become groundless and increasingly individualised, disclosure alone can contribute little to how we resolve collective social or moral conflicts. If in a pluralist society disclosure cannot secure ethical or aesthetic agreement, even less can it secure moral agreement. Its import lies instead in the affective and aesthetic resources it can provide, the imaginative facility that feeds the cognitive filtering of experiences through communicative action:

> If aesthetic experience is incorporated into the context of individual life-histories, if it is utilized to illuminate a situation and to throw light on individual life-problems – if it at all communicates its impulses to a collective form of life – then art enters into a language game which is no longer that of aesthetic criticism, but belongs, rather, to everyday communicative practice.

It then no longer affects only our evaluative language or only renews the interpretation of needs that color our perceptions; rather it reaches into our cognitive interpretations and normative expectations and transforms the totality in which these moments are related to each other (1985: 202).

Habermas therefore argues that critics miss the point when they object to the abstract and cognitivist nature of communicative action and the fact that it appears to ignore the affective, aesthetic substance of social life. They introduce a substantive theory of ethics into the debate far too quickly, and attempt to apply sociological and ethical concerns to what is a formal-pragmatic theory of action (1991: 233). The fact that his theory eschews substantive questions does not mean that they are deemed unimportant. Morality only takes precedence over ethics from the standpoint of moral theory:

> communicative rationality precisely does not amount to the sum total of its moral-practical components.... Such an ethics cannot exhaust the rational content of everyday communicative practice, but can grasp it only in terms of one aspect, and only within the framework of a normative theory (1991: 219).

Habermas's intent is to distinguish the aesthetic, monological model of knowledge as disclosure from his cognitive and intersubjective approach which emphasises both participants' acts of evaluation as well as the critical distance permitted by language as a symbolic system. Thus, for him, the post-conventional world emerges in the course of dialogue. It is not a pre-existing, packaged whole, any more than it comes from individual learning experiences. Nor is the validity of meaning simply a matter of lifeworld usage. It is grounded in intersubjective processes of argumentation.

Conclusion

From my reading, Habermas presents us with a genuinely dialectical understanding of modernity. Communicative action is not a mere 'ethos' but a communicative enactment of understanding that acknowledges the tension between culture and reason, affect and reflexivity. Such a dialectic can be kept alive on the sole condition that neither cognitive reason nor aesthetic interpretations *alone* can resolve moral disputes.

The impartiality of rational judgement cannot *replace* the lifeworld's interpretative depth, it must transcend it. Our interpretative capacities, whether mediated through time or space or with an immediate dialogical partner, requires an *imaginative as well as rational understanding* of the conditions of its possibility.. A speaker's intended meaning, lifeworld knowledge and particular experience all act as 'evidence' for understanding and evaluating a claim (1984: 115-116). This is not to claim that we become – at will – purely rational beings. The attitude of hypothetical impartiality will not always be devoid of strategic interests, and the lifeworld may be a distorting force on rational discourse. Nevertheless the principles of communicative reason are *regulative* ideals which *in certain circumstances* – moral discourse in a communicative setting – call into question in a rational manner our everyday interpretative actions and values. These circumstances include, for example, if only on occasion, the familiar rhetoric of legislative, judicial and electoral arenas.

Habermas is striving to escape from what he sees as thought's helpless oscillation between the belief that knowledge is either simply given *to* the subject, or it is produced *by* the subject. In both cases language is mistakenly conceived 'either as a vehicle for the creation of meaning or as something that happens behind our backs. Either way, the connection between the disclosure of the world and mundane learning processes is excluded' (Outhwaite, 1994: 33).

There is, then, a dialectical process between disclosure, argument and will-formation that reveals, shapes and transfigures participants' beliefs. The end result of rational discourse cannot amount to what is *disclosed*, for this would be a foreclosure of dialogue, simply the acceptance of what is. Rather, disclosure is *one* step in the process of rational reflection, a process of ongoing interaction, self-reflection and intersubjective communication within the lifeworld as well as in communicative action contexts. This is no mystical 'General Will'. The common good is not 'out there' waiting to be revealed through dialogue, but formed *through* it.

By articulating explicit and latent interests, listening to those of others, hearing new viewpoints and perspectives, arguing about their respective merits, we undergo a learning process. Our beliefs are transfigured, irrational and strategic interests exposed, common interests recognised, or compromises settled. If we remain in the world of ethical concerns, arguing about what is good for you and me, we are in no danger of losing a proper concern for our own happiness. In turn, we cannot reconcile that interest with what is right or just if the sacrifice of price is *another's* happiness (1996b: 23-24). What is subjectively meaningful for just the two of us, should we chance to agree, nevertheless does not determine validity. Rather, in postconventional morality, meaning is endowed through the process of validation itself. In that sense the objective of communicative action is to disclose what lies beyond the lifeworld, that is, in universally shared principles of social action.

Notes

[1] Aesthetic in the sense that knowledge is not grounded on objective, rational or universal principles but is viewed as a product of human creativity, and is therefore a contingent product of human societies.

[2] For purposes of brevity, all parenthetic references to Habermas's work in the text will omit his name, and simply indicate relevant publication date and page number.

[3] Martin Seel explains the nature of aesthetic claims as follows: 'statements are *aesthetic* if they are asserted and justified with a view to lending the *object* of these statements validity as a reason for adopting world-shaping views' (Seel, 1991: 41).

[4] A society or individual that has achieved a certain level of moral reasoning, namely, the ability to detach itself from its particular context and apply universalisable principles of moral conduct, along the lines of Lawrence Kohlberg's developmental model of moral psychology. See Habermas (1993) and Benhabib (1992).

[5] For a brief and reasonably accessible account of Habermas's understanding of language and disclosure in his own words, see his 'Actions, Speech Acts, Linguistically Mediated Interactions and the Lifeworld' (1994). Also 'A Reply', especially pp. 214-28 (1991). Outhwaite (1994) provides a good general introduction to Habermas's work.

[6] Non-consensual strategic or instrumental action, or even argumentation, cannot be equated with communicative discourse, for the aims of the former extend outside the linguistic world; that is, they are oriented not towards an ideal of communication but to an ulterior purpose, realising values or ends that have *already* been decided (Outhwaite, 1994: 112).

[7] This does not mean that we live our lives pondering the validity of every speech act. The role of interpreter and actor are not identical, Habermas insists. The rational justification of validity claims can only occur when we 'suspend the validity naively imputed to value standards, facts, norms, and experiences, and instead deal *hypothetically* with the validity claims which have been *left open*' (1991: 227).

[8] In Habermas's words: 'Value standards and the corresponding evaluative utterances can be validated only indirectly, namely by means of authentically world-disclosing productions. Things are different in the case of factual, normative or experiential utterances. Here, their justification aims at proving the existence of factual matters, the acceptability of modes of action or norms, and the transparency of subjective experiences' (1991: 227).

[9] 'Manifestations display the same grammatical features as expressive speech acts – they are linked to claims of sincerity, truthfulness, or authenticity, but not to truth claims' (Habermas 1996: 11). In his *Theory of Communicative Action*, aesthetic validity is not dependent on the assent or agreement of all participants. Rather, the reasons given must be intelligible, and the motivations 'authentic' (1984: 16-20).

[10] On this point see especially Bernstein (1995) and Taylor (1991). See also Benhabib (1992) and Richard Bernstein's collection of critical essays (1985).

[11] Habermas recognises that the theoretically neat distinction between universal and particular knowledge, form and substance, cannot be sustained in practice. Although he insists on the primacy of universalist principles, somewhat akin to a deontological right over a teleological good, in practice how a norm is *applied* must be compatible with the social good; it must fulfil the needs and expectations of all those involved in a context sensitive manner, or else the norm is itself neither universalisable nor just. Any moral point, therefore, contains the two moments of normative universality and ethical-aesthetic particularity. While justification works at an abstract, universal level, application demands the integration of all spheres of knowledge, including world-disclosing modes. Several critics have pointed out that justification depends for its validity on the process of application, implying the reversal of the universal-particular hierarchy. Equally, however, the moment of justification cannot be lost, for without it knowledge loses the external criteria necessary for distinguishing between what a group of people *think* is right and what *is* right (see Habermas, 1993).

[12] Thus it might be observed that the often problematic distinction between the ethical and the moral is most clearly observed where conflict over values demands the intervention of moral, or universalisable, procedures.

[13] This is exemplified in Kant's moral imperative, which requires not the agreement of rational wills but an (individual) act of reason.

[14] See, for instance, Rousseau's *Discourse on Inequality* and Marx's *On the Jewish Question*.

[15] *The Weekend Australian*, 6-7 March, 1999.

[16] See Habermas, *Between Facts and Norms* (1996a).

References

Benhabib, S. (1990), 'Afterword' in S. Benhabib and F. Dallmayr (eds), *The Communicative Ethics Controversy*, MIT Press, Cambridge, Mass., pp. 330-369.

_____ (1992), *Situating the Self: Gender, Community and Postmodernism in Contemporary Ethics*, Polity Press, Cambridge.

Bernstein, J. (1995), *Recovering Ethical Life*, Polity Press, Cambridge.

Bernstein, R. (ed.) (1985), *Habermas and Modernity*, Polity Press, Cambridge.

Cooke, M. (1995), *Language and Reason: A Study of Habermas's Pragmatics*, MIT Press, Cambridge, Mass. and London.

Cronin, C. (1993), 'Preface' in J. Habermas, *Justification and Application*, Polity Press, Cambridge, pp. i-xxxi.

Eagleton, T. (1990), *The Ideology of the Aesthetic*, Blackwell, Oxford and Cambridge, Mass.

Günther, K. (1990), 'Impartial Application of Moral and Legal Norms: A Contribution to Discourse Ethics' in D. Rasmussen (ed.), *Universalism vs Communitarianism: Contemporary Debates in Ethics*, MIT Press, London and Cambridge, Mass., pp. 199-206.

Habermas, J. (1994), 'Actions, Speech Acts, Linguistically Mediated Interactions and the Lifeworld', *Philosophical Problems Today*, vol. 1, pp. 45-74.

_____ (1996a), *Between Facts and Norms: Contributions to a Discourse Theory of Law and Democracy*, W. Rehg trans., Polity Press, Cambridge.

_____ (1996b), 'Coping with Contingencies: The Return of Historicism' in J. Niznik and J.T. Sanders (eds), *Debating the State of Philosophy: Habermas, Rorty and Kolakowski*, Praeger Press, Connecticut, pp. 1-30.

_____ (1993), *Justification and Application*, C. Cronin trans., Polity Press, Cambridge.

_____ (1985), 'Questions and Counterquestions' in R. Bernstein (ed.), *Habermas and Modernity*, MIT Press, Cambridge, Mass., pp. 192-216.

_____ (1991), 'A Reply' in A. Honneth and H. Joas (eds), *Communicative Action*, Polity Press, Cambridge, pp. 214-264.

_____ (1984), *Theory of Communicative Action*, vol. 1, T. McCarthy trans., Beacon Press, Boston.

How, A. (1995), *The Habermas-Gadamer Debate and the Nature of the Social*, Avebury Press, London.

Larmore, C. (1996), *The Morals of Modernity*, Cambridge University Press, Cambridge.

Outhwaite, W. (1994), *Habermas: An Introduction*, Polity Press, Cambridge.

Rorty, R. (1996), 'The Notion of Rationality' in J. Niznik and J.T. Sanders (eds), *Debating the State of Philosophy: Habermas, Rorty and Kolakowski*, Praeger Press, Connecticut, pp. 84-88.

Schnädelbach, H. (1991), 'The Transformation of Critical Theory' in A. Honneth and H. Joas (eds), *Communicative Action*, Polity Press, Cambridge, pp. 7-22.

Seel, M. (1991), 'The Two Meanings of 'Communicative' Rationality: Remarks on Habermas's Critique of a Plural Concept of Reason' in A. Honneth and H. Joas (eds), *Communicative Action*, Polity Press, Cambridge, pp. 36-48.

Taylor, C. (1989), *Sources of the Self: The Making of Modern Identity*, Harvard University Press, Cambridge, Mass.

_____(1991), 'Language and Society' in A. Honneth and H. Joas (eds), *Communicative Action*, Polity Press, Cambridge, pp. 23-35.

3 Baring All: Self-Disclosure as Moral Exhortation

MARION MADDOX

Introduction: bared for action

Moral action, when we consider others' needs and experiences, takes us beyond ourselves. Politics also extends our concerns to the community of 'others'. A precondition for both encounters is difference. If there were no different needs, or if needs could be satisfied equally, moral action would have no meaning. Moral virtues such as sympathy and empathy would need no cultivation. Denunciation of moral vices such as selfishness would lose much of its sense. Politics, too, would be non-existent. Without the virtue of moderation, negotiation, diplomacy, leadership and compromise would be impossible. Political vices – for example, slander, bribery, bullying, blackmailing and ballot-rigging – would find no fertile ground.

We become aware of otherness through disclosure: from unconscious revelations through our body language, dress and gesture, to deliberate statements of experience or demands, or violent outbursts and political uprisings. Without the disclosure of difference, the situation is stable. I may think I know your needs, aspirations, resentments or desires; or I may be indifferent to them; or it may not even occur to me that your world exists for my consideration. When the process of disclosure begins, the situation becomes unstable: even if I do not change my perception of you, or my actions towards you, your attempts to have me know you surely disrupt the equilibrium in which we previously hung. I, in turn, wittingly or not, am impelled to some kind of action, whether to respond to your difference or to try to regain the prior stability.

Any communication – from a casual touch to 'I love you', from 'Pass the salt' to 'You are standing on my foot' – has many levels of meaning in its expression, complexities in its transmission, and confusions in its receipt. These difficulties assume an even greater intensity when making and receiving the disclosures of ultimately impassable difference which unleash the instability out of which moral and political action arise. You take my green shirt to be a simple fashion statement, until someone mentions that I am an Irish nationalist, but all the time I meant you to notice its pairing with purple trousers and that today is International Women's Day. My account of suffering, which I give as the basis of a demand for justice, you may hear as a potential threat, a selfish demand, empty whining, or perhaps not at all.

Given the convolutions through which all kinds of communication, inadvertent or deliberate, must pass, perhaps 'disclosure' with its connotations of sudden revelation and one-way communication is altogether too hopeful a term. If difference lies at the heart of moral and political enterprises, at the heart of difference lies mystery. Encountering others through their self-disclosure, we encounter also the realisation that self-disclosure is only ever fragmentary. Self-disclosure knows no final closure.

Put another way, the uncertainty and ephemerality of self-disclosure make the undertakings of moral or political engagement inherently optimistic: we know the gulf between our self and others, and we know it to be, at many levels, impassable, yet we try to make something out of it for our own or others' ends. Moral and political activity start from the premise that right can be discovered (or why look?), that empathy can be achieved (or why listen?), that negotiation can succeed (or why start?), that lives can be improved (or why try?). Reveal yourself to us: what do you want? what do you need? what is it like to be you? Or notice me revealing myself: through my placard, street parade, hunger strike, novel, poems, silence, illness, bearing, business card, suit, mobile phone. Then, surely, you will know what I want you to know about what it is like to be me. Then, surely, you will respond in the ways I want you to respond.

The language of moral and political discourse has undergone a sea-change in the closing decades of the twentieth century, moving away from the search for certainty and closure towards an appreciation of the moral and political challenge of inevitably fragmentary and ephemeral self-disclosure. This chapter charts this change by exploring two examples of moral discourse which appeal not to universal norms or generalisable principles but to self-disclosure as a means of moral motivation: World Vision's advertisements for child sponsorship and the World Council of Church's method of ecumenical moral reasoning.

Baring all for the best

In formal systems of moral philosophy and theology, disclosure has traditionally sought a private place. In the confessional, penitents disclose wrong-doing, while the priest reveals the remedy. In private prayer, devotees examine their conscience, baring their troubles to the divine. Disclosure is from the penitent to God (with or without an intermediary), and back again, in the form of appropriate penance or direct revelation. The casuistry of pre-Vatican II Roman Catholic ethics details penances for every conceivable misdeed and Protestants undergo relentless self-examination, painfully aware of their place in fallen humanity. Each set of pastoral and practical traditions issues in a system of moral theology whose aim is to ease the task of individuals and institutions in determining what is right and wrong. Secular moral philosophy also provides various systems to activate or train the mind to disclose the right to oneself through reason.

Over the last thirty years, these individualised approaches in formal systems of ethics have been challenged by a different kind of morally-oriented disclosure. Mutual self-disclosure among narrative partners has taken over from disclosure to and from the divine, or disclosure within the rational self.

In the 1960s and 70s, 'situation ethics' valued unmediated apprehension of a situation of moral choice, to be met by spontaneous response (Fletcher, 1966; Cox, 1968). My encounter with others and my empathy with their situation would provide the necessary framework for moral decision.

The revival of 'virtue ethics' in the 1980s provided a more complex story about what makes a virtuous person or a good citizen. 'Virtue ethics' points to the qualities I should cultivate, the attitudes I should develop, and the attentions I should bestow on others (Foot, 1978; MacIntyre, 1981; Pence, 1984).

In the 1980s and 1990s, 'narrative ethics' emphasises the communal nature of this moral development, hoping that the shared telling of stories will provide a path to moral conclusions. Narrative, through its multifarious development of metaphor, allusion and analogy, provides a means both to reveal and reflect on the experience of otherwise unknowable others (Brenner, 1994; Charon, 1994; Frank, 1995; Hauerwas, 1994; Montello, 1995; Newton, 1995; Roe, 1994).

Storytelling and intuitive responses have always had an important place in moral discourse from the Hebrew prophets' parables, which were told to kings and their subjects to inspire repentance, to the nineteenth-century literary denunciations of Charles Dickens or Harriet Beecher Stowe. While narrative and virtue ethics, at least, aim for more subtle accounts of moral dilemmas than is often given in literary polemic, one can look to the works of Charlotte Brontë and Anthony Trollope for examples of multifaceted moral conundrums in nineteenth-century literature. The flourishing of moral theory based on inter-personal disclosure in the late twentieth century, then, could be understood partly as a revival of what has long been a popular medium of moral thought, but one which has been suppressed within formal moral philosophy and theology.

Despite any continuities, however, it is important to note that the older traditions of moral storytelling also differ from the various kinds of 'disclosure ethics' which have emerged since the 1960s. Prophetic parables, hortatory epics and normative novels might adopt a first-person voice, but they still share the characteristic of being told from the outside. They are, as it were, mediated disclosures. Dickens was not himself a poor Londoner, nor Beecher Stowe a slave. For that matter, there is no indication that the prophet Nathan had personally suffered from the death of Uriah the Hittite, nor Amos from Israel's 'trampling on the poor'. Tellers of stories in this 'prophetic' moral tradition take up verbal cudgels on others' behalf.

The strands of ethics which have emerged since the 1960s, by contrast, are more likely to emphasise first-person disclosure.[1] In situation ethics, the focus remains on the individual making a moral decision, but that person's choices are seen to be formed by circumstances. The motive for disclosure is no longer either internal to the deciding person, or a communicative act between that person and the divine, but comes partly from an individual's apprehension of the situation. My decision about what to do, as in older forms of ethics, remains internal to myself, but part of the crucial disclosure which makes that decision possible comes from the world, potentially destabilising established principles. No two situations are exactly alike: the world will not speak to me the same way twice.

In narrative ethics, stories become the means by which a community thinks through various moral possibilities, weighing competing principles and anticipating a range of outcomes. Along the way, participants may disclose elements of their own experience which contribute to a bigger picture; ultimately, the community's collective mind sees possibilities which lone thinkers could not envision.

Virtue ethics takes this appreciation for the social dimension of individuals' moral decisions beyond the collective moral story to embrace the individuals who contribute to it. No-one becomes virtuous on their own: moral personality is formed in community, as members shape and condition one another's visions of what it means to be a good person, a good family member, a good professional, a good citizen and a member of a good society. Morally efficacious disclosure has taken on a public dimension: no longer alone with God or wrestling within one's own reason or conscience, moral personality is formed through conversation.

Two utopias: deliberative and communicative disclosure

I began by arguing that moral action and political engagement, and the kinds of reflection which accompany them, are rooted in difference. Formal debates about discerning right action have shifted away from their traditional, private assumptions about the structure of moral decision, towards seeing disclosure within a community or in the context of a specific situation as a driving force in moral choice. Across barriers of difference, disclosure provides enough instability for change to begin. A political parallel to the developments in ethics which I have been describing has come in an upsurge of attention to the conditions for democracy.

Democratic theory and practice attempts to institutionalise ways for conversation to be carried out, for disclosures to be made. Citizens engage in mutual disclosure of their needs, wishes, fears and resentments through the ballot box, on the street, at local meetings and in letters to the editor. Proponents of deliberative democracy argue for more of these encounters: reveal more of yourself, hear more of others' revelations, transparently and sincerely expressed, rationally offered and fairly heard, in a free public square. By following the rules of deliberative communication, we can overcome differences in background and assumptions enough to reach a common starting-point. The process of communication which lies behind models of deliberative democracy rests on the streak of hope that if we only had enough disclosures of the right kind, which are derived by following fair procedural rules, the ground would be laid out for fruitful moral action and successful political interaction. Ultimately, we can reconcile differences: a difference disclosed is the first step to mutuality.

In 'Communication and the Other: Beyond Deliberative Democracy', Iris Young (1995) shares the call for more disclosure, but her charter goes further than the architects of deliberative democracy. More rational sharing of experience and information is not enough: that sharing must come in more varied kinds, with more flexible rules of procedure.

Young suggests that deliberative theorists' calls for transparent communication between free and uncoerced communicative partners are a good first step to democracy. Such disclosure 'creates a public, citizens coming together to talk about collective problems, goals, ideals and actions'. Rather than simply insisting on their own interests, players in the deliberative forum 'are careful to sort out good reasons from bad, valid arguments from invalid.' The game of deliberative democracy has rules: 'The interlocutors properly discount bad reasons and speeches that are not well argued, and they ignore or discount rhetorical flourishes and emotional outbursts' (1995: 135).

But Young wants us to be suspicious. The utopia drawn by theorists of deliberative democracy, where all citizens communicate freely and rationally, and without concealment, is a country in which not everyone can be a citizen. The country's publicists are those theoreticians who invite us in to experience rational discourse and feel 'the force of the better argument', until we reach consensus or, failing that, majority conclusions in which everyone has been heard. No inequality of wealth or political clout will prevent you speaking in our town squares, they entice. But, Young cautions, there are other factors than political and economic power which might turn potential immigrants back at the borders:

> the social power which can prevent people from being equal speakers derives...also from an internalised sense of one's right to speak or not to speak, and from the devaluation of some people's style of speech and the elevation of others (1995: 137).

She warns that truly democratic conversation needs room not just for the measured tones of the deliberative theorists, but for styles of communication which are often devalued. If the deliberative country is a utopia, its origins and traditions reach back into *topoi* – commonplace themes and motifs – we know and can identify. The 'institutional forms, rules, rhetorical and cultural styles' valued by deliberative theorists are those of Western society's most powerful institutions: 'scientific debate, modern Parliaments and courts'. These, in turn, have a pedigree 'in ancient Greek and Roman philosophy and politics and in the medieval academy'(1995: 135). The deliberative utopia brings its border guards from those familiar places: they are 'norms of deliberation' which 'privilege speech that is dispassionate and disembodied':

> They tend to presuppose an opposition between mind and body, reason and emotion. They tend falsely to identify objectivity with calm and absence of emotional expression. Expressions of anger, hurt or passionate concern discount claims and reasons they accompany. Similarly, the entrance of the body into speech – in wide gestures, nervous movements or physical expressions of emotion – are signs of weakness that cancel out one's assertions or reveal one's lack of objectivity and control. Deliberative norms also tend to privilege 'literal' language over figurative language such as hyperbole, metaphor and so on (1995: 139).

Whether or not one agrees with Young's characterisation of deliberative democracy and its theorists, her next step takes us into challenging territory. Young effectively proposes her own utopia: a communicative democracy in which different styles of communication, and the communication of difference, can be equally valued. Immigrants to this utopia could include not only those proficient in the valued, typically masculine form of 'assertive and confrontational' speech which 'is formal and general, that proceeds from premise to conclusion in an orderly fashion', but also those whose speech follows the typically feminine form of being 'tentative, exploratory and conciliatory' (1995: 138-39). Those culturally given or personally inclined to dramatic, passionate, or emotional speech could be citizens alongside the rational, the calm and the ordered.

In Young's utopia, critical argument is only one common language; speakers must also master the forms of greeting, rhetoric and storytelling. Greeting, depicted by Young as 'the vice of flattery' in Plato's *Gorgias*,[2] is recast as a virtue which smoothes the rocky progress of communication across difference with 'gestures of politeness and deference', together with 'non-linguistic gestures that bring people together warmly, seeing conditions for amicability: smiles, handshakes, hugs, the giving and taking of food and drink' (1995: 145). Rhetoric orientates speech to its listeners by constructing the situations of speaker and hearer, and by luring the listener through the workings of desire (1995: 146). Storytelling gives speaker-citizens a way of sharing the particularities of experience across the barriers of difference: 'narrative exhibits subjective experience to other subjects. It can evoke sympathy while maintaining distance because it also carries an inexhaustible latent shadow, the transcendence of the Other, that there is always more to be told' (1995: 147). In Young's utopia, difference is neither a hurdle to be jumped over before communication can take place nor a barrier to be torn down in the process of deliberation, but a resource for the political enterprise, preserved even as the participants arrive at a point of mutual 'understanding' (1995: 143).

Bearing witness: disclosure as exhortation

Young's utopia recalls real-world movements for greater understanding through storytelling as a spur to moral action on the part of listeners. Having charted a shift to interpersonal disclosure in moral and political theory, I wish to turn to two popular, relatively informal sources of moral discourse which parallel moves towards less private forms of disclosure-oriented ethics. In part, each may owe something to the Christian revival movements of the nineteenth century in which personal testimony became a significant and, importantly, unchallengeable source for moral and religious reflection. These popular movements use a distinctive method based on self-disclosure by people in situations of poverty and oppression. In each case, such self-disclosure is meant to awaken the consciences of people in wealthy countries, sensitising them to global injustice. But spurring those in wealthy countries to create a more equitable world in the future is not the only aim. In each case, a distinctive method uses elements of communication which match up well with aspects of Young's communicative utopia. Through their characteristic use of interpersonal communication, each aims to create just economic and human relationships in the present.

The first example uses disclosure about the details of individuals' lives to elicit moral action on the part of other individuals. World Vision International (WVI) has, over the last half-century, developed a highly recognisable style of moral discourse in which potential donors are told a little about the life of a suffering third world child to lure them into closer interaction. The relationship begins with the donor sending money to alleviate the child's distress and develops through an exchange of letters and photographs. This relationship, with the expectation of ever-increasing amounts of mutual self-disclosure between donor and recipient, is seen by the agency not just as an educational exercise which is personally fulfilling for both parties, but importantly as a key to maintaining the donor's moral motivation.

In my second example, the focus shifts from individual moral motivation to collective action with a political direction. The World Council of Churches (WCC) is an international, ecumenical body of Christian churches founded in 1948 but with roots extending well back into the nineteenth century. Although it has an aid and development unit, the WCC's main objective is to foster Christian unity and greater social justice through the twin activities of doctrinal negotiation and collective action by churches, both locally and internationally. The self-disclosure style of moral discourse characteristic of the WCC since the 1960s is the product of a long attempt to find a method which could provide a common starting point for people who would otherwise begin their reflections from an almost prohibitively wide range of cultural, theological and philosophical positions. Unlike World Vision donors, delegates to WCC conferences are likely to have formal theological or philosophical qualifications which are rooted in their particular cultural, academic and religious traditions. When positions are so highly diverse, the task of arriving at mutually acceptable conclusions is made all the more difficult. A method of moral discourse based on personal disclosure thus became the substitute for an agreed theological or philosophical base among conference delegates.

Both WVI and the WCC have large organisational structures which include theological units to provide formal moral and, in the WCC's case, political theory. My examination here, however, focuses on activities designed to evoke a response in lay people that does not require acquiescence to a formal theological position. In this respect both have been influential purveyors of a distinctive kind of popular moral or political discourse: 'sponsor a child' programs are widely recognised and imitated by some aid agencies, while a number of the WCC's social justice programs have drawn international attention to a range of human rights, environmental and social issues.

Each example illustrates a different way of developing moral discourse out of the disclosure of otherness. Nevertheless, they share striking similarities: each has developed, in practice, a tendency to focus on suffering as the crucial matter of self-disclosure. Because both emphasise something like personal interaction (albeit mediated through a range of institutional structures) as source material for moral and political reflection, they help to illuminate some dimensions of the multi-levelled communication across difference which this kind of disclosure entails. They also draw attention to various possibilities and pitfalls which accompany the precarious task of disclosure across difference.

Bare facts: sponsoring a child through World Vision

World Vision International provides aid to communities in the third world from donors in the first world. From a potential donor's first contact with the agency through advertisements in newspapers and magazines, stories of suffering children are intended to spur people to put their hands in their pockets. 'In Australia, a pot belly often means *too* much beer,' admonishes a typical advertisement in a women's magazine. It goes on to inform us that '[i]n Africa, it usually means severe malnutrition – a disease caused by lack of protein'. Next to the text, a child stands with her dress pulled up under her chin, while the copy continues:

> For Monica, who lives in Zambia, this is only the beginning of the trouble. She has contracted a parasitic flatworm from contaminated water. Her brothers and sisters have been sick with malaria and malnutrition. Her family will soon run out of food and their house is falling to pieces.

> Fortunately, a World Vision Child Sponsorship program has meant Monica and all the children in her village will now get regular medical check-ups and healthcare. Monica's family is receiving supplementary food, and her father has received fertilizers and agricultural training. Her mother is going to nutrition classes. The community will also have clean water.

> But thousands of other desperate children in Africa, Asia and Latin America do not have sponsors yet. Please help one (*New Idea*, 1987).

Information on how to become a sponsor is followed with the promise: 'We'll send you a photo and history of a child, followed by progress reports. And you can correspond.'

Monica's story illustrates a kind of discourse for which WVI has been widely criticised. Throughout the 1970s and 1980s, in particular, a number of overseas aid organisations argued that such stories and photos exploit the children and deceive donors. Critics claimed that individual child sponsorship isolates aid beneficiaries from their communities, privileges some while leaving their neighbours unaided, perpetuates a view of poor people as everlasting helpless victims, and promotes a relationship of dependency between child and sponsor. At the same time, such advertising misleads donors as the concentration on the plight of a single child obscures the political and social dimensions of famine and poverty.

In response, World Vision changed some of its practices. While World Vision Australia's *1996 Annual Report* still devotes four glossy pages to 'Our Focus: The Child', the organisation has also, at least since the mid-1980s, supplemented its assistance to individual children with increasing attention to 'community development'. The promotional magazine *World Vision News* includes stories of former sponsored children now grown up and doing well, and stories of present beneficiaries of sponsorship, but it also tells of families who, although their children do not have an overseas sponsor, still benefit from the sponsorship program operating in their district (World Vision Australia, 1997b).

At the same time, other World Vision programs have developed a more political edge. Projects with indigenous Australians begun in 1979 to foster 'Christian leadership' now include 'health care, education, business development and appropriate technology' (World Vision Australia, 1996: 13), while a 1997 issue of World Vision's *Action News* begins a feature on 'reconciliation' with a quotation from indigenous activist Pat Dodson, then chair of the Council for Aboriginal Reconciliation. Inside, subscribers can read an account of the politically fraught Australian Reconciliation Convention, where disillusioned delegates dramatically turned their backs during the Prime Minister's address. The last page offers advice on framing a petition to Members of Parliament (1979a: 1-8).

Although World Vision has modified its practice in response to criticism of ethical problems with the 'one child at a time' approach, it continues to promote itself as though nothing has changed. The shift may become apparent to donors once they have joined the organisation and become recipients of internal publications like World Vision's *Action News*, but advertisements still exhort unfledged donors to join up in return for photos, progress reports and personal letters from 'their' child. The reason is simple: the quasi-fiction of individual child sponsorship draws funds like no other marketing technique. Advertisements show a child gazing appealingly up at the reader. The text emphasises personal connection by calling the child by his or her given name and addressing the reader directly: '*You* can be the lifeline!' As emotions translate into donations, the figures demonstrate the effectiveness of this Gorgias-like rhetoric. The *1996 Annual Report* draws readers' attention to the fact that '[p]rograms funded through Child Sponsorship remain World Vision Australia's major contribution to development needs overseas' with Child Sponsorship donations leading the 'Revenue' list in the columns of figures headed 'Operating Highlights' (World Vision Australia, 1996: 15).

The Report further details the programs funded by these child sponsorship dollars 'includ[ing] smaller community development projects, larger area development programs and some projects catering for groups' special needs'. But a potential donor, to find this out, would need knowledge well beyond anything contained in the advertisements. A *World Vision News* story called 'On A New Learning Curve' carries the telling strap: 'World Vision Child Sponsors in Australia are playing a part in bringing real benefits to remote Indonesian villages *in ways they probably never imagined*' (World Vision Australia, 1997b: 18; my emphasis). Nevertheless, in newspapers and magazines, on billboards and television, celebrities continue to cuddle famished African or Asian children and enthuse about how this meeting changed their life, how it can also change a child's life, and how you, too, can share the feeling of changing a life, for thirty-one dollars a month.

Baring children

Monica's story, like the stories of Tendai, Tawanda, Sarlotha, Sarun and countless others in a range of media, is told in the third person. Rather than the child's own voice, it offers a rhetorically-structured account generic in World Vision advertising (Maddox, 1993). Yet once a donor has clipped the coupon, communication is meant to become more spontaneous: you can expect a real disclosure of subjective experience, progressively opening up as you advance in intimacy, from looking at a photo and reading a history to engaging in correspondence.

This is certainly how donors, at least, appear to read the promise that 'you can correspond'. A child does not simply eat, learn and is thereby cured. Regular letters and photos inform the sponsor how many inches the child has grown, how far he or she has progressed at school and how his or her state of health has improved. This reflects a somewhat clinical style of revelation, or 'laying bare', pervasive in World Vision images of its beneficiaries in advertising photos of near-naked children, the heavy emphasis on health information about particular programs, and communications between the organisation and donors. In this process of 'laying bare', the child's body itself becomes a site of disclosure (Maddox, 1993).

Critics, especially during the 1980s, argued that this objectification, together with one-to-one contact between financially dependent children and their adult benefactors, seemed to invite the donor to demand intrusive amounts of information and to intrude alien values and expectations upon recipient children. Indeed, critics have pointed out that sponsors' letters often work hard to elicit personal information, from 'are you studying hard?' to questions about Christian faith. 'Mind your own business' – even politely euphemised – is likely to be a hard thing to say to someone who is providing you with clothing, food, education and health care which you would not otherwise have.

World Vision, not surprisingly, sees this process of disclosure in a different light: for example, *World Vision News* offers encouragement to donors to engage in correspondence which fosters genuine disclosure. One issue not only recounts donor stories, but reprints an award-winning letter first published in a mass-circulation women's magazine, in which a donor describes the feelings evoked by sponsoring a 'little Thai boy', Jirasak:

> I loved getting his letters and hearing about his life, seeing him grow stronger and more handsome in every photograph. Knowing I was helping this child improve his life through education and even helping his village was very fulfilling ('M. L.', 1997).

Such stories are common, but the struggle for disclosure and the donor's sense of its importance are seldom as poignantly documented as in Pamela Blower's 'Our Child in Haiti'. Her eventual feeling of fulfilment was achieved only with the exercise of great patience in developing 'this long-distance, strangely intimate relationship':

> We were encouraged to develop a close relationship with the child, and it hasn't been easy. Our personal letters frequently met with impersonal, even evasive replies. It's nice, of course, to know that Mucianie is praying for us. We do that for her. But I so much wanted to hear the little things she got up to. Maybe that's selfish – our giving tainted by wanting to take – but it's human. On the other hand, when the breaches in the barriers did start to happen, our delight was all the greater (Blower, 1987).

Eventually, Mucianie provided the kind of personal revelation the Blower family was hoping for: 'At Christmas, we received a special surprise: some first rather wobbly attempts at writing. Were we ever proud!' Readers are not told the words which Mucianie wrote. Nevertheless, the family clearly felt this move from mediated self-disclosure (through a letter-writer) to direct self-disclosure (in her own writing) was a significant step in their relationship. At the same time, the Blower family experienced this process as an emotional journey from thwarted desire (to 'hear the little things she gets up to') through delight to pride.

Why should the donors be *proud* of 'their' child's writing? WVI goes to some lengths to foster a feeling of 'family' between donors and children. For example, one advertising brochure presents snapshots of unsponsored children in a mocked-up family album, with the captions, 'Could your family be MISSING one of these children?' and 'A hurting child like one of these is simply a family member you don't know yet!' Donors' pride in 'their' children's achievements is surely like any parent's pride in their child.

Yet these children are already members of families. The fine print in the 'Photo Album' advertisement reveals, for example, that Khothatso's family 'lives in a rural area where life is a constant struggle against poverty'; Daice's 'father barely earns enough to support the family'; Lovena's 'mother struggles to give Lovena essentials we take for granted in Australia'; and Sajith's 'family earns such a low wage that they cannot provide for Sajith'. Presenting 'hurting children' as being in need of families echoes WVI's origins in caring for orphaned children after the Korean war (WVI, 1997). When the children so presented are not orphans, however, the picture that is painted in such personal terms might be read as the parents' failure, rather than the result of international inequality which makes the parents' task impossible.

In contrast with the apparent failure of the children's parents, the Blower family has a very clear, itemised knowledge of what their money buys for Mucianie's education: 'tuition, books, teaching aids, school clothes, health care and lunch, which may be the only proper meal she gets' (Blower, 1987). In light of such an inventory, Mucianie's wobbly writing begins to seem less her own achievement than that of her donor family.

Who bares what to whom?

World Vision makes available not only stories of what it is like to be a sponsor, but also reflections by children who have grown up and cut loose from the donor relationship. Their recollections emphasise a different kind of intimacy:

> My sponsor (an Australian lady)...encouraged me in my studies. She taught
> me to leave my future in God's hands, for Him to direct. Her
> letters...contained a wealth of Christian faith and values. She shaped me and
> put me on the right path (cited in World Vision Australia, 1997b: 23).

The sponsor's Christian faith was conveyed not only through her
letters but also by the mediating organisation: under World Vision's care,
the child received 'moral and spiritual training' along with 'educational
benefits'. Such accounts bear out Stalker's (1982) observations about
donors' attempts to inculcate a value system through letters and donations.

World Vision donors, as they clip the coupon, embark on a journey.
They begin as readers of a third person story in a magazine advertisement.
On payment of thirty-one dollars a month, they begin the possibly
demanding process of eliciting responses in a one-to-one relationship
structured around the expectation of the disclosure of subjective
experience. Occasionally sponsors make the physical journey to meet their
child, but the main focus of the relationship remains on correspondence,
perhaps intensifying the pressure for more and more epistolary self-
disclosure from 'their' child. In return, the child also sets out on a journey
into regular communication with someone from outside their community,
frequently someone motivated by a strong value system. The relationship is
superficially like having a pen-friend in another country. However, the fact
that one partner is supplying the other with the means of subsistence means
the relationship, billed in the 'Photo Album' brochure as 'a deeply personal
and satisfying act of caring', can never proceed on anything approaching
grounds of mutuality. While one ubiquitous theme in World Vision
advertising is the idea of sponsorship as 'relationship', 'communication'
and 'personal caring', it runs in parallel with another theme which
promotes the donor's feelings of potency compared with the child's
powerlessness: 'You can be the lifeline!'; 'Your *love* will give them hope!'
'This opportunity puts *power in your hands* to change a child's life'.

Unfortunately, much less is known about the personal disclosures
donors make to 'their' children than about what donors hope to elicit from
them. Donors reveal their own faith and values, but do they write about 'the
little things they get up to' or tell their child about the difficulties in their
own lives? Critics of child sponsorship programs have pointed out that such
reciprocity might not be a good idea:

> Manuel...lives in a squalid slum on the edge of a Latin American city. The
> regular letters he gets from his sponsoring family give accounts of their
> interesting lives – of skiing holidays in Austria, for example. For the
> European family this correspondence might offer an interesting educational

experience for their own children. What Manuel gets from it, apart from a vague feeling of inferiority, is much less clear (Stalker, 1982: 8).

Some sponsorship charities discourage long and detailed correspondence for precisely such reasons (Australian Consumers' Association, 1983: 12). Donors' accounts of their side of the relationship do not disclose enough about their letters for us to know what, or how much, they disclose to 'their' children.

Baring hearts

The disclosures fostered by World Vision's child sponsorship program are designed to elicit a specific moral response. Confrontation with another's needs draws a direct connection from heart-string to hip-pocket. It is clear from both the program's success compared to other kinds of overseas aid donor programs and World Vision's responses to its critics over a sustained period that the 'starving child' genre of advertising moves donors who are not moved in other ways. For example, a report on the costs and benefits of child sponsorship quoted a World Vision official:

> We try to approach people on a level that challenges them to give. Once they've responded we can begin to show them through articles in our publications that people in Third World countries have great dignity and they are resourceful. But if you don't talk to people in terms of what they believe about the Third World and human needs, in many instances what you're trying to say just goes right by them (Australian Consumers' Association, 1983: 14).

Presumably, many people who become child sponsors have already passed by the more sustained arguments about the political causes of poverty, or the moral responsibility of those in the developed world presented in other agencies' advertisements.[3] Donors typically describe their decision to join the child sponsorship program in terms of a split-second impulse produced by an emotionally moving advertisement or World Vision documentary. 'The photograph was of a skeletal child, very close to death', reports Jirasak's sponsor of the picture which inspired her. 'I was sitting in my office when I saw it and just cried and cried. I cut out that picture and hung it on my office wall and right then and there decided I had to do something to help these wretched children'. She sent the coupon immediately; 'one of the best decisions I have ever made' ('M. L.', 1997).

In Young's model of the communication of difference, the initial moral trigger is a form of disclosure in which critical argument is likely to be the least important element. In the case of 'M. L.', the visual spur possesses a dramatic and emotional appeal. Young's categories of greeting, rhetoric and storytelling are prominent in the text accompanying this visual representation. Storytelling elicits a response of compassion and a desire to 'do something'. Headlines and copy address the reader directly: 'Your impact on a needy child is staggering'; 'You can give them happy childhood memories and a dream of a future'. Once the correspondence is established, greeting would incorporate both the conventions of letter-writing such as 'Dear Mucianie' and more specific indications of care: 'We are praying for you'.

'Desire', in Young's sense, is the rhetorical component of communication which orients the content towards the listener. It is activated in a number of ways. First, there is the immediate appeal of a child's gaze. Visual techniques usually emphasise both the subject's dependency and otherness. The sense of dependency is heightened, for example, by the child looking up at an adult-height camera, while the subject's otherness is enhanced by cutting around the child's outline so that no background or context is shown beyond the advertising text contoured around it (Maddox, 1993). Secondly, there is the promise of immediate rewards: 'You'll receive a photo, detailed background information, history and progress reports'. Finally, there is the prospect of long-term personal fulfilment: 'Your life will change too'; 'You'll have the satisfaction of knowing that you've helped a child'.

Many of WVI's critics object to the interlocutor's rhetoric in these advertisements. However, if the function of the relationship from WVI's point of view is to stimulate and sustain the sponsor's compassion, an emphasis upon correspondence is an effective way to 'seduce' (Young, 1995: 146) both parties into the developing relationship. Both the sense of an unfolding relationship and awareness of another's circumstances are developed through storytelling. The effectiveness of this kind of communication is demonstrated in World Vision's unparalleled share of private overseas aid donations.

The kind of storytelling which Young advocates as part of her extended model of deliberative democracy is one which 'can evoke sympathy while maintaining distance because it also carries an inexhaustible latent shadow, the transcendence of the Other, that there is always more to be told' (1995: 147). The inequalities of both wealth and rhetorical position which are inherent in the exchange between donor and child have the potential, however, to mask the shadow, at least from the donors' point of view. While there might be 'always more to be told' about the details of 'their' children's lives, the construction of donors as omnipotent saviours deflects inquiry about the reasons for the child's poverty or possible solutions. Mucianie's sponsors' realisation that 'there is always more to be told' challenges them to elicit more and more personal information, rather than acting as a reminder that we can never know all about another person or their situation.

The elements of greeting, rhetoric and personal disclosure of intimate details stimulate and maintain a response in the form of moral action by the donor. Certainly, the inequalities of the respective participants' positions, the unavoidably constrained nature of relationships mediated through an institution, and the deferral of critical reflection about the power relationships involved mean that the interactions take place very far from Young's democratic utopia. Nevertheless World Vision's success in eliciting donations through its style of advertising and promise of personal correspondence underlines the effectiveness of using such personal elements in attempting to elicit moral action.

Widening the dialogue: disclosure in the World Council of Churches

Member churches of the World Council of Churches (WCC) are among WVI's critics. The WCC's primary focus is not on direct aid programs, but on the promotion of Christian unity. An important part of this effort is directed towards achieving united action for social justice. At international conferences, consultations and hearings, and through publications, WCC delegates and adherents of member churches are invited to hear personal disclosures of subjective experience of suffering. The aim is to move them to try actively to alter the circumstances of this suffering. The WCC's disclosure-based method of social ethics has a long and complicated history.

The WCC's birth in post-war Amsterdam in 1948 saw the incorporation of two pre-existing ecumenical organisations, the World Conference on Faith and Order and the Universal Christian Council on Life and Work (UCCLW). Under new names, they now constitute major streams in the WCC's structure. The Faith and Order Commission, as the former World Conference became, concentrates on matters of doctrine, while the WCC's Subunit on Church and Society inherited the UCCLW's emphasis on the quest for greater social justice along with its slogan, 'Doctrine Divides, Service Unites'. It was not that the social reformers thought doctrine unimportant. Rather, they saw potentially intractable doctrinal disagreements eased, in many cases, by the experience of working together across difference to achieve political or social results.

This tradition remains. Less durable, however, was the method for ethical reflection originally developed by UCCLW to decide which issues should be addressed, what kind of social action should be taken and how it could best be carried out.

Dialogue, difference and reason in the community of nations

For the century leading up to the WCC's formal foundation, the ecumenical organisations shared a commitment to dialogue as a means to achieve unity between churches, peace among nations, an end to child labour, and greater justice between classes, races and sexes (Rouse and Neill, 1986). This passion for dialogue arose from a greater recognition of difference which was a feature not only of the ecumenical movement but a range of social movements at the end of the nineteenth century.

Transportation by steam made international conferences feasible. European Christians, at least, got to encounter a degree of difference face to face. Through the burgeoning international missionary movement, European and North American Christians met people whose lives would otherwise have remained largely unknown to them. At the same time, different churches found themselves effectively as trade rivals in the mission fields. Unable to help noticing that this rivalry was an anomalous position for preachers of love and unity, they were spurred to pursue paths of greater cooperation and understanding with one another.

This wave of optimism about the world-changing potential of communication and solidarity was not limited to ecumenical bodies. While the WCC's predecessors in Christian socialist movements were consolidating themselves, the First International inaugurated in 1864 was bringing together socialists from the major countries of Western Europe to declare their common interests and strategies. From 1887 proponents of Esperanto hoped a common language could foster mutual understanding. Early in the twentieth century, embryonic secular peace movements advocated international unity and cooperation, and the Industrial Workers of the World advocated One Big Union to break the power of exploitative capital. Meanwhile, in 1910, churches from Germany, Belgium, France, England, Italy and Switzerland formed *La Fédération Internationale des Chrétiens Sociaux* to be followed, when the political pressures of 1914 suggested a new focus, by the World Alliance for Promoting Peace Through the Churches. The ecumenical fervour for dialogue across barriers of difference in the nineteenth and early twentieth centuries blew with the spirit of the times.

Yet, from its earliest tremors through the WCC's formal inauguration in 1948 to the 1960s, the ecumenical movement for all its cosmopolitan enthusiasm remained dominated by European and North American Protestant churches. Devoting a great deal of its time and attention to questions of social ethics, the movement found comparatively little difficulty in developing methods and procedures to which all participants in the international conversation could subscribe. The Protestant heritage of almost all participants along with their common theological traditions, a shared commitment to empirical methods of problem-solving, and their faith in the products of secular reason provided a solid foundation for unified action for economic, industrial and social progress.

Out of this shared intellectual and historical background the ecumenical movement developed a distinctive method for 'doing' social ethics, retrospectively named the 'Oldham Method' after its founding father, J.H. Oldham (1874-1969). The method involves four distinct steps:

1. To discover the men and women who can best help the churches understand the nature of the crisis of society;
2. To arrive with the help of these men and women at a definition of the fundamental issues with which the churches should be concerned in order to render their witness to society;
3. To promote an interdisciplinary approach between theologians and lay people;
4. To present the results to the churches for study and action (Visser't Hooft, 1985: 3-9).

Protestant to its bootstraps, this method emphasises study, discussion and the testimony of secular 'experts'. Faced with a social issue, Oldham's way to address it was to bring together a committee of theologians, social scientists and natural scientists, and preferably some United States' Senators, United Nations representatives and entrepreneurs with funding potential. Oldham's method was sometimes summarised in the quip, 'find out where the power is, and lunch with it'.[4]

The Oldham method emphasised academic analysis of social ills, consultation with experts in various fields, and study and action by the churches who receive their reports. This method was used for a good many decades and allowed the ecumenical movement to consider a range of questions which were revolutionary in their day. It worked well in a social and intellectual milieu in which the advice of experts and academic reasoning are valued, and there is general agreement about what a good, or at least better, society would look like. With its emphasis on reasoned argument, mutually respectful debate and adherence to the rules of procedure, the Oldham method had much in common with deliberative democracy.

From knowing all to baring all

The WCC learned more of what it meant to be ecumenical at its 1961 New Delhi Assembly where it received its first Pentecostal member churches and a large influx of third world churches. It also received the Russian Orthodox church into full membership the same year. This burgeoning of cultural, economic and theological diversity, encapsulated in the slogan, 'widening the ecumenical dialogue', had major ramifications for the ecumenical movement, particularly in the area of social ethics. The Oldham method's generally Protestant emphasis on secular authority made little sense to the Orthodox. Its appeal to scientific and social scientific expertise made even less sense to delegates from the third world where liberation movements were starting to suggest that Western technological and scientific dominance had created many of their social problems in the first place.

A new way of talking about social ethics had to be found. Inspired by developments in the sociology of knowledge but also in response to the pressing practical exigencies of an increasingly confrontational, diverse and unwieldy ecumenical field, the WCC evolved more flexible methods. The new focus was on direct political action in place of often drawn-out theological and sociological study, and on the experience of the victims of social ills rather than on the analysis of experts. No longer were the churches to address questions of social ethics mainly by asking an 'expert' opinion. The appropriate method for social ethics, now, was to 'listen to the victims', and the task of the churches was to be 'the voice of the voiceless'. In the widened ecumenical field, canonical pronouncements, traditional authority and expert opinions were open to question.

Consequently, from the 1960s ecumenical writing on social and political issues saw a shift in the locus of authority to personal disclosure of the lived experience of victims of oppression. Phrases such as 'the epistemological privilege of the poor' came to encapsulate the idea that both religious insight and ethical competence arise, first of all, out of the experience of suffering. Such concepts became the dominant meta-ethical theme running through the WCC's post-1960s writing on social ethics. The 'epistemological privilege of the poor' became the tool by which all other norms and principles could be relativised: a moral position would stand or fall not by its abstract logic, universalisability or congruence with doctrine, but by its consonance or dissonance with the perspective of 'the poor'. First-person narratives of suffering thus became pivotal to the structure of ecumenical moral reasoning.

Baring burdens

The ethical focus on the 'victim' is indebted to the influence of third world theologies such as Korean *minjung* theology which emphasises the special role of 'the poorest of the poor'. At a seminal WCC conference in 1979, Korean theologian Kim Yong-Bock advocated a 'theology of victims' (Kim, 1986a: 50), a point which he put even more strongly in an article for the WCC's Subunit on Church and Society:

> The victims of power and technology hold privileged knowledge not understood by the experts, the scientists, the academics. For they hold an epistemological advantage. The victims have a special knowledge and experience of history, real history, of which those who are in control are completely unaware (Kim, 1986b: 2).

Among frequent discussions of this idea came a report of the WCC's 1981 Consultation on Political Ethics:

> As followers of Jesus Christ, the suffering servant, the churches in the ecumenical community are called upon to share in the pain of the world. The incarnation of God in Christ found its fulfilment on the cross, which is the symbol of the power of love against the love of power; ecumenical solidarity can take the form of an 'incarnational' participation in the suffering of the people as they seek to transform their political predicament. The suffering of the people constitutes in itself a witness against the illegitimacy of power, crying out not only for its rectification but for a fundamental transformation (World Council of Churches, 1982).

Here is a stark contrast to the rugged optimism about the human place in the created order and the prospects for human betterment which characterised the Protestant-dominated period of ecumenical social ethics up until the late 1960s. Certain human beings were now seen to hold an epistemological and even spiritual advantage by virtue of their 'victim' status.

A striking example of this post-1960s style of moral deliberation can be found in the WCC's 1990 convocation at Seoul on the theme of 'Justice, Peace and the Integrity of Creation'. Before the convocation, delegates received a number of preliminary documents, including *Between the Flood and the Rainbow* (World Council of Churches, 1989). Its opening section, a striking example of the 'victim' emphasis, recalls the ecumenical movement's Protestant, empirical tradition by opening with the subheading, 'The Realities We Face'. Yet it deals with those 'realities' in ways that relegate the Oldham method to a distant echo. The five 'realities' identified are 'The Reign Of Injustice', 'The Reign Of Violence', 'The

Disintegration Of Creation' and 'Interconnecting Dimensions Of Our Crisis'. Each of these is further divided into subsections. For example, 'The Reign Of Injustice' is divided into 'The Scandal of Poverty', 'Violations of Human Rights', 'The Sin of Sexism' and 'The Tenacity of Racism'. Each subdivision offers a barrage of statistics reminiscent of the Oldham method but, importantly, the statistics are followed in most cases by a first-person narrative by someone represented as a victim of the scandal, violation, sin or tenacious evil under discussion.

'The Scandal of Poverty' opens with UNICEF statistics on hunger and economic resource distribution and International Labour Organisation statistics on income levels of third world people. This data is followed by four descriptive paragraphs outlining the effects of poverty on its victims. For example:

> To be poor is to live daily on the edge of despair. Poverty mutilates the human spirit. It makes people refugees in their own homes, alienating them from one another and conditioning their communal, familial, and personal existence at every turn.... In the end poverty begets fatalization. For those exposed to prolonged states of poverty, the only resolution seems to be resignation.... Poverty thus becomes a psychic state, an outlook, even a world view. The powerful anticipate and capitalize on this development amongst the poor. Political and economic systems assume it! Such systems enshrine a permanent paternalism in relation to the poor, thus completing a vicious cycle of dependency and fatalization (World Council of Churches, 1989: 4).

The descriptive material is followed by a first-person narrative in either prose or poetry recounting the person's experience of the evil in question. The section on 'The Reign of Violence' explains how self-disclosure is an essential mode of moral discourse:

> as with injustice, so with war: we must cease reducing it to an abstraction! Only those who can feel the pain and anguish of warfare are likely to become peacemakers. Again we must listen to the victims! (World Council of Churches, 1989: 10).

Immediately following this explanation is a poem. The reader is informed in a footnote that it was written by 'Gabrielle Dietrich in memory of her friend Rajini who was martyred in Jaffna, Sri Lanka, on 22 September 1989':

> ...The long oval of your face
> with eyes sparking fire
> was with me all night
> your eloquent hands

your emphatic voice
the seashells speaking of life's beauty
from pink to mother of pearl.

They can bump off a few of us but not all
if we are many
You paid the price for nurturing fearlessness
in all of us.

...

but your voice rings out to raise the skeletons
from the killing fields of your island.
(World Council of Churches, 1989: 10)

Rajini's martyrdom means that she is silenced, except insofar as her death spurs the living to action. The silencing is intensified by Rajini being identified only by her given name, an indication of personal intimacy, while the public identity of the poet is enhanced by the disclosure of her full name. Dietrich's use of Rajini's first name both reveals a bond of personal intimacy and intensifies the feeling that Rajini has ceased to play an active role in the affairs of her country, thus engaging the intimate emotions of those who hear about her death and must now act on her behalf. The emphasis on the fatalistic and dehumanising effects of oppression means that the 'oppressed' emerge as 'victims' who can disclose their suffering, but who cannot actually change their situation themselves.

A section called 'The Disintegration of Creation' follows a similar pattern. A description of present and potential environmental disasters is proceeded by the explanation:

The data of environmental deterioration is readily available, and no-one today can avoid its impact. It needs, however, to be supplemented by testimony of a more immediate nature (World Council of Churches 1989: 12).

The needed supplement is duly provided:

My name is Anna. I am from the Marshall Islands. My people have traditionally treasured our lands and lagoons, sources of our food. My people are a sharing people who live in close interdependence not only with one another but also with our atoll homes. Now, however, we are troubled.... Our land no longer feeds us. The more we eat of its fruit and of the fish in our lagoons, the sicker we become. What has happened to my people? What has happened to our land? (World Council of Churches, 1989: 12).

Here again we see how the first-person narrative form combines rational argument with elements that, as Young noted, appeal to the reader at a more emotional level. At times, Anna presents scientific data: 'From 1946 to 1958, nuclear tests were held in our atolls. Some of these atolls have simply disappeared. Others are still slowly releasing radioactivity into our waters….' But her information is framed by greeting ('My name is Anna…') and interlocutor orientation ('What has happened to my people? What has happened to our land?'). Together, these elements have the effect of moving the reader to become active in Anna's defence.

The structure, moving from a presentation of statistical data through a description of the debilitating effects of this objective reality to a poetic evocation of the horror it represents, is repeated throughout 'The Realities We Face'. It is an effective way of combining the 'rational' element of debate with rhetorical characteristics more likely to engage the readers' emotions and possibly motivate them to action. Here, it would seem, is a mode of moral discourse which brings together Young's various elements of genuinely democratic communication with the aim of producing action to change the circumstances in which people are presently oppressed. Yet, as in the case of WVI, this mode of moral discourse illustrates not only the creative possibilities in disclosure-based ethics but also the ways in which familiar, intractable inequalities intrude into even the most careful efforts to communicate difference.

Anna, by contrast with Rajini, speaks in her own voice and is a living presence. Her first-person account of her people's history and troubles gives us the impression that we are indeed 'listening to the victims'. In fact, however, her story came to Seoul delegates as an edited account quoted from the written proceedings of an address given at a meeting held in Norway, a year before the Seoul convocation. In this instance, the Seoul text uses the genre of an individual's self-disclosure to construct itself as providing interpretation-free, unmediated personal experience. Yet the narrative's location within an edited text means that Anna herself remains distant from the delegates who read her story. They are called to action, while she remains a supplicating voice confined to the printed page.

Here is a paradox. As the 'Reign of Violence' commentary declares, 'only those who can feel the pain and anguish' are able to take action to alleviate it. But to be a victim is to become 'fatalised', 'dehumanised' and 'powerless', an interpretation of victimhood which is only strengthened by the textual presentation of victims' voices. The document's rhetorical structure proposes a solution: 'the pain and anguish' of 'the victims' can be experienced by those who are not victims. They can be drawn into the experience by reading a poem or a paragraph of first-hand self-disclosure. They can 'feel the pain and anguish' and become motivated to work for its eradication. Agents of change are produced not by *actually* experiencing a situation of oppression because then you are 'dehumanised', 'fatalised' and 'powerless', but by reading a poem about one, or hearing a narrative of self-disclosure.

Vicarious suffering: how much can a victim bare?

Through a poem or first person narrative, readers and listeners gain access to an oppressed person's 'epistemological advantage' and 'privileged knowledge' without also being trapped by that person's 'fatalization' and 'dehumanization'.[5] The WCC is certainly aware of the difficulties of inclusion and exclusion that concern Young. Its disclosure-based method of social and ethical inquiry arose partly out of its attempts to address those very difficulties. Indeed, in conference after conference, the WCC has engaged in soul-searching about the distribution of power relations in its own practices as well as in the world it seeks to change. It 'listens to the victims' not in a quest for donations – at least in the first instance – but because that is the approach which, over the years, has seemed best able to hold together a common sense of purpose in an organisation in danger of disintegrating over internal differences. Its most stringent critics have included its own third world delegates who saw the earlier methods of moral reflection as further manifestations of the very hegemony it sought to oppose.

Yet the familiar inequalities intrude. Even as disclosure of subjective experience acts as a spur to moral action and political engagement, its textual mediation constructs a particular set of power relations which are not necessarily very different from those which the use of self-disclosure aims to challenge. In trying to invert existing power relations by privileging the 'voice of the voiceless', a first-person narrative offers itself as an act of genuine disclosure. But these voices are heard in an 'encounter' that is actually a carefully mediated communication between people who normally would never meet. They are neither face-to-face nor one-to-one, but take place in the formal and constraining setting of a conference presentation. In *Between the Flood and the Rainbow* the 'speaking' is never more than a metaphor: the first person narratives are circulated in pre-convocation material to be read by delegates before their arrival. Incorporating stories of people who speak from a position of powerlessness into a professionally edited document produced by a historically first-world organisation for the purpose of motivating readers to moral and political action is inevitably an appropriation of their voices.

My argument here is not that, every time the less powerful speak, their words are doomed to reinforce their subordinate position in the distribution of power relations. Rather, when their words are appropriated into a text disseminated by an organisation which speaks from a position of power,[6] the disclosure invests the text with an added authority. Such a text now bears not only the stamps of scientific expertise, ecclesiastical authority and international consensus, but the additional authority conferred by a 'genuine' self-disclosure. Yet, paradoxically, this process of textual incorporation reduces the immediacy of first-person speech to a mediated voice.

In this context the speaker's experience of suffering becomes a textual construct whose function is to stimulate ecumenical delegates to political action. At the same time, the text's structure together with its descriptions of victimhood as disempowering portray the speakers as lacking the capacity to act on their own behalf. The same structures that give us the impression that we are receiving an authentic disclosure of subjective experience by an oppressed person also conceal the power relations which the text encodes. The WCC's mode of social ethics is the product of more than a century's sustained reflection by Christian socialist and peace movements about how to equalise power imbalances in an unjust world. Yet the dynamics in its use of self-disclosure recall, if less overtly, WVI's picture of powerful donors intervening to change the life of a hopeless child. In both cases the image denies the 'victim' agency. By attempting to sensitise hearers to power imbalances, the WCC's emphasis on first-hand narrative leading to first-hand experience becomes, paradoxically, a denial of difference. Victims cannot act for themselves because their situation leaves them 'fatalised', 'dehumanised', 'powerless' and seeing, as in Anna's story, 'no hope for the future'. But having heard their stories, we 'share' their experience and act for them.

Young's view of storytelling in the process of moral and political reflection offers some clues here. Her argument differs significantly from the idea that to hear another's story is to share the suffering. On the contrary, for Young, storytelling maintains and indeed intensifies the participants' appreciation of their difference. She takes the example of people in wheelchairs telling stories 'of their physical, temporal, social and emotional obstacles' to able-bodied colleagues in a bid to have their special needs recognised:

> It would be a mistake to say that once they hear these stories the others who can walk will understand the situation of the wheelchair-bound to the extent that they can adopt their point of view. On the contrary, the storytelling provides enough understanding of the situation of the wheelchair-bound by those who can walk for them to understand that they cannot share the experience (1995: 146).

Aware that they can never feel their colleagues' feelings or share their situation, the able-bodied listeners realise that the wheelchair-bound can be the only experts on their own situation. The task of others is to express solidarity with them when requested. The speakers do not lose their agency. They only ask that others become collaborators in a common cause. This example suggests a different view about the structure of moral motivation from that which informs the WCC's approach. While feelings such as sympathy and empathy still play an important part in eliciting moral action from the listeners of such stories, they do not allow these moral agents to take over the emotions and reactions of the people whom their moral action is supposed to benefit.

Disclosing diversity

When the WCC's narratives mentioned above are presented as interpretation-free experience and objective fact, the stories perform a further role, namely, to offer a victim's-eye legitimation of the documents in which they appear. When privileged insight comes not from ecclesiastical authority or scientific expertise but from the duly disclosed experience of 'victims', victim's imprimatur lends credence to textual authority. Whether as ecclesiastical works, doctrinal statements or recommendations to member churches, WCC's documents on social ethics present themselves as a voice of moral exhortation. By reading Anna's story ('My name is Anna. I am from the Marshall Islands....'), I imagine that Anna is here, now, standing beside my desk and so to argue with the points being made (by the text, but using her voice) would be not only difficult but positively impolite. Consequently, my emotional reaction to Anna's story provides a basis for united action among people with whom I might otherwise share little philosophical, theological or cultural ground.

In an earlier era, Protestants of a more or less common cultural heritage sought to solve the world's problems using generally uncontested methods and models of moral theology. After the 1960s, the podiums of WCC conferences saw Biblical hermeneutics jostle with divine command ethics, and situation ethics contest the ground with natural law, while Asian and African theologies tended to view them all as examples of what they were trying to overcome. A method based on disclosure of subjective experience of suffering was a starting point. It circumvented the need for theological and ideological debate and enabled remote voices and difference stories to be heard. If someone proposes, 'Here is the correct moral theory and appropriate method; we will proceed this way', it is easy to disagree: 'No, my tradition has a better one'. If someone says, 'This is my experience, here is my suffering, share my grief', it is much harder to disagree. Caught up in a newly found whirl of diversity which threatened to engulf the ecumenical movement's vision and achievements, the disclosure-based method enabled much to be done when otherwise nothing might have been possible.

Conclusion

The two examples I have explored do not take place in Young's deliberative utopia, but in and between the everyday *topoi* of international inequalities. They illustrate attempts in good faith, by people painfully aware of those inequalities and moved by them, to move others in a quest for greater justice. They do this by confronting their respective audiences with disclosures of various kinds of suffering.

Although neither case meets all of Young's conditions for free and open disclosure, each exhibits a number of the ingredients with which she wants to leaven the dry uniformity of existing theories of deliberative democracy. While these cases do not illustrate the full working out of Young's model, they nevertheless alert us to some potential difficulties worthy of consideration in the ongoing quest for greater mutual understanding. Whereas Young no less than the deliberative theorists she challenges both speak in the utopia of theoretical debate, my examples draw attention to the constraints which attend any real world effort to realise utopia. Our quest for greater justice does not begin on a theoretical blank slate but must be built up, piece by painful piece, out of the unequal world we now inhabit and whose imprints persist in our attempts to transcend it.

Notes

[1] The shift of moral focus from the admonitory voices of dissenting members of élites to cries for justice from those who suffer oppression reflected the wider shift apparent in many academic disciplines such as the movement known as 'history from below' (Wolf, 1982). Wolf attributes this change to 'the intellectual reassessments that marked the late 1960s' (1982: x). The movement involving studies 'from below' owes much to the Frankfurt-School-inspired South American-based theorists such as Freire, Illich and Gutièrrez, who formulated their approaches during this period. For a discussion of the connection between oppression and epistemological privilege, see Narayan (1988) and below. Beyond changing academic fashions, we might associate the shift to personal disclosure with the shrinking world of 'reality' television, global communication, cheap air travel and postmodern sensitisations to the

'other' involved in the rise of feminism, civil rights, the politicisation of disability, gay rights, natural birth, alternative therapies, etc.

[2] Contrary to Young's claim, in Plato's *Gorgias*, Socrates employs the phrase 'the vice of flattery' with reference to oratory, or rhetoric, which is specifically designed to persuade an audience irrespective of the validity of the argument. The question of greeting is not addressed. Eds.

[3] For a deliberately provocative example of such an appeal see the brochure produced by Community Aid Abroad (an Australian affiliate organisation of Oxfam) which, when the 1980s criticism of child sponsorship was at its height, featured head-and-shoulders photos of an adult and child with the caption 'Don't waste your charity on people like these: there are better ways to help'. Inside, readers were presented with an argument about the need for long-term political change in the relations between rich and poor countries, as opposed to one-to-one handouts. They were invited to join CAA's regular giving program AWARE, which provides support to third world community and cooperative ventures, usually developed and planned by the recipients.

[4] I have been unable to find a definite source for this saying, which lives in ecumenical folk lore.

[5] This view is in marked contrast to that of Foucault, who regards 'hierarchical observation' of the experience of an oppressed person as a means not of sympathetic identification but of control (1979: 170-74). Indeed, the recounting of experience as a means of control over the speaking subject is a recurring theme in Foucault's work (see also 1981, Chapter 1). This argument has been developed by others in studies of visual representation of oppressed people, e.g. Green (1985). It can also be convincingly extended to the 'incitement to discourse' in which the relationship between powerless and powerful actors are constructed as between speaker and listener. Foucault goes so far as to call this kind of relationship 'pastoral power' (1982: 214-15), which he associates with the traditions of the confessional. Foucault's model of 'transferring ...desire...into discourse' (1981: 23) is not intended to stand alone, but is an example of other means by which Western culture controls experience by transforming it into discourse. This synergy of means of control may prove telling in understanding how the post-1960s WCC method of disclosure-based ethics seems to have the unintended consequence of perpetuating its subjects' 'victim' status.

[6] That is, economic and social power in a first world country and as the representative body of member churches; but consider also the element of spiritual and moral authority claimed by WCC texts, and owed in part to the validating function within the texts of these very 'stories'. For a discussion based on Foucaultian field-theory of textual expressions of various kinds of religious power, see Chidester (1986: 8).

References

Australian Consumers' Association (1983), 'Sponsoring a Child: What Really Happens When you Clip that Coupon?', *Choice*, July, pp. 11-16.
Blower, P. (1987), 'Our Child in Haiti', *Australian Women's Weekly*, July, p. 210.
Charon, R. (1994), 'Narrative Contributions to Medical Ethics: Recognition, Formulation, Interpretation, and Validation in the Practice of the Ethicist' in E. DuBose, R.P. Hamel and L.J. O'Connell (eds), *A Matter of Principles? Ferment in U.S. Bioethics*, Trinity Press International, Valley Forge.
Chidester, D. (1986), 'Michel Foucault and the Study of Religion', *Religious Studies Review*, vol. 12, no. 1, pp. 1-9.
Cox, H. (ed.) (1968), *The Situation Ethics Debate*, Westminster Press, Philadelphia.
Cunningham, R.L. (1970), *Situationism and the New Morality*, Appleton-Century-Crofts, New York.
Fletcher, J. (1966), *Situation Ethics: the New Morality*, Westminster Press, Philadelphia.
Foot, P. (1978), *Virtues and Vices and Other Essays in Moral Philosophy*, University of California Press, Berkeley.
Foucault, M. (1979), *Discipline and Punish: the Birth of the Prison*, A. Sheridan trans., Penguin, Harmondsworth.
____ (1981), *The History of Sexuality*, vol. 1, R. Hurley, trans., Penguin, Harmondsworth.
____ (1982), 'The Subject and Power', Afterword to H. Dreyfus and P. Rabinow, *Michel Foucault: Beyond Structuralism and Hermeneutics*, Harvester Press, New York, pp. 208-66.
Frank, A.W. (1995), *The Wounded Storyteller: Body, Illness, and Ethics*, University of Chicago Press, Chicago.
Green, D. (1985), 'On Foucault: Disciplinary Power and Photography', *Camerawork*, 32.
Hauerwas, S. (1994), *Dispatches from the Front: Theological Engagements with the Secular*, Duke University Press, Durham.
Kim, Y-B. (1986a) 'Justice, Peace and the Integrity of Creation: An Asian Perspective' in *Technology from the Underside: Report of the Consultation of New Technology, Work and the Environment Sponsored by the World Council of Churches Sub-unit on Church and Society and the National Council of Churches in the Philippines January 10-15, Manila, Philippines*, Geneva, WCC, Geneva and NCCP, Quezon City, pp. 48-57.
____ (1986b) in *Church and Society Newsletter*, 4 January.
MacIntyre, A. (1981), *After Virtue*, University of Notre Dame Press, South Bend.
Maddox, M. (1993), 'Ethics and Rhetoric of the Starving Child', *Social Semiotics*, vol. 3, no. 1, pp. 71-94.
Montello, M. (1995), 'Medical Stories: Narrative and Phenomenological Approaches' in M.A. Grodin (ed.), *Meta Medical Ethics: the Philosophical Foundations of Bioethics*, Kluwer Academic Publishers, Boston.

'M. L.' (1997), 'A Great Idea', *World Vision News*, September, p. 23 (reprinted from *New Idea*, 24 May 1997).

Narayan, U. (1988), 'Working Together Across Difference: Some Considerations on Emotion and Political Practice', *Hypatia*, vol. 3, no. 2, pp. 31-47.

New Idea (1987), World Vision International display advertisement, 21 April.

Newton, A.Z. (1995), *Narrative Ethics*, Harvard University Press, Cambridge, Mass.

Pence, G. (1984), 'Recent Work on the Virtues', *American Philosophical Quarterly*, vol. 21, pp. 281-97.

Roe, E. (1994), *Narrative Policy Analysis: Theory and Practice*, Duke University Press, Durham.

Rouse, R. and Neill, S.C. (eds) (1986), *A History of the Ecumenical Movement*, vol. 1, *1517-1948*, 3rd ed., WCC, Geneva.

Stalker, P. (1982), 'Please Do Not Sponsor this Child', *New Internationalist*, May, pp. 7-9.

Visser't Hooft, W. A. (1985), 'Oldham's Method in Abrecht's Hands', *The Ecumenical Review*, vol. 37, no. 1, pp. 3-9.

Wolf, E. (1982), *Europe and the People Without History*, University of California Press, Berkeley.

World Council of Churches (1982), 'Ecumenical Perspectives on Political Ethics', Report of Consultation, Cyprus, October 1981, *The Ecumenical Review*, vol. 34, no. 4, October, pp. 403-11.

____ (1989), *Between the Flood and the Rainbow: Second Draft Document for the World Convocation on Justice, Peace, and the Integrity of Creation*, Seoul, Korea, 6-12 March 1990, WCC, Geneva.

World Vision Australia (1996), *1996 Annual Report*, World Vision Australia, South Melbourne, Vic.

____ (1997a), *Action News*, September, World Vision of Australia, Melbourne, Vic.

____ (1997b), *World Vision News*, September, World Vision of Australia, Melbourne, Vic.

World Vision International (1997), 'Understanding Who We Are', http://csde. aces.k12.ct.us/friends/wvision/WHOAREWE

Young, I.M. (1995), 'Communication and the Other: Beyond Deliberative Democracy' in M. Wilson and A. Yeatman (eds), *Justice and Identity: Antipodean Practices*, Allen and Unwin, St Leonards, N.S.W., pp. 135-52.

4 Shifting Policy Frameworks: Disclosure and Discipline

CAROL BACCHI

Introduction

Scenario one: The atmosphere is gloomy. There have been several murders but few clues. The forensics people have done their work, and done it well. Traces of body hair, an identified blood group, a single finger print. Inspector Osborne is asked to take on the case and the gloom lifts. Here is the mind who will sift through the facts and put them together. Through trials and tribulations, near death experiences and sleepless nights, she will solve the case. We, the murder mystery readers, travel with her, probing the evidence, discovering links. If well-written, the 'answer' will be disclosed before we, the readers, discover it. That after all is the nature of the entertainment.

Scenario Two: The atmosphere is gloomy. The blow-out in the budget deficit headlines all the major metropolitan papers. The figures are presented, the suspects identified – over-expenditure on welfare, welfare cheats, single mothers exploiting the system. We, the readers, wait for the experts to comment, to disclose the answer. That after all is the nature of the entertainment.

I have set out these two parallel scenarios to highlight the similarities between a 'Who done it?' and the way policy issues are often presented. The common impression in most discussions of policy, as in our detective story, is that 'solutions' to 'puzzles' are discovered. The parallel suggested itself to me when Catherine Belsey (1980: 70) described how, in the classic realist novel, there is a puzzle which is resolved when some vital piece of information is *disclosed*. Then all the pieces of the puzzle fall into place. In this chapter I will be suggesting that dominant models of policy analysis assume a similar approach. The task of policy makers and their advisers[1] is to disclose 'solutions' to 'puzzles'.

Belsey makes an important point here. In her view, the classic realist novel 'moves inevitably towards closure which is also disclosure, the dissolution of enigma through the re-establishment of order.' Belsey is using 'disclosure' here in the sense of revelation. Her point is that disclosure, in this instance of the culprit in a detective novel, closes off further analysis; in effect, it closes the case. I will be suggesting that dominant models of policy analysis similarly imply that a policy recommendation is a genuine attempt to 'solve' some readily identifiable problem, and that this closes the case. A story is told, questions are asked, and answers are provided. The crucial difference, of course, is that in a novel the fabricated character and shape of a plot is anticipated and accepted. In policy analysis, by contrast, we are led to believe that what is revealed is all that needs to be revealed. We neither expect nor would we accept that what is on offer is a story with an author or authors.

My argument proceeds in three stages. First I illustrate that the dominant models of policy analysis are disclosure models which produce closure by suggesting that puzzles have been solved, that answers to 'problems' have been revealed. Next I offer competing models, including an approach I develop which I call 'What's the problem (represented to be)?', which open up a space to consider the constructed nature of policy narratives (Roe, 1994).[2] Finally I comment on what is at stake in these debates.

Rationalist approaches to policy: disclosure as closure

Most policy analysis adopts a discovery/response description of policy making which I argue is analogous to Belsey's closure/disclosure model of plot resolution in realist fiction. In this view, social problems are readily identifiable and the task of the analyst is to disclose solutions to those problems. Rob Watts (1993/94: 116) identifies 'the deep-seated assumption found in both social liberal and radical readings of the modern state that in state policy intervention there was/is a discovery process which uncovers "real" social problems as a prelude to state policy interventions.' Policy analysts are assigned the role of detecting the vital pieces of information which allow policy makers to resolve those problems. Different schools of policy analysis, however, identify those pieces of information differently. 'Comprehensive rationalists', for example, concentrate on scientific and technical information. 'Political rationalists' offer political information. Despite their differences, both technical and political rationalists tend to argue 'that the techniques of policy analysis can contribute to democracy by generating usable knowledge for decision-makers.' This 'usable information' is what they will disclose. The principal antagonism between the two schools, as Mary Hawkesworth (1988: 13) identifies it, arises from a disagreement over 'what sort of knowledge is most useful – technical or political.'

The comprehensive rationalist views policy making simply as a matter of problem-solving. The process is set out in clear-cut stages: formulation (of the problem), implementation (of the solution), evaluation. This approach harbours an assumption that there is some readily identifiable socio-economic problem that needs to be addressed and that policy makers must get together and do their best to discover a policy to solve or ameliorate this problem. The task is to disclose the solution. A further assumption is that policy makers will approach this task rationally and will produce the 'best' solution within the given cultural, political and economic constraints. The emphasis on measurement and technical expertise leads to the labelling of this approach, in some accounts, as 'technical rationalism'. Marshall Dimock (Braybrooke and Lindblom, 1963: 38) articulates such a viewpoint:

> First, there are always the problems and the issues. Second, there are the facts and analyses that need to be applied to the issues. Third, there is the setting forth of alternatives and the pros and cons applicable to each possible solution – all this in the light of larger institutional objectives. Fourth, there is the decision proper, which depends upon choosing among alternatives....

Values, in this vision, stand outside the purview of policy advice, as is implied in Dimock's unquestioning acceptance of 'larger institutional objectives.' Today we might call these 'mission statements'. In similar fashion, Herbert Simon, a prototypical exponent of the comprehensive rationalist approach, stipulates that policy advisors can examine and judge only 'whether the appropriate *means* to particular objectives have been selected.' Ethical premises are simply given. These values, carefully identified as organisational objectives, must be explicit so that 'their degree of realization in any situation can be assessed.' In his view, 'rational behavior' refers to 'behavior that is evaluated *in terms of* the objectives of the larger organization' (Simon, 1961: 41; my emphases). For the policy analyst the problem is a given: it is defined by the institution. The 'solution' to a problem merely requires the disclosure of a 'means' to attaining the institution's objectives.

Political rationalists such as Charles Lindblom, David Dery, Aaron Wildavsky, Martin Rein and Donald Schön challenge the premises of technical rationality. They present themselves as democrats unhappy with an over-reliance on bureaucracy and technocracy. Commonly characterised as pluralists, they stress the importance of participation rather than expertise. In Lindblom's words (1980: 27), they 'substitute interaction for analysis'. We see here a move to a more democratic polis at one level.

There is a definite call for the voice of the people to become part of the analysis.

It also seems, at first glance, that Lindblom is challenging the discovery/response model of policy making. He states, for example, that '... for most policy decisions there can never be any final solution, and that the problem will remain unresolved whichever policy is implemented.' However, he continues to maintain that policy makers will work incrementally 'toward improving the situation'. While the process may not be as straight-forward as the comprehensive rationalists imply, the goal is much the same: *moving towards* the solution of a problem. Braybrooke and Lindblom (1963: 123) describe their approach to problem-solving as 'successive approximation'. So, despite the attempt to incorporate the voices of the citizenry, those offering policy advice are still positioned as those who know *how* to improve the situation and who have the task of disclosing this information.

This is not to deny the importance of the distinction between the ways comprehensive rationalists and political rationalists approach 'problems'. Technical rationalists assume that there is a discrete phase at the outset of the policy process in which values and objectives are revealed and clarified. They call this a 'decision space'. These accounts convey the idea that this is a relatively uncomplicated process, and that the real work, as it were, begins in finding solutions, often technical solutions, to the problems which have been identified. Political rationalists, by contrast, engage in depth in the analysis of problem definition. The literature here, for example Dery (1984), makes the case that this is indeed a difficult task and tries to suggest how to do it better. Political rationalists see problems as 'too complex for the human brain; hence, their trust in any one analyst or policy maker does not go very far' (Lindblom, 1980: 35). It follows that 'policy-making responsibility should be shared by a plurality of interacting policy makers and analysts'. Here is the pluralist rationale for providing input from citizen groups and political actors outside the technocracy.

Indeed, some political rationalists demonstrate a keen awareness of the importance of problem definition in policy analysis, and how particular definitions of problems lead necessarily to certain kinds of solutions. There is a sensitivity here to the closure exerted in the process of problem definition. For example, Rein and Schön (1977: 235) challenge the technical rationalists on their easy dismissal of the key importance of problem definition. They criticise the notion that the process of policy development begins with 'a shared articulation of the problematic situation'. This, in their view, excludes 'the most crucial aspect of the policy process.... [I]n policy development one seldom starts from a consensual definition of the problem to be solved....' They go on: 'policy development is essentially about a process of *problem setting ...*'. In a similar vein, Dery (1984: 4) states clearly that 'each solution seems to have a different problem in mind.'

Nevertheless, their pragmatic approach assigns the task of problem definition to policy advisors. Dery (1984: 38) declares: 'our interest is unashamedly "applied"'. Hence, he insists that for political science any approach 'not normally concerned with the production of administratively workable and politically realistic ideas for solving problems' is, quite simply, inadequate. The goal of the analyst, therefore, is precisely to define problems in such a way that something can be done about them: 'an intervention model requires a problem to be defined in one way only, one that will promote its solution (amelioration or transformation).' Despite the critiques of comprehensive rationalism, then, we are still offered a model in which policy analysts are responsible for disclosing solutions to problems. The only difference here is that the constructed nature of the problem is admitted.

Wildavsky (1979: 3) clarified this position: 'in public policy...creativity consists of finding a problem about which something can and ought to be done. In a word, the solution is part of defining the problem.' He tells a story to illustrate his approach:

> Mike Teitz tells about a soldier in New Zealand who was ordered to build a bridge across a river without enough men or material. He stared along the bank looking glum when a Maori woman came along asking, 'Why so sad, soldier?' He explained that he had been given a problem for which there was no solution. Immediately she brightened, saying 'Cheer up! No solution, no problem'.

What all this means for teaching policy, according to Wildavsky (1979: 3), is that it is better taught backward:

> Instead of beginning by formulating a problem, considering alternative solutions, developing criteria, applying criteria to data, and so on, students' work improved when exercises went the other way around. The best way to begin learning was to apply strong criteria to good data, go on to create criteria and discover alternatives, and, after numerous trials, formulate a problem at the end.

The reference to criteria as if this information stands outside the analytical process indicates a positivist bias in political rationalism, a point pursued below.

Because problems, for political rationalists, can never be *finally* 'solved' – all that is possible is 'successive approximation' – the task of the analyst is to define problems which permit *some movement* toward an 'improvement in the situation'. This is the 'political information' which policy analysts need to disclose to policy makers. Of course, the presumption here, as with the comprehensive rationalists, is that it is quite clear in which *direction* 'improvement' lies. Hence, despite all the sensitivity to problem definition, there is no suggestion that policy proposals might be proceeding in the wrong or in a questionable direction. Problems in the sense of broader contingencies and long-term goals, therefore, remain exogenous to the political rationalist's problem/solution analysis.

Moreover, despite some sensitivity to the role of values in policy analysis and policy making, political rationalists assume that analysts can, in the words of Rein and Schön (1977: 238), stand back from their values, their 'tacit frames'. It is interesting, given the parallel between policy analysis and narrative fiction developed in this chapter, that these authors suggest storytelling as a way of discovering the 'tacit frames that underlie our problem settings'. They argue that this approach permits storytellers to ask what they have left out of the account. In other words, storytelling is a way of disclosing our 'tacit frames' – our values and preconceptions – to ourselves, enhancing our capacity to be objective. With this potentially distorting information disclosed, the analyst can move on to offer sound, scientific advice. According to Rein and Schön (1977: 239), '...stories do permit partial objective social assessment and this allows a scientific debate to take place'. So in this account, our tacit frames can be uncovered and subjected to critical self-reflection. Disclosure of one's values to oneself is seen as a precondition for the adequate disclosure of solutions to problems. We can see here a link with the view of Frank Fischer discussed in the next section.

Postpositivist approaches to policy: refusing closure

At its most basic, postpositivist policy analysis challenges the fact-value distinction explicit in technical and political rationalists' appeals to data and criteria. Beyond this, postpositivists vary widely both in the nature of their critique of traditional policy analysis and in their recommendations regarding how to proceed. A number of theorists can be seen as transitional in the move to postpositivism, raising questions which the disclosure models described above have difficulty answering. For example, some (Bachrach and Baratz, 1963; Kingdom, 1995) draw attention to the ways in which items are kept off political agendas and how this necessarily imposes limitations on the character of the policy solutions analysts provide. Their argument is that suggested solutions to problems will be limited if vital information is missing, for example, the effects of pollution or of passive smoking on the health of the general population. Other authors (Fischer, 1980, 1990; Drysek, 1990) place at the forefront of consideration the value commitments, acknowledged or otherwise, of policy analysts. Their aim is to find a way to allow normative analysis to be incorporated into policy design to produce 'a more comprehensive rationality' along Habermasian lines. As with Rein and Schön, the idea here is to put our values 'on the table' and discuss them.

Fischer, for example, describes the postpositivist challenge as 'an effort to move beyond the calculation of efficient means to include an assessment of the substantive ends of policy, that is, the rationality of goals, values, and attitudes towards various ways of life' (Fischer, 1990: 216). He specifies that this involves confronting 'positivism's most fundamental principle, namely, the strict separation of facts and values'. In Fischer's view, this requires analysts to surmount a 'narrowly gauged commitment to the analysis of means by integrating empirical and normative criteria in a more comprehensive concept of rationality.' Like Rein and Schön, he believes that analysts can disclose their values to themselves and to others, and then move on to a rational resolution of competing values.

The major distinction between Fischer and the political rationalists emerges in his criticism of the 'process approach' to policy (1980: 80). The determination of goals is left to political processes. The analysis cannot escape the narrow limitations implicit in the political rationalist view that problems need to be defined in ways which permit solutions. Recall here Wildavsky's soldier and the bridge example. To Fischer, this defining of problems to match available solutions is sadly inadequate. In his view, a procedure must be found to allow 'an assessment of the *outcomes* of the decision-making process (my emphasis).' For Fischer it would be unthinkable to 'do policy backwards' as Wildavsky (1979) recommends. Rather, assessment must 'aim at determining the "right" or "good" decision.' There is a determination here to move beyond pragmatism, to reveal frankly and honestly institutional objectives and goals through conversation.

When it comes to setting the criteria for making these judgements, however, some of Fischer's suggestions sound familiar. For example, he insists (1980: 193-212) that there must be a 'potential basis for normative consensus in policy deliberation.' Analysts are *to be provided* with a 'framework of ideals' which are considered to be uncontroversial, for example, economic progress and political freedom. The analyst is then invited to try his or her hand at 'political consensus formation'. The passive voice in the phrase 'to be provided' is significant, as is the suggestion that 'ideals' can be uncontroversial. The lack of critical scrutiny of commonly accepted social norms is highlighted here. To put it simply, Fischer (1990: 88) believes that the ends of policy, or the 'problems' policy is to address should and can be discussed and decided upon beforehand, and that ways can be found to allow 'an assessment of the outcomes of the decision-making process'. We are still working here with a discovery/response model. Although the complexity and value-laden character of the procedures of 'discovery' are acknowledged, the analyst will disclose 'solutions' which effectively propose closure.

Problems as constructed narrative

An alternative version of postpositivist policy analysis, which I advance below, as I have elsewhere (Bacchi, 1996b, 1999), challenges the discovery-response model of policy analysis which presumes analysts are outside that process, merely responding to 'problems' or trying to make 'improvements'. This alternative version of postpositivism insists upon the *constructed nature of policy problems* and challenges the ability of analysts to stand back and analyse their own values and frames of cultural reference. This postpositivist approach undermines the view that analysts can disclose solutions to problems in the way that a crime fiction novelist reveals a solution to a murder mystery. Moreover, it illustrates how such a 'disclosure model', for the policy analyst, imposes closure. The 'problem/solution' approach rules out alternative perspectives and framings of problems, constraining and disciplining the options for social change. Of particular concern is the way in which disclosure models defined within the narrow constraints of the rationalist approaches canvassed so far, ignore the role of policy analysis in constituting the subjects of policy as 'winners' and 'losers', as 'heroes' and 'villains'.

Murray Edelman (1988) was among the first to draw attention to the constructed nature of policy problems. He makes the case that social problems do not exist 'out there' waiting to be discovered but that, in a sense, they are 'created' by the policy community. By this, Edelman means that a 'problem' will assume a particular shape, depending upon how it is thought about and represented. It follows that the specific policies recommended to 'solve' the problem will reflect and follow from the particular way in which a problem is construed. He notes, for example, that racism and racial segregation existed in the United States long before they were 'called' problems. This insight directs attention to the processes of problem construction, asking how these and other problems are characterised and what follows from these characterisations. This approach is clearly a challenge to the view that the way forward is simply to disclose 'solutions' to readily identifiable problems. From this perspective, policy recommendations become, not solutions to puzzles, but part of a constructed narrative with a predetermined character. The analogy with the author of a detective novel is apt.

It is interesting that political rationalists actually advocate this very model of policy analysis as an ideal. Wildavsky's recommendation to do policy backwards is precisely such a proposal: a constructed narrative with a predetermined character. However, as mentioned earlier, political rationalists describe this approach as a necessarily pragmatic way to move towards 'an improvement in the situation'. There remains in this understanding an assumption that what it means to 'improve' a situation is patently clear, the flip side of an assurance that the 'problem' is also patently clear. Despite the creative role assigned policy analysts by political rationalists, their role in constituting the problem (in terms of an end-point for their 'improvements') is unacknowledged. Their proffered advice still takes the form of a revelation or disclosure designed to close the case. The solution, even if only a proximate one, is presumed to be unambiguous because the problem is unambiguous.

Marie Danziger (1995: 438) draws attention to the non-innocence of the framing of problems with a lovely example from Neil Postman's (1992) *Technopoly*. Postman relates the story of two priests who were having difficulty deciding about the appropriateness of a certain behaviour and wrote to the Pope for a definitive answer:

> One priest asks, 'Is it permissible to smoke while praying', and was told that it is not, since prayer should be the focus of one's whole attention. The other priest asks, 'Is it permissible to pray while smoking', and was told that it is, since it is always appropriate to pray.

Postman's point, as Danziger says, is '...that the form of a question may block us from seeing solutions to problems that become visible through a different question' (Postman, 1992: 126). Unless we pay heed to the multitude of factors involved in the ways we construct or represent problems, we constrain, foreclose and, as in the priests' questions above, literally 'predicate' the responses of political analysts.

Michael Shapiro (1992: 99) makes exactly this point. He reflects upon the framing of the 'problem' of 'traffic congestion' as a way of illustrating the effects of 'the typical passive grammar of decision makers "faced with problems", rather than, for example, a more politically astute version that would inquire into the way public policy thinking tends to remain within certain narrow modes of problematization.' As an example, he describes 'traffic congestion' as a middle-class problem, which already accepts the '...segregation, housing, and shaping of the labor force that has arisen from the structures of real estate speculation, work-force creation, city planning, and so on'. Shapiro's purpose is to show that, in the very labelling of a problem, like 'traffic congestion', there are in-built premises about what is acceptable and what needs to change. Traffic congestion becomes a given; the factors constituting it remain unexamined. The task we are left with is 'dealing' with the problem. The implication here is, not simply that we cannot expect to 'solve' the problem if our analysis is inadequate, but that the understanding of policy analysis as disclosing solutions to problems masks the multitude of considerations that go into our framing of the problem in the first place.

To highlight the contrast between postpositivist and rationalist/ disclosure models of policy analysis, consider the way in which Eugene Bardach (1981: 164), a technical rationalist, discusses the 'problem' of traffic congestion. In his view, analysts need to be trained not to overestimate or underestimate 'problems' such as 'auto congestion in downtown Berkeley'. In this account, all that needs to be considered is quantification. What remains unasked in accepting traffic congestion as a 'problem' – the wider context of housing developments, land use, traffic patterns or the use of private automobiles – are issues he neither addresses nor feels the need to address. The task is simply to keep the 'problem' within limits.

Along lines similar to Shapiro's, I would suggest that the second scenario which introduced this chapter – the news report of a blow-out in the budget deficit – contains a 'problem' representation which invites interrogation. *Who defines* this as a problem? *What kind* of a problem is it represented to be? Could it not in another account be presented as the *solution* to poverty and distress, if we accepted that government expenditure to relieve distress was legitimate? With 'deficit' defined as the 'problem', political analysis is constrained to offering ways to *reduce* it. This becomes the information which needs to be disclosed. Other kinds of questions about the purposes of government expenditure remain unasked. Hence they are assumed to be unimportant. The idea that governments should constrain expenditure stands as an unexamined backdrop to the analysis. The point here is that the way a problem is defined or simply identified forecloses the scope of questioning.

Problematic representations

I have argued (Bacchi, 1999) that a postpositivist approach to policy analysis should highlight the ways in which policy problems are 'created' within the terms of proposed solutions. When we ask, with analytical persistence, 'What's the problem (represented to be)?', the argument's presuppositions are clearly exposed. Put simply, every policy proposal necessarily contains a problem representation. Every policy proposal by its nature assumes that it is helping to 'solve' a problem.

A simple example captures my central premise. Consider the case of a facility which introduces water-timed showers to reduce water consumption. The 'solution', water-timed taps, constructs the problem as consumer indulgence in water use. Alternative problems, such as the possibility of faulty taps or leaking mains pipes, are not considered. The nature of the problem – wasteful over-use – is contained in the proposed solution. As another example, consider two different responses to the increase in ex-nuptial births. A recommendation that morals teaching be introduced in schools constructs the problem as 'promiscuity'. By way of contrast, a suggestion to increase access to contraception produces the problem as 'unwanted pregnancy'. The recommendations become disclosures, solutions to problems. The different ways in which the recommendations construct the problem go unexamined.

It follows that policy proposals necessarily assume a causal linkage which is inadequately discussed. The purpose of a 'What's the Problem?' approach is to bring these assumed causal linkages to the surface in order to scrutinise them. The point is not simply to suggest that one problem representation is more accurate than another, but to tease out the implications of different problem representations. We need to identify, for example, who is designated as responsible for 'problems' in particular representations, and what this leaves unproblematized. The point is to draw attention to the silences in problem representations and hence to the narrow constraints imposed in much policy analysis on our understanding of worrying social conditions.

Problem analysis is centrally concerned with the discursive construction of policy proposals (Watts, 1993/94; Fulcher, 1988; Danziger, 1995; Ball, 1990). Theorists who examine the discourse of public policy draw attention to the ways in which language or, more broadly, bodies of knowledge, conceptual and interpretative schema define the terrain and complicate attempts at change. Discourse is understood as a way of speaking which sets limits on what can be said. Stephen Muecke (1992: 15) usefully describes discourse as 'publicly available ways of speaking or writing.' Discourses, then, are frames which provide ways of viewing issues (Bové, 1990: 56; Frank, 1992, 110). Applied to the policy field, an interest in discourse becomes an interest in the ways in which arguments are structured, 'problems' are created, and objects and subjects are constituted in language and conceptual schema (Bacchi, 2000).

When an issue or policy-making task is addressed by asking 'What's the problem?', of central concern are the ways in which groups are assigned position and value within problem representations. Nowhere is the creative side of policy analysis clearer than in the ways subjects are constituted within it. For example, consider the effects of labelling some groups as 'needy' (Fraser, 1989), or as 'disadvantaged' (Eveline, 1994; Bacchi, 1996a). This positioning ascribes the power to define 'need' and 'disadvantage' to those designing the policy. Such ascriptions can also disempower groups who are thus reduced to supplicants. For example, Gillian Fulcher questions the discourse surrounding education policy and disability which, she argues, construes disabled children as the 'problem', distracting attention from the disabling structures which surround them. With the 'disabled' children constructed as the problem, change can be kept within limits. There is also the implication of beneficence among those who 'attend' to their 'needs'. The ways in which buildings and social services accommodate the able-bodied are kept silent. The interplay of disclosure, closure and silencing is clear.

Policies often construct the 'victims' of adverse social circumstances as 'problems'. This illustrates the non-innocence of policy analysis which aims only to disclose 'solutions' to 'problems'. Consider, for example, how much of the early literature describing inequality in girls' education focused upon *their lack* of self-esteem and *their need* to be encouraged into non-traditional areas of study. But a focus upon the ways in which non-traditional studies exclude or are even hostile to women, or the need for boys to enter non-traditional areas such as art and literature, would produce very different 'problems' and very different agendas (Bacchi, 1996b). Attention might then be directed to the nature of the hostility women and girls face, and to the presumption that only subjects which encourage economic growth are important. 'Solutions' then are not simply disclosures; they construct the problem in ways that need to be analysed. Interpretations have programmatic effects (Fraser, 1989: 166-75). What we represent to be the problem will determine what we propose to do about it, and what we propose to do will contain unexamined assumptions, or perhaps wilfully negligent attitudes, about the nature of the problem.

Another example of how policy analysis *creates* problems rather than discloses objective solutions to problems is the focus on the individual as the cause of problems. The policy implications which flow from this are significant. Responses to sexual harassment, for example, usually offer grievance procedures as a solution, ignoring how this response creates the 'problem' as deviant *individuals* instead of considering harassment as one symptom of an environment in which women are unwelcome and are treated as such (Bacchi, 1998). Again, with domestic violence, the dominant models of explanation focus upon either 'deviant' (drunken, lower-class) males or 'problem families', ignoring how family structures and gender dynamics construct situations which produce violence (Gordon, 1988). In this regard Muecke (1994: 30) notes how 'familiar responses to problems of Aborigines and alcohol, Aborigines and work, are made in terms of their being genetically incapable of tolerating either of these ("can't handle the grog", "can't hold a steady job", "go walkabout")'. As Muecke goes on to explain, 'by locating a problem at a genetic level, any explanation or resolution in terms of social-economic forces lapses'. We are left, in the words of Colin Gordon (1991: 38), with 'sick people' rather than a 'sick society'. In each case the 'problem' is isolated and individualised. Roger Sibeon (1996: 117) concludes that 'political and policy discourse constructs an object – crime, marriage, the welfare state, or whatever – in such a way that it can be governed.'

Sarah Nettleton's insights into the construction of a 'new paradigm of health and medicine' are useful here. Acknowledging the inadequacy of a biomedical model which encourages the patient to adopt the 'sick role' and which empowers doctors to 'make them well', she directs attention to nuances in the crafting of the new preventative health paradigm. She notes that in the literature which privileges prevention over cure 'health has increasingly come to be seen as something that is within the control of the individual' (1994: 39, 47, 45). The prevention paradigm 'exhorts that individuals can them*selves* ensure and maintain health'. This representation of the problem has a number of effects. In Nettleton's view, it ultimately 'individualises health issues' and 'may operate as more subtle forms of social control'; it sits rather too comfortably for Nettleton with the 'aims of voluntarism and consumerism'; it creates the conditions for 'blaming' individuals if they fail to 'keep themselves healthy'. This last effect is of particular concern to women who are thereby held responsible not only for their own health but also for the health of others, their children in particular. In the end such an approach directs attention away from the possibility that working conditions or environmental conditions may be what is making people ill. A 'Life Be In It' advertising campaign sponsored by the Australian government to encourage physical exercise would appear to be expedient and less of a political risk than legislating stricter pollution controls.

The point of a 'What's the Problem?' analysis then is to draw attention to the non-innocent framing of problems which lodge within policy proposals, and to consider the effects of those frames. Policy proposals, it is argued, necessarily include problem representations, while the language of conventional policy analysis makes it appear that solutions are offered to problems which exist *outside the analytical process*. Hence, it is implied that we need only to disclose the solution, in the same way as the detective finds the culprit. Focussing on the discursive construction of problems shows that problem representations are implicit in proposals and that problem representations constitute problems in ways which either delimit or encourage structural change. A 'What's the Problem?' approach encourages us to reflect upon which of these goals, either the delimiting or encouraging of structural change, is implicit in policy proposals and their problem representations.

Rhetoric and the policy process

The focus upon language and discourse has led a number of postpositivists to emphasise the role of rhetoric in policy formulation (see Pal, 1996; Majone, 1989). In these accounts rhetoric is rescued from its pejorative characterisation as dissimulation and manipulation to become an important tool in communication and persuasion. If we accept that problem construction (inherently a linguistic act) places boundaries on problem 'solutions', then it is important to be aware of the ways in which the framing of problems work. This involves a study of rhetoric. Moreover, if policy texts are seen as political narratives, students of policy need to learn how to construct convincing ones. This, however, would be inadequate unless we also educate our students to understand the profound social implications of policy analysis. Danziger (1995) agrees that, far from encouraging students to see themselves as disclosing 'solutions' to obvious problems, we need to teach our students 'the conflicts' in society, thus opening up for examination complex issues which are not readily resolvable (Graff, 1992).

There is clearly a vast distance between this proposal and Wildavsky's suggestion that policy students learn to 'do policy backwards' by deciphering policy documents to identify goals and advise whether or not specific proposals will yield 'an improvement in the situation'. By contrast, postpositivists encourage policy analysts to focus on and decipher problem representations and formative features of policy recommendations, because the 'problem', as constructed, will be the effective lens though which any goal is perceived. Thus postpositivist policy analysts seek to 'open up' policy texts to examine the tensions and contradictions within them, reflect upon the problem representations they contain and discuss their plural meanings. The task is to draw attention to the absences and silences which make some readings more likely than others. While this move might be described as a reinvestment in even more disclosure, there is no sense here of a resolution to a story or a closure that brings the curtain down on further questioning. Whereas the rationalist disclosure models examined in this chapter seem to be intent upon revealing 'solutions' to 'close the case', my argument urges that we keep the curtain up and the conversation going.

The stakes

The contrast drawn in this chapter between rationalist and postpositivist models of policy analysis is meant to highlight the political implications of approaches to teaching and 'doing' policy analysis. Rationalist models position the state and policy analysts, in both their individual and professional capacities, as benign, objective, neutral. This aspiration to present themselves as merely 'responding' to 'identifiable problems', or defining problems pragmatically in order to 'improve the situation', neglects their active role in shaping the issues and setting priorities for policy analysis.

The effect is often to reinforce the status quo. With Deborah Stone (1988: 194), I would insist that 'portraying a problem as a decision is a way of controlling its boundaries'. Rationalist, goal-oriented models encourage students of policy to confine their analysis to 'workable solutions' to 'resolvable' problems, thus discouraging the questioning of larger political objectives. It is in this sense that these 'detect the culprit' analyses or, in Belsey's sense, 'disclosure/closure' narratives constrain and distort social analysis.

These approaches to policy 'create' heroes and villains. Torgerson (1996: 278) identifies what is at stake when the active role of policy analysts in constructing citizen groups and their problems is not acknowledged: 'Attention is deflected not only from important difficulties arising from contemporary economic developments, but also from the questionable privileges intrinsic to the prevailing alignment of power.' Thus analysts' power to constitute 'heroes' and 'villains' goes unanalysed. The narrow constraints of rationalist concepts and empirical methodology subvert the complex social narrative, substituting a sketchy 'Who done it?' plot with its deceptive but satisfying closure and simple assumptions of guilt.

Policy formulation and analysis so conceived is depoliticising. The discovery/response model offers the promise of closure. All that can be done is being done. Solutions *will be* found. Villains *will be* revealed.

Hidden from consideration is the productive side of problem creation, the closure exerted through the assertion that solutions to 'problems' will be found or, at the very least, policy will contribute to an 'improvement in the situation'. The public is not encouraged to reflect upon the problem representations encapsulated in policy proposals, nor upon the implications which would flow from competing problem representations. Instead, they must simply wait to read the next instalment.

Notes

[1] A good deal of the literature discussed in this chapter refers to the training of policy advisors. I use the broader term 'policy analysts' in an attempt to talk about all those who position themselves as offering 'solutions' to 'social problems'. Here I would include newspaper reports and academic analyses of 'social problems'. It is important to remember that all these commentators are embedded in time and place and that their analyses are likely to reflect some of a range of social values. The lack of recognition of this embeddedness is one theme pursued in this chapter.

[2] I borrow the language of 'policy narratives' from Emery Roe (1994: xi-xii) but, unlike Roe, in using his words, I suggest 'taking narrative analysis to its logical conclusion'.

References

Bacchi, C. (1998), 'Changing the Sexual Harassment Agenda' in M. Gatens and A. Mackinnon (eds), *Gender and Institutions: Welfare, Work and Citizenship*, Cambridge University Press, Cambridge, pp. 75-89.

_____ (1996a), *The Politics of Affirmative Action: 'Women', Equality and Category Politics*, Sage, London.

_____ (1996b), 'What's the Problem? An Approach to Women and Education' in J. Gill and M. Dyer (eds), *School Days: Past, Present and Future. Education of Girls in 20th Century Australia*. An edited collection of papers from the Conference at the Research Centre for Gender Studies and the Faculty of Education, University of South Australia, Adelaide, pp. 11-16.

_____ (1999), *Women, Policy and Politics: The Construction of Policy Problems*, Sage, London.

_____ (2000), 'Policy as Discourse: What Does it Mean?', *Discourse: Studies in the Cultural Politics of Education*, vol. 21, no. 1, forthcoming.

Bachrach, P. and Baratz, M.S. (1963), 'Decisions and Nondecisions: An Analytical Framework', *American Political Science Review*, vol. 57, pp. 632-43.

Ball, S. (1990), *Politics and Policy Making in Education: Explorations in Policy Sociology,* Routledge, New York.

Bardach, E. (1981), 'Problems of Problem Definition in Policy Analysis' in J. Crecine (ed.), *Research in Public Policy Analysis and Management*, vol. 1, Jai Press, Greenwich, Connecticut, pp. 161-71.

Belsey, C. (1980), *Critical Practice*, Methuen, London and New York.

Bové, P.A. (1990), 'Discourse' in F. Lentricchia and T. McLaughlin (eds), *Critical Terms for Literary Study,* University of Toronto Press, Toronto.

Braybrooke, D. and Lindblom, C.E. (1963), *A Strategy of Decision: Policy Evaluation as a Social Process*, The Free Press, Collier-Macmillan Ltd, London.

Danziger, M. (1995), 'Policy Analysis Postmodernized: Some Political and Pedagogical Ramifications', *Policy Studies Journal*, vol. 23, no. 3, pp. 435-50.

Dery, D. (1984), *Problem Definition in Policy Analysis*, foreword by A. Wildavsky, University Press of Kansas, Lawrence, Kansas.

Drysek, J. (1990), *Discursive Democracy: Politics, Policy and Political Science*, Cambridge University Press, Cambridge.

Edelman, M. (1988), *Constructing the Political Spectacle*, The University of Chicago Press, Chicago.

Eveline, J. (1994), 'The Politics of Advantage', *Political Theory Newsletter*, vol. 5, no. 1, pp. 53-67.

Fischer, F. (1980), *Politics, Values and Public Policy: The Problem of Methodology*, Westview Press, Boulder, Colorado.

_____ (1990), *Technocracy and the Politics of Expertise*, Sage, Newbury Park.

Frank, M. (1992), 'On Foucault's Concept of Discourse' in T.J. Armstrong trans. *Michel Foucault Philosopher*, Routledge, New York, pp. 99-116.

Fraser, N. (1989), *Unruly Practices: Power, Discourse and Gender in Contemporary Social Theory*, University of Minnesota Press, Minneapolis.

Fulcher, G. (1989), *Disabling Policies? A Comparative Approach to Education Policy and Disability*, The Falmer Press, London.

Gordon, C. (1991), 'Governmental Rationality: An Introduction' in G. Burchell, C. Gordon and P. Miller (eds), *The Foucault Effects: Studies in Governmentality*, University of Chicago Press, Chicago, pp. 1-52.

Gordon, L. (1988), *Heroes of Their Own Lives: The Politics and History of Family Violence: Boston 1880-1960*, Viking, New York.

Graff, G. (1992), *Beyond the Culture Wars: How Teaching the Conflicts can Revitalize American Education*, W.W. Norton, New York.

Hawkesworth, M. (1988), *Theoretical Issues in Policy Analysis*, State University of New York Press, Albany.

Kingdom, J. (1995), *Agendas, Alternatives and Public Policies*, 2nd ed., Harper Collins, New York.

Lindblom, C.E. (1980), *The Policy-making Process*, 2nd ed., Prentice-Hall Foundations of Modern Political Science Series, New Jersey, Prentice-Hall.

Majone, G. (1989), *Evidence, Argument and Persuasion in the Policy Process*, Yale University Press, New Haven.

Muecke, S. (1992), *Textual Spaces: Aboriginality and Cultural Studies*, University of New South Wales Press, Kensington, N.S.W.

Nettleton, S. (1996), 'Women and the New Paradigm of Health and Medicine', *Critical Social Policy*, vol. 16, no. 3, pp. 33-54.

Pal, L. (1996), 'Missed Opportunities or Comparative Advantage? Canadian Contributions to the Study of Public Policy' in L. Dobuzinskis, M. Howlett and D. Laycock (eds), *Policy Studies in Canada: The State of the Art*, University of Toronto Press, Toronto.

Rein, M. and Schön, D. (1977), 'Problem Setting in Policy Research' in C. Weiss (ed.), *Using Research in Public Policy Making*, Lexington Books, Lexington, Mass., pp. 235-51.

Roe, E. (1994), *Narrative Policy Analysis: Theory and Practice*, Duke University Press, Durham.

Shapiro, M. (1992), *Reading the Postmodern Policy: Political Theory as Textual Practice*, University of Minneapolis Press, Minneapolis.

Sibeon, R. (1996), *Contemporary Sociology and Policy Analysis: The New Sociology of Public Policy*, Tudor Press, Wirral, Merseyside.

Simon, H. (1961), *Administrative Behavior: A Study of Decision-Making Processes in Administrative Organization*, 2nd ed., Macmillan, New York.

Torgerson, D. (1996), 'Power and Insight in Policy Discourse: Post-Positivism and Problem Definition' in L. Dobuzinskis, M. Howlitt and D. Laycock (eds), *Policy Studies in Canada: The State of the Art*, University of Toronto Press, Toronto, pp. 266-98.

Watts, R. (1993/94), 'Government and Modernity: An Essay in Thinking Governmentality', *Arena*, vol. 2, pp. 103-57.

Wildavsky, A. (1979), *The Art and Craft of Policy Analysis*, Macmillan, London.

5 Therapeutic Self-Disclosure: The Talking Cure

PAUL CORCORAN

> And ye shall know the truth, and the truth shall
> make you free.
>
> *St. John*, 8:32

> ...the patient only gets free from the hysterical
> symptoms by producing the pathogenic
> impressions that caused it and by giving
> expression to them.... The therapeutic task
> consists solely in inducing him to do so....
>
> Sigmund Freud
> *Psychotherapy of Hysteria*

Introduction

The act of confiding personal feelings, intimate experiences and closely
guarded memories to another person has long been considered an effective
therapy for troubled and sorrowing minds. Wise counsel encourages us to
find words for experiences we have shamefully hidden from others or even
tried to suppress in our own minds. The benefits of self-disclosure come
from speaking of these hidden aspects of our lives in the presence of a
sympathetic person. The underlying idea is that revealing ourselves to
others, openly and honestly, is healthful and therapeutic: a release from the
grip of harmful thoughts and emotions. Long before Freud attempted to
establish psychoanalysis as a science, spiritual, religious and philosophical
traditions advocated self-disclosure as a means of treating mental and
emotional turmoil and its painful consequences.

The idea that language has 'magical powers' appears to be at odds
with modern science, and might easily be dismissed as a reversion to
superstitious beliefs in charmed phrases, curses, spells and incantations.
'Saying it', the sceptical adage reminds us, 'doesn't make it so'.

Nevertheless, today there are many advocates of self-disclosure who insist upon the power of speech to effect healthful change in the mind and body.

Preconceptions about magic aside, we have no difficulty accepting the findings of linguists, philosophers and clinical psychologists that language is essential to human consciousness and thought. Without language, *Homo Sapiens* would not be the species it is. There is a fairly broad scientific consensus that we do not simply think *with* language, but that in the normal human being language is *essential* to thought: we think *in* language (Black, 1972: 86-94; Chomsky, 1976: 3-13). It follows that our ability to form ideas into articulate language is not simply an end-product or a superfluous extra skill, but is rather an essential ability – an actual behaviour and function – necessary for normal life.

Consequently, it is *not* a reversion to superstition to suggest that a person who is profoundly inhibited or incapable of giving voice to memories, experiences and self-identity – *'I just can't talk about it. Don't ask! There's nothing to say, really.'* – has lost not only the power to speak but, in some senses, the ability to feel. If that person can be brought to the point of speaking about those sequestered, painful or shameful things, this 'restoration' of language is itself a retrieval of the power of 'normal functioning' and an enhanced capacity *to think about one's life*. The *inability* to talk about one's life – one's self – therefore amounts to a mental impairment that might well be repaired by self-disclosing speech.

The benefits of self-disclosure

The importance of self-disclosure to health and well-being is widely acknowledged in both specialist and popular literature. Professional psychologists and psychotherapists have used non-technical language to make this case, pointing out that people often try to 'conceal' themselves in order to seek protection against criticism, hurt and rejection. 'This protection is purchased at a steep price. When we are not truly known by the other people in our lives, we are misunderstood', and by this means we lose touch with our 'real selves' (Jourard, 1964: iii). There is an alternative:

> through my self-disclosure, I let others know my soul. They can know it, really know it, only as I make it known. In fact, I am beginning to suspect that I can't even know my own soul except as I disclose it. I suspect that I will know myself 'for real' at the exact moment that I have succeeded in making it known through my disclosure to another person (Jourard, 1964: 10).

In contemporary society the healthful effects of self-disclosure – for one's physical, moral and even professional well-being – are recognised and promoted by an expanding range of therapies. Books, audio and video tapes, personal growth seminars, leadership training and management courses promise self-discovery and self-improvement. Serious academic researchers as well as exponents and practitioners of popular psychology make confident claims about the benefits of disclosure.

> Most therapists agree that talking about an upsetting experience is psychologically beneficial. The agreement ends there. Some think that talking about a trauma is primarily valuable in achieving catharsis by getting the person to express pent-up emotions. Others believe that talking helps [to] attain insight into the causes and cures of the difficulties with the trauma (Pennebaker, 1990: 38).

Inhibitions to openness operate as the 'cumulative stressors on the body, increasing the probability of illness and other stress-related physical and psychological problems.' However, the beneficial effects of speech, with its consequence of self-understanding, are deemed to be self-fulfilling.

> When we talk a great deal in a group, we claim that we enjoy it and learn from it. After confessing a crime, our minds and bodies appear to be relaxed. *Once we understand* the link between a psychological event and a recurring health problem, *our health improves* (Pennebaker, 1990: 20-21; my emphasis).

Self-disclosure, then, is both a 'symptom' of a healthy personality and 'at the same time a means of ultimately achieving healthy personality'. Those who disclose themselves to others find a personal identity that at once distinguishes and binds. 'They learn the extent to which they are similar one to the other, and the extent to which they differ from one another in thoughts, feelings, hopes, reactions to the past, etc.' (Jourard, 1964: 3).

By contrast, an inability to disclose leads to alienation from others and 'makes a farce out of one's relationships with people', such that one 'can never truly love or be loved'. The stakes are high, and extend from social alienation to life-threatening illness. 'When a man does not acknowledge to himself who, what, and how he is, he is out of touch with reality, and he will sicken and die' (Jourard, 1964: 5):

> in the effort to avoid becoming known, a person provides for himself a cancerous kind of stress which is subtle and unrecognized but none the less effective in producing not only the assorted patterns of unhealthy personality which psychiatry talks about, but also the wide array of physical ills that

have come to be recognized as the stock in trade of psychosomatic medicine (Jourard, 1964: 24-26).

Freely expressing our emotions serves an important communicative function. Self-disclosure enables us to attain 'insight into our own thoughts and feelings', thus enhancing our ability to avoid stressful situations, accommodate them, or at least be able to anticipate them (Pennebaker, 1990: 39-40).

Although self-disclosure is widely praised as empowering and therapeutic, another important benefit of self-disclosure is that it enables us to perceive and accept our inevitable or insurmountable limitations. 'The more we can accept the many aspects of our humanity, the less troubled we are by them, and the more surely we will feel a sense of self-control and self-confidence' (Kennedy, 1975: 28). In the absence of this acknowledgement, we 'act our way through life, finding the right expression and learning the correct manoeuvres that enable us to save face and look good.'

> One of the troubles with living this way – aside from the amount of energy it demands – is that it kills our freedom and spontaneity, two of the most important qualities needed for a healthy attitude towards ourselves. We cannot be free when we are bound by the expectations of other people, when being ourselves might meet with disapproval and social failure.... There is not much room left for ourselves – or for even finding out who we are – when impressing others becomes our basic style in life (Kennedy, 1975: 18).

The risk required to 'be ourselves', Kennedy claims, 'is the key to entering life more deeply, experiencing it in a happier and fuller fashion'. Moreover self-disclosure offers the benefits of enhanced personal creativity.

> Sharing private perceptions with one another appears to afford the only real means by which human beings can construct a more complete picture out of their separate visions and correct the distortion that confound efforts to perceive the real world. Communication also provides...the conditions that stimulate human creativity, for out of the expression of differences new thoughts and new possibilities are born (Barnlund, 1975: 115-16).

These gains are at least in part the result of relinquishing adult hypocrisy and rediscovering a child-like honesty and innocence, in which all emotions, from joy to pain, are expressed spontaneously and directly. Yet from the moment of birth there are always compulsions to 'behave' in ways appropriate to the formed manners of a public self. Pennebaker

(1990: 23) observes that '[m]any of our truly natural behaviors, such as sex and aggression...must be controlled for the good of society. Inhibition, then, is the Scotch tape of civilization.' *Formation*, a French synonym for *education*, is an inescapable pressure that stifles even as it attempts to foster good manners and civil behaviour:

> societies oppose [the] 'childish' impulse to say what one thinks and share what one feels, and by adulthood an inner split is accomplished and the self is 'compartmentalized.' But this division, necessary or not, is bought at a price. It takes immense psychic energy to monitor inner reactions constantly, carefully segregating what can be revealed from what must be concealed. This inner guardedness makes it difficult for people to 'let go,' to experience events deeply, makes them ultimately suspicious and afraid of their own impulses. They must constantly stand guard over their own lives, sensitively weighing public reaction to every word and gesture. The results may not merely alienate people from each other but from themselves as well. While all societies erect some boundaries between what people may think and what they may say, there is a reason to question how extensively this repression can be practiced without damaging the personality (Barnlund, 1975: 158).

Self-awareness

Despite the illusive nature of self-conscious mental powers, it is intuitively obvious that the mind not only senses its physical embodiment in present consciousness but at the same time apprehends the data of sensation, continuity of experience, emotion and memory. Indeed, there is a second level of mental apprehension, self-conscious self-consciousness. When we blush with embarrassment, for example, it is clear that we are intensely self-conscious of the very state of self-conscious awareness. These complex mental processes, referred to by psychologists as 'metacognition', are casually taken for granted and casually described as self-awareness or self-consciousness (Goleman, 1996: 46; Kabat-Zinn, 1994). We easily apply these terms to ourselves and to others in moments when these qualities or states are, for example, vividly present in a nervous actor or strikingly absent in a child at play.

> This quality of awareness is akin to what Freud described as an "evenly hovering attention," and which he commended to those who would do psychoanalysis. Such attention takes in whatever passes through awareness with impartiality, as an interested yet unreactive witness. Some psychologists call it the "observing ego," the capacity of self-awareness that allows the analyst to monitor his own reactions to what the patient is saying,

and which the process of free association nurtures in the patient (Goleman, 1996: 46-47).

Yet at the very moment we acknowledge such remarkable capacities of self-consciousness we become aware of its limitations. We know that memory may be distorted, fragmented or it may fail altogether. Connected experiences are lost, obscured or confused with disparate associations. Memories come spontaneously to mind, or suddenly vanish. To extend the metaphor of the mirror, far from the mind's transparency and reflective power being the chief characteristics of human consciousness, we are often impressed, or indeed frustrated, by how the mind operates 'on its own' in an obscure, partly murky, partly lost or suppressed, field of awareness. From ancient times we have been reminded that we see through a glass darkly.[1]

In 397 AD, St. Augustine's *Confessions* described memory as a landscape of his inner self where some things spring 'flirtatiously' into view while others, submerged, must be fished up from a dark sea:

> I venture over the lawns and spacious structures of memory, where treasures are stored – all images conveyed there by any of our senses, and, moreover, all the ideas derived by expanding, contracting, or otherwise manipulating the images; everything ticketed, here, and stored for preservation (everything that has not been blotted out...and buried in oblivion). Some things, summoned, are instantly delivered up, though others require a longer search, to be drawn from recesses less penetrable. All the while, jumbled memories flirt out on their own, interrupting the search for what we want, pestering: "Wasn't it us you were seeking"? My heart strenuously waves these things off from my memory's gaze until the dim thing sought arrives at last, fresh from the depths.[2]

Just as there are inhibitions, dangers and taboos that govern the act of uncovering the body – before whom, when, for what purposes – so too are there fears, constraints and shame involved in the exposure of the mind and its memories, emotions and feelings to others and to one's conscious self. Self-awareness, then, is a capacity of the human mind, but it is also one that may be weak or dysfunctional.

It is interesting that psychologists link the inability to be emotionally self-aware – to 'have feelings' and to show emotion – directly to the inability to disclose ourselves to others. One such patient, Gary, told his therapist: 'I don't naturally express my feelings. I don't know what to talk about; I have no strong feelings, either positive or negative." Gary's therapist diagnosed this 'emotional flatness' as *alexithyma* (Swiller, 1988), a Greek term meaning 'lack of words for emotion'. The condition was given its first description in 1972 (Sifneos, 1991). Goleman (1996: 50, 52) describes how alexithymics lack the important tie between self-awareness and self-disclosure:

> Such people lack words for their feelings. Indeed they seem to lack feelings altogether, although this may actually be because of their inability to express emotion rather than from an absence of emotion altogether. Such people were first noticed by psychoanalysts puzzled by a class of patients who were untreatable by that method because they reported no feelings, no fantasies, and colorless dreams – in short, no inner emotional life to talk about at all. The clinical features that mark alexithymics include having difficulty describing feelings – their own or anyone else's – and a sharply limited emotional vocabulary.... And that is the nub of the problem. It is not that alexithymics never feel, but that they are unable to know – and especially unable to put into words – precisely what their feelings are. They are utterly lacking in the fundamental skill of emotional intelligence, self-awareness....

It has not escaped the self-awareness of psychologists, communication theorists and the many advocates of 'personal growth' that alexithymia charts the territory for promoting therapies which promise to enable you to 'get in touch with your self'. Goleman (1996, 1998), it should be noted, has written best-sellers with chapter titles such as 'Know Thyself', 'Emotional Awareness' and 'The Courage to Speak Out'. Self-disclosure has been enthusiastically embraced in popular psychology and self-help therapies (Jourard, 1971; Chelune, 1979; Thandi, 1993; Pennebaker, 1990).

Self-disclosure has become not only an indicator of personal health and well-being, but has also been normatively incorporated into social mores as a standard of ethical action. Kennedy (1975: 35-36) affirms that 'the risk of letting out the truth of ourselves makes that truth available to others. They respond immediately and positively. What attracts people is not what we pretend to be but what we are.' Fitzpatrick (1988: 177) finds that in the late twentieth century 'the sharing of personal feelings and information about the self has become for some members of our culture the hallmark of a close relationship. The gradual exchange of intimate information about one's inner self is considered the major process through which relationships develop between people.'

The value of intimate disclosure has been occasionally challenged. Some critics contend that 'the emphasis on self-disclosure and expressivity is actually harmful to the satisfaction and stability of relationships' (Fitzpatrick, 1988: 177). For example, Richard Sennett (1978: 259) launches a rare but strong attack on the 'tyranny of intimacy' and rejects the assumption that 'social relationships of all kinds are real, believable, and authentic the closer they approach the inner psychological concerns of each person. This ideology transmutes political categories into psychological categories. This ideology of intimacy defines the humanitarian spirit of a society without gods: warmth is our god.'

What Sennett abhors is the loss of objectivity and the structured, cosmopolitan, impersonal, urbane life of the city's civilised 'public culture' – 'the mould in which diversity and complexity of persons, interests and tastes become available as social experience' (1978: 339). The tyranny of intimacy arises from 'the measurement of society in psychological terms:

> we have come to care about institutions and events only when we can discern personalities at work in them or embodying them. Intimacy is a field of vision and an expectation of human relations. It is the localizing of human experience, so that what is close to the immediate circumstances of life is paramount. The more this localizing rules, the more people seek out or put pressure on each other to strip away the barriers of custom, manners, and gesture which stand in the way of frankness and mutual openness. The expectation is that when relations are close, they are warm; it is an intense kind of sociability which people seek out in attempting to remove the barriers to intimate contact, but...[t]he closer people come, the less sociable, the more painful, the more fratricidal their relations (Sennett, 1978: 338).

Freud's 'talking cure'

In the late nineteenth century, Freud and several other European physicians, in an age optimistic about the beneficial effects of science, collaborated in developing a science of the mind, psychology. They produced not only a theory of the human mind – its organic powers, mechanisms and developmental stages – but also what Freud specifically advocated as a scientific method of diagnosing and treating its pathologies. Interestingly, this new contribution to 'self knowledge' – literally a science of the psyche – was seen as a breakthrough for the inward journey long considered to be a path leading to inner peace, emotional stability and well-being. This destination required a careful tour of what Freud called the 'contents' of the mind. This was not, however, primarily an inspection of one's mental acuity or one's store of memories. Of chief interest was the sedimented, intertwined, often submerged materials pressed down or camouflaged in the 'subconscious' or 'unconscious' regions of the mind. Knowledge of one's self, therefore, required a process of bringing into present consciousness the things that are only supposed to be 'forgotten' but which are in fact, in Freud's view, repressed and hidden away, or diverted and falsely projected in one's thoughts, behaviour and 'symptoms'. This is an enormous burden carried through life at great cost to one's mental and physical health, and to one's ability to live normally in society.

More than meditation or inner reflection was needed to achieve this self-knowledge. It required one to speak by engaging in a slow, painstaking dialogue with a therapist trained in psychoanalysis. Patients had come to Freud's attention with painful or disabling symptoms that could not be explained physiologically and they had therefore been diagnosed as 'hysterics' or 'psychotics'. Freud's therapeutic response was to develop psychoanalytic techniques that enabled patients to find, put in words and disclose the events, conflicts, sufferings, shames, delusions, fears, anger and guilt of their lives, all the way back to earliest childhood. A patient, with the help of a knowledgeable listener, must locate, describe and expose what had been long and destructively repressed.

The therapeutic value of this self-disclosure, it was believed, was obtained in the disclosure itself. One simply had to bring to consciousness and actually *speak* about 'the material' (as Freud called it) whose repression was causing all the 'neurotic' symptoms. It was the best imaginable application of the injunction that 'the truth shall make you free'. However, getting at the truth and enabling the patient to voice it required a complex 'analytic' procedure.

The psychoanalytic therapy of self-disclosure was summed up with admirable conciseness as 'the talking cure' in the first published case study by Freud and Breuer (1974: 95). Much later in his career, in *The Question of Lay Analysis*, Freud (1970 [1926]) remained optimistic about the simple principles underlying the talking cure: 'The analyst agrees upon a fixed regular hour with the patient, gets him to talk, listens to him, talks to him in turn, and gets him to listen.'

'The Impartial Person', Freud's fictitious companion in the dialogue he wrote to explain psychoanalysis to sceptics, pretends amazement: 'Nothing more than that? Words, words, words, as Prince Hamlet says? ... So it is a kind of magic...: you talk, and blow away his ailments?'

Freud's reply is disarmingly candid in his acceptance of magic as an analogy for the methods he struggled all his life to establish as a science. The admission turns out to be both erudite and canny in acknowledging the assistance of a mysterious element:

Quite true. It *would* be magic if it worked rather quicker. An essential attribute of a magician is speed.... But analytic treatments take months, and even years.... And incidentally do not let us despise the *word*. After all, it is a powerful instrument; it is the means by which we convey our feelings to one another, our method of influencing other people. Words can do unspeakable good and cause terrible wounds. No doubt 'in the beginning was the deed'[3] and the word came later, in some circumstances it meant an advance in civilization when deeds were turned into words. But originally the word was magic – a magical act; and it has retained much of its magic power (Freud, 1970: 96).

Freud and Josef Breuer (1974), published their early cases and methods of analysis for the 'talking cure' in 1895. It was their stated intention to bring both palliative relief for their patients' neurotic symptoms and ultimately a therapeutic resolution. This was to be achieved by the patient's confrontation with personal traumas, resulting in an understanding and acceptance of both normal and pathological mechanisms of personality development. The essential function of self-disclosure in the talking cure was the release of 'pent-up emotions' – although more impressively re-labelled as *cathexis* and *catharsis*.[4]

Once a picture has emerged from the patient's memory, we may hear him say that it becomes fragmentary and obscure in proportion as he proceeds with his description of it. *The patient is, as it were, getting rid of it by turning it into words* (Freud and Breuer, 1974: 365).

In their earliest collaboration in 1892, Breuer and Freud (1974: 57) were enthusiastic about the effects of self-disclosure:

For we found, to our great surprise at first, that *each individual hysterical symptom immediately and permanently disappeared when we had succeeded in bringing clearly to light the memory of the event by which it was provoked and in arousing its accompanying affect, and when the patient had described that event in the greatest possible detail and had put the affect into words.* ... The psychical process which originally took place must be repeated as vividly as possible; it must be brought back to its *status nascendi* and then given verbal utterance. Where what we are dealing with are phenomena involving stimuli (spasms, neuralgias and hallucinations) these re-appear once again with the fullest intensity and then vanish forever.

More recent analysts have been less bold in their description of the therapeutic effect, but the central role of self-disclosure is still acknowledged. Stricker (1990) writes: 'Self-disclosure lies at the heart of psychotherapy, the talking cure. It can be defined, somewhat tautologically, as a process by which the self is revealed.' Weiner (1978), in discussing self-disclosure as a therapeutic technique, puts the matter succinctly:

Psychoanalysis aims to modify personality structure through introspection, based on the premise that the greater one's awareness of his unconscious ego defense mechanisms and of his unconscious fantasies, the freer one is to deal with reality. Symptomatology is seen as the end-product of the ego's defense against anxiety, which in turn signals the presence of unconscious conflict.

Transference and self-disclosure

The talking cure was not, indeed, magic, and not only because it lacked speed. Analysis was likely to be an emotional roller-coaster ride, complete with the risks and resistance, exciting ups and downs, circuitous routes and sudden reversals. Weiner coolly describes the 'treatment process' of overcoming neurotic symptoms through self-disclosure as 'the *development* and resolution of the transference neurosis. The resolution comes through interpretation of the transference neurosis' (Weiner, 1978: 11; my emphasis). In this crucial phase the auditor of one's self-disclosure – the analyst – becomes an interactive participant in locating, exposing and releasing the hold of the unconscious on the patient's life, but only after the development of a new problem.

Transference, in classical psychoanalytic theory, is the process by which emotions and desires originally felt for a parent or sibling are unconsciously shifted to the analyst. This emotional investment may be positive or negative, but in either case it is a cathartic expression of repression and trauma whose origins date to early childhood. Typically, transference develops as an intense affective relationship between the therapist and the patient. In effect, the patient 'transfers' love, anger or aggressive dislike toward the therapist in what the psychoanalyst assumes to be a re-creation of the patient's repressed and traumatised emotional history.

Freud's first published use of the term transference, in *The Psychotherapy of Hysteria* [1895] (Freud and Breuer, 1974: 389-92), reflects a frank familiarity with the transference relationship.

> In not a few cases, especially with women and where it is a question of elucidating erotic trains of thought, the patient's cooperation becomes a personal sacrifice, which must be compensated by some substitute for love. The trouble taken by the physician and his friendliness have to suffice for such a substitute. If, now, this relation of the patient to the physician is disturbed, her cooperativeness fails too.... In my experience this obstacle arises in three principal cases.
> (1) If there is a personal estrangement – if, for example, the patient feels she has been neglected, has been too little appreciated or has been insulted.... This is the least serious case....
> (2) If the patient is seized by a dread of becoming too much accustomed to the physician personally, of losing her independence in relation to him, and

even of perhaps becoming sexually dependent on him. This is a more important case, because its determinants are less individual. The cause of this obstacle lies in the special solicitude inherent in the treatment. The patient then has a new motive for resistance....

(3) If the patient is frightened at finding that she is transferring on to the figure of the physician the distressing ideas which arise from the content of the analysis. This is a frequent, and indeed in some analyses a regular, occurrence. Transference on to the physician takes place through a *false connection*....

The therapist must overcome the patient's 'psychical force of resistance' to remembering, articulating and confronting the source of the traumatic experiences, long-buried by neurotic repressions, underlying the symptomatic expressions:

It is impossible to carry any analysis through to a conclusion unless we know how to meet the resistance arising in these three ways. But we can...if we make up our minds that this new symptom that has been produced on the old model must be treated in the same way as the old system. Our first task is to make this obstacle [the transferred 'dependence'] conscious to the patient....

   To begin with I was greatly annoyed at this increase in my psychological work, till I came to see that the whole process followed a law; and I then noticed, too, that transference of this kind brought about no great addition to what I had to do. For the patient the work remained the same: she had to overcome the distressing affect aroused by having been able to entertain such a wish [of 'personal relations' with the physician] even for a moment; and it seemed to make no difference to the success of the treatment whether she made this psychical repudiation the theme of her work in the historical instance [the original trauma] or in the recent one connected with me. The patients, too, gradually learnt to realise that in these transferences onto the figure of the physician it was a question of a compulsion and an illusion which melted away with the conclusion of the analysis. ...If I had neglected to make the nature of the 'obstacle' clear to them I should simply have given them a new hysterical symptom – though, it is true, a milder one....

Far from the emotional attachment being a distraction or derailing of the therapeutic strategy, it is regarded as an essential and inevitable phase of treatment. Describing it as a 'transference neurosis' reflects Freud's view that the transference process is not a solution or resolution of the patient's primary repressive symptoms (Freud and Breuer, 1974: 388-92). In effect, it is merely an externalised reassignment of this burden onto the therapist as intimacy, trust, dependence and emotional dependency evolve in the course of the patient's self-disclosure to the analyst. The patient's 'love' for the therapist, as it is often experienced, is a 'bond' between patient and therapist that arises in the course of successful analysis. But this must be overcome through 'counter-transference', in which the 'spell' of the transference neurosis must be broken.

At this stage of the analysis the therapist's own self-disclosure to the patient is a potentially powerful factor. Opponents of therapist self-disclosure argue that the therapeutic relationship is necessarily intense and intimate, despite the significant differences in power, sophistication and emotional exposure between the two parties. The therapist is in a position of authority and trust while the patient is likely to be vulnerable and emotionally distraught. Should the therapist strive to be a 'neutral' auditor, simply a perfect mirror or sounding-board for the patient's self-disclosure? Or should the therapist be supportive, warm and sympathetic, in order to encourage and provide a humane and supportive environment for the patient's difficult and painful task? The preponderance of professional opinion holds that the therapist's self-disclosure to the patient is inevitable at some minimal level of humane empathy, and there is an obvious need to be supportive and encouraging in the relative intimacy of the analytical setting. Beyond that minimal level, however, there is a clear, though not unanimous, consensus that therapists should not engage in active, open, calculated self-disclosure to manipulate or 'lead' the patient. However, some have advocated that the therapist should touch, show affection and even enter into sexual enactments, thus serving, in effect, as an active participant in the necessary phase of transference (Lum, 1988; Langs, 1976). An early paper by Weiner (1969) explicitly confronts the latter view: 'Nudity versus neutrality in psychotherapy'.[5]

The critical, often traumatic, phase of transference in the process of analysis must be resolved in such a way that a patient understands the mechanism and history of his or her repressive struggles and, thus enlightened, accepts and takes responsibility for this self-understanding. In this sense, the analysis is 'educative'; the patient, as it were, is cured through a process of guided self-understanding.

The journey of self-disclosure and 'resolution'

In vastly oversimplified Freudian terms, the analytic process affords the patient the opportunity to:

• confront and, with the therapist's aid, self-disclose the libidinal forces and repressive counterforces of one's unconscious

- appropriate the therapist as a temporary substitute for one's own governing super-ego
- reappropriate this rebuilt super-ego as one's own.

In brief, the therapeutic dialogue yields a 'resolution' of the transference neurosis. The critical assumption is that *interpretation* is the path to *resolution* in the final healing phase of transcending the transference neurosis – that is, in layman's terms, 'getting over' the emotional strains of the treatment itself.

It needs to be underscored that analysis is a mutual undertaking. For the patient, self-disclosure is the means, the very substance and process, of the therapy. The patient's self-disclosing speech provides the grist for the mill of the therapist's illuminating interpretation. Self-disclosure enables the patient to 'usurp' the therapist by interpreting his or her own symptomatology. The effect is a cathartic 'resolution' and a liberation from the mechanisms and the symptoms of psychic self-oppression. This is, in sum and substance, the talking cure. One's 'truth' – the voice of self-disclosure – will make you free.

The scope of the patient's self-disclosure is extremely broad. It involves a gradual, unhurried unravelling of one's life, literally a return journey in which one strives to remember, revive and recreate all the contents of one's past, beginning almost anywhere, and ideally leading everywhere. Freud (Freud and Breuer, 1974: 378-79) was keen to point out that the therapist should take care to look for gaps and weak spots, rather than the 'complete and self-contained' account produced by the patient's path of recollection and reconstruction. The patient's attempt to give a straight and systematic narrative will be a 'wall which shuts out every prospect'. Thus the narrative should be occasionally distracted and thrown off track by a question about a trivial or possibly irrelevant detail, or noting some event or person on the margin of the account being given: 'it is quite hopeless to try to penetrate directly to the nucleus of the pathogenic organization'. The analyst pays careful attention to slips of the tongue (Freud, 1975) and may also initiate 'directed' provocations by pursuing apparent minutiae in a patient's story that eventually open up memories, break through resistances and circumvent barriers to reach repressed material.

A patient in the normal course of a classic Freudian analysis is led back through memories and dreams to childhood and one's earliest parental, sibling and kinship experiences, as well as to other relationships, conversations, experiences, acquaintances, memorable places and events. One's journey in such an analysis is a gradual regression into the sub-conscious and the unconscious mental landscape of one's life, all the way back, ideally and theoretically, to earliest infancy and inevitably to one's earliest traumas and repressive reactions. The vehicles for this journey of self-disclosure include dream interpretation and techniques to 'induce' the recollection of lost or truncated memories: free association, word association, hypnosis and the heuristic use of language devices such as analogy, metaphor, symbolism and mythological archetypes. Freud was also enthusiastic about a method he developed after losing confidence in the effectiveness of hypnosis. He simply 'fooled' his patients by suggesting that when he pressed his hands firmly on their forehead they would suddenly retrieve a blocked memory or visualise a significant image. Freud claimed this invariably worked (Freud, 1994: 354, 360-62).

The critical reaction

Freud's theories of the complex web of psychic barriers erected to prevent or distort disclosure of the origins of traumatic repression survive as background hypotheses of an entire gamut of psychoanalytical theory, clinical practice and popular psychology. Although Freud's theories of personality development are no longer widely accepted as scientifically credible, the technique of assisted self-disclosure remains a central tenet of diagnostic and therapeutic strategies in both professional and popular therapies. Freud's acceptance of self-disclosure as a method of discovery and recovery has survived the relentless attack upon his ideas from feminist theory, the medical profession and social theorists generally (Burck and Speed, 1995; Klages, 1995; Crews, 1995; Masson, 1984, 1986; Mitchell, 1975; Hale, 1995).

The 'classical' framework of Freudian theory and practice has been hotly contested from its earliest publicity in the late nineteenth century. The most vehement opposition came in reaction to Freud's claims of infantile and childhood experiences of sexual desire and gratification. But there was also widespread resistance from defenders, already challenged by Darwinian science, of Enlightenment ideas, classical values and Christian doctrine. The rational mind, human virtue, the assumptions of a natural moral harmony and spiritual equilibrium in normal mental life were, in the face of Freudian theory, swept aside as naive deceptions of the repressive super-ego. Freud offered, instead, a mechanistic theory of consciousness that presupposed mental life as a maelstrom of conflicting and destructive forces, including a wholly irrational and self-destructive egoism, a pervasive sexuality, destructive libidinal fixations, a 'normal' life based on conflict and unnatural controls, and to top it all off, the 'death wish'. Traditional concepts of the 'normal' individual, the justly tempered society and 'progressive' civilisation must now be explained as the conquest, repression and the displacement of unruly natural instincts and self-destructive psychic forces.

Within the psychoanalytic tradition itself there have always been internecine warfare, revisions, rival schools, scandals, neo-Freudian theory, and major reconceptualisations by Carl Jung, Melanie Klein, Karen Horney, Jacques Lacan and numerous others (Wolman, 1984). For the past three decades, psychoanalysis and psychiatry have been condemned by philosophers, historians and philosophers of science. Recent archival investigators have argued that important elements of Freud's theories, case reports and clinical methods, and those of his collaborators and early rivals, were suppressed, grossly distorted or simply fraudulent (Masson, 1984, 1988 and 1991). The profession of psychoanalysis at large has been repeatedly accused of being unscientific (Rosenfeld, 1970; Hillman and Ventura, 1992; Crews, 1995). Theories about the mind's mechanisms, forces, processes and pathologies have been dismissed as tautological or simply imaginary. It has been claimed that an adequate empirical grounding of Freudian psychoanalysis is impossible in principle and its clinical 'findings' are based on a narrow selection of affluent, middle class, predominantly female patients.

Psychoanalysis has also faced ideological critiques. Freud's work was accused by the Nazis for being un-German, immoral and simply Jewish. In recent decades it has been condemned as bourgeois, individualistic, Eurocentric, patriarchal and misogynist (Greer, 1971: 90-98; Mitchell, 1975). In some cases, Freud's own theories have been turned against him with the intention of displaying how his interpretative biases and symbolic schemes are clear evidence of his own fixations and neurotic thought and behaviour.

Modernism and the psychotherapeutic culture

Despite these harsh verdicts, Freudian thought has profoundly influenced Western thinking about sexuality, the makeup of the human mind, the psychic depth of religion, art and literature, and how we understand human behaviour and motivations. Perhaps no less influential has been the adoption of Freudian theory, symbolism and interpretative methods in literature (both creative and critical), biography, history and the popular and fine arts. Freudian concepts and terminology to describe the operation of the mind have unquestionably entered into common discourse and modes of popular representation, as have Freudian theories of the thoroughly sexual formation and expression of the human personality.

It is easy to get lost in the complex theories and esoteric practices of psychoanalysis. Yet at the same time psychiatry has produced stereotypes so familiar that they serve as easy clichés for the cartoonist. Who has not seen a cartoon of the psychoanalyst, bearded, cigar smoking, aloof, invariably seated behind the couch? The fraught patient lying on the couch is anxiously struggling to come to terms with childhood memories, neurotic 'complexes', and mind-boggling Oedipal traumas. Popular culture has long provided a repertoire of exotic ideas that make us vaguely 'knowing' about sexual imagery, 'Freudian slips' and suggestive lyrics, sung with girlish sauciness and Oedipal overtones, that 'my heart belongs to Daddy!' Freudian nomenclature has entered into everyday speech, literature and the dialogue of television sitcoms and talk shows (Adams and Williams, 1995; Berman, 1985; Shattuck, 1996). Psychosis, neurosis, sublimation, projection, oral fixation, anal retentiveness, narcissism and numerous other terms are integral to the æsthetic of modernism (Boone, 1998). Shulamith Firestone's 1970s critique (1973: 46) paid tribute to Freud as 'the one cultural current that most characterized America in the twentieth century':

> There is no one who remains unexposed to his vision of human life, whether through courses in it ('psych'); through personal therapy, a common cultural experience for children of the middle class; or generally, through its pervasion of popular culture. The new vocabulary has crept into our everyday speech, so that the ordinary man thinks in terms of being 'sick', 'neurotic', or 'psycho'; he checks his 'id' periodically for a 'death wish', and his 'ego' for 'weakness'; he takes for granted that he has a 'castration complex', that he has a 'repressed' desire to sleep with his mother, that he was and maybe still is engaged in 'sibling rivalry', that women 'envy' his penis; he is likely to see every banana or hotdog as a 'phallic symbol'.... The spectacled and goateed little Viennese dozing in an armchair is a (nervous) cliché of modern humour.... Freudianism has become, with its confessionals and penance, its proselytes and converts, with the millions spent on its upkeep, our modern Church.

At the end of the Freudian century, the situation has not changed. People who have never read a word of Freud or Jung have some idea about the psychological complexity of sexual fantasies and dream symbolism. We accept that dreams are not 'just dreams'. Jokes about phallic symbols no longer make people blush. When a feminist critic slams a 'masculinist' cityscape, we assume she is ridiculing architects' fascination with 'thrusting skyscrapers'. In an argument with friends, we may breezily ignore matters of fact and slyly observe that they are *obsessed, projecting, sublimating* or *in denial*. Someone who insists upon a special point of logic is likely to be met with the put-down, 'Oh, stop being so anal!' Such repartee is all part of modernist language and humour.

These few anecdotes reflect a popular absorption of Freud's theories of the unconscious mind. It is a teeming cauldron of libidinal fantasies. This brew has produced in each of us a personality that betrays shameful repressions of things we have seen, thought, touched, experienced and dreamed from earliest infancy. It may be that the bantering use of Freudian ideas is a technique by which we concede a small point in order to draw a discreet veil of silence over still powerful taboos: the hatred and abuse of siblings, Freud's infamous theory of penis envy, Oedipal incest and violence, the death wish. Anxiously, we may feel some things are still *best left unsaid*.

Granting that there are extremes of experience, more or less nurturing families and varying degrees of personal strength, some individuals will suffer more than others from the tensions of keeping the lid on that 'cauldron' of unconsciousness. Some will be disabled more than others from functioning 'normally' as a result of this effort. In such cases, it follows that the 'talking cure' is a means of lifting that lid, gradually and under expert care, to release the tension by articulating these inner thoughts for the first time ever in language, narratives and coherent accounts to another person. One way to exorcise demons is to take them out for an airing in the full light of day.

Despite the successive efforts to 'debunk' the Freudian tradition, a broad consensus, indeed enthusiasm, about the beneficial nature of self-disclosure has formed.[6] Thus people in serious personal difficulty are likely to hear – from counsellors, friends, television talk show hosts, ministers of religion and personnel advisors in the workplace – that you should 'open up'. It is an inspirational message that has escaped the calm of the psychoanalyst's office and taken to the streets in the aggressive swagger of rap music: *'Spress yo'self!* Candour, openness, self-disclosure, and confession constitute the expressive modality of the mature, well-adjusted, strong and outwardly engaged individual.

The post-Freudian therapeutic culture

Advances in medical technology, bio-chemistry and pharmacology in the past half-century might suggest to some that scientific claims for the 'talking cure'[7] as a therapy for mental and physical disorders are merely quaint and retrograde. However, in recent decades optimism about the 'miracles of science' and 'wonder drugs' has palled, not least because of fears, as well as evidence, of the harmful side effects of medications and 'nutritional additives'. This reaction has given rise to a wide range of 'alternative' and 'natural' therapies – for example, herbalism, reflexology, flotation tanks and Reiki massage – to treat organic diseases and recover psychic and spiritual well-being. In this context, therapies involving professionally guided self-disclosure are neither extreme nor lacking in rational appeal. Therefore despite powerful assaults on the ramparts of Freudian and neo-Freudian psychoanalytic theory and psychiatric practice in recent decades, there remains a widespread conviction and a considerable body of literature defending the diagnostic and healing powers of 'the talking cure' (Vaughan, 1997; Wolman, 1984).

Therapeutic techniques that employ self-disclosure have multiplied in recent decades even as the practice of classical psychoanalysis has declined. Assertiveness and sensitivity training, empowerment courses, self-esteem seminars and group therapy for alcoholism, drug dependency, domestic violence, depression, stress and trauma are, in whole or part, talking cures (Toukmanian and Brouwers, 1998). 'Pastoral care' is a newly bestowed responsibility of academics in their collegial, pedagogical and supervisory roles. Personnel and management training courses employ techniques to achieve 'openness' and mutual disclosure. Everyone, it seems, is encouraged to 'open up' and be 'out front'. Being 'comfortable' as a human being is equated with one's ease in revealing private things in 'safe' and confidential speech settings.

Popular therapies seldom embrace or even acknowledge Freudian theory and methods (Beier and Young, 1984). Nevertheless, despite the diminished credibility of scientific positivism and the abandonment of mechanistic theories of the mind, it is clear from the professional literature and promotional advertising that many therapies and 'services' are heavily influenced by Freudian theory, vocabulary and methods. Whether simply called counselling or promoted as movements or proprietary techniques – for example, the violently named 'Primal Scream Therapy' – they tend to use Freudian terminology. Freud's special terms, such as *libido, id, ego, superego, repression, fixation* and *sublimation* are now casually used in therapeutic discourse. The Freudian influence on therapeutic discourse is evident in New Age psychoanalytic analogies: dream interpretation, memory recovery, 'voicing', autobiography (Smith and Watson, 1996), 'dumping' and 'letting go'.

These techniques encourage a patient's disclosure of memories, dreams, fears, emotions and traumatic experiences to a professional auditor or a clinical group. With or without a Freudian idiom, the contemporary patient may be described as suffering from stress, depression, personality fragmentation or a 'decentred' and 'conflicted' personality. Indeed, many pathological 'disturbances' are virtually meaningless outside of an implicit framework of Freud's theories of infantile personality development, libidinal repression, neurosis, and trauma. The same is true of widely used analytic and therapeutic techniques involving guided self-disclosure through dream symbolism and interpretation, thought and word associations, hypnosis and other means of 'confronting' deeply embedded, gradually penetrated childhood experiences and memories.

The common thread that runs through these techniques is the imperative of self-disclosure and the belief that self-understanding offers a path of liberation from the painful and disabling efforts required to keep things hidden from the self and others. The healing potential of self-disclosure, although rarely linked to Freudian psychoanalytic diagnoses, is now routinely expressed in standard clinical terms. Similarly, inhibitions against self-disclosure are thought to offer insights into physical and organic disorders. One psychologist argues that 'actively holding back or inhibiting our thoughts and feelings can be hard work.'

> Over time, the work of inhibition gradually undermines the body's defences. Like other stressors, inhibition can affect immune function, the action of the heart and vascular systems, and even the biochemical workings of the brain and nervous systems. In short, excessive holding back of thoughts, feelings, and behaviours can place people at risk for both major and minor diseases (Pennebaker, 1990: 13-14).

This is a view that has entered into folk wisdom, even if it has been theorised in esoteric bodies of theory. Revealing phrases from the vernacular show how these insights have been encouraged from ancient times. How many times have you encouraged others, or received their encouragement, to 'make a breast of it' and 'get something off your chest'? Such injunctions harken back to the Homeric idea that the 'true self' resides in the heart or the vital organs of the chest and abdomen. But the meaning survives quite clearly. The idea is to 'come clean' and reveal oneself to others for the good it will do all concerned:

> ...confronting our deepest thoughts and feelings can have remarkable short- and long-term health benefits. Confession, whether by writing or talking, can neutralize many of the problems of inhibition. Further, writing or talking about upsetting things can influence our basic values, our daily thinking patterns, and our feelings about ourselves. In short, there appears to be something akin to an urge to confess. Not disclosing our thoughts and feeling can be unhealthy. Divulging them can be healthy (Pennebaker, 1990: 13-14).

The Socratic background: the psyche and the 'knowing self'

Contemporary therapies emphasise the values of self-awareness and openness to others, but they also underscore how discipline is required to achieve them. This should remind us that important schools of thought from ancient times have emphasised that self-disclosure is not only socially desirable but is essential to spiritual well-being and one's effectiveness as a fully functional member of society. Indeed the role of self-disclosure in psychoanalytic theory and practice cannot be fully appreciated without exploring how its deeper roots in philosophy and religion have nourished the modern ideas.

Long before the development of modern psychology, the *self* has been considered to be a philosophically and morally significant object of knowledge. It is not surprising that knowledge of such a kind would be difficult to acquire. How, and under what conditions, could knowledge of the 'self' ever be transparent to the knowing subject? Indeed, if it be supposed that knowledge of the self will effect a transformation in one's life, does this not logically imply that 'self-knowledge' is in principle impossible, or at best solipsistic? Even to pose the injunction, 'Know thyself' – calls to mind the image of looking into a mirror, or indeed finding the 'self' in a hall of mirrors. Reflexivity, self-reflection, contemplation of the contemplating self, *self-disclosure*: such phrases seem hopelessly bound up in a paradox of the 'self-knowing self'.

'Know thyself', a moral admonition associated with Socrates in the fifth century BC, indicated the path to spiritual harmony and wisdom. It was the essential foundation for virtuous action. *Self-knowledge*, the goal of many philosophies and religions, has been sought by meditation, contemplation, prayer and various ecstasies achieved through self-induced pain, hunger or mind-altering drugs. These disciplines are supposed to illuminate the path of an inward journey of discovery in which the conscious self becomes both the guide and the spectator of one's past and present mental landscapes.

If Plato's dialogues from fourth-century Athens are to be trusted, the Socratic injunction is the earliest, and certainly the most concise, theory of self-disclosure. It proved controversial and, for Socrates, ultimately fatal. Modern scholars credit Socrates, or blame him, for enjoining us to examine our mortal souls rather than worship the divinities or aspire to solve the riddles of the universe.

Scholars also argue that Socrates in effect 'discovered' the soul or psyche as it has been understood ever since, namely, as the seat of consciousness, intelligence and individual personality (Cornford, 1974: 50-53; Taylor, 1953: 134-40). Anyone today who is surprised at such a claim need only remember that *courage* and *love* (charity, *caritas*) are derived from the Greek word for heart (*kear*). We still 'know' what is most certain in our hearts, especially love. Poetry, if we know it truly, we recite 'by heart'. Socrates overturned this archaic understanding of the bodily location of the 'true self'. What had been for his predecessors the mere spark of conscious life or a shadow of the body, the *psyche* was, for Socrates, the force that distinguishes the human from other creatures and constitutes each individual as unique: intelligence, language, volition and the desire to know. *But what ought we to know?*

The great pre-Socratic thinkers of the Ionian enlightenment had, for several centuries, speculated about the origins of the universe (Smith, 1965). They propounded ingenious theories about the fundamental elements of physical matter and the appearance of change and diversity in the natural world. Though well-versed in these theories as a youth, Socrates concluded that what any truly wise person would want to know is the purpose – the *telos* or end – of human life and how to live it well and truly. This is the task of one who seeks true wisdom, the philosopher. It is instructive that Plato's dialogues (*Gorgias, Republic, Sophist* and others) repeatedly described the philosopher, and the philosopher ruler, as a 'physician of the soul'.

For Socrates, knowledge of the origins and underlying principles of the· universe was trivial and useless compared with the knowledge necessary for living the good life. He reasoned that certain, true, real knowledge of how one ought to live could not be gained from following the gods' licentious examples nor from mere conformity with the opinions and customs of one's fellow citizens. Rather, this special wisdom required the soul's awakening to the knowledge that one's truly informed – that is, one's *real* – desires are in harmony with justice. Knowing this is to know the real Good. The task of Plato's metaphorical physician of the soul – the original 'psychologist' – is to diagnose undernourished and diseased souls suffering from ignorance (the absence of self-knowledge). This deficiency of the soul has corrupting consequences for the body and the body politic, causing them to seek counterfeit pleasures – sensuous confections and superficial cosmetics – instead of a nutritious diet and physical training.

The physician's method of 'treating' the sick is to draw them out, engage them in dialogue and reveal their false opinions and blindness to their true interests. In the dark cavern, they must be 'turned around', disabused of the shadowy images and made to face up to the initially painful sunlight streaming down from the mouth of the cave. Only then will the shadows be exposed as insubstantial and reality gradually revealed in its true dimensions.[8]

This emphasis on self-knowledge was very far from pre-Socratic speculations about stability and change in the cosmos, and its fundamental elements: air, earth, fire and water. Moreover, Socrates' view was scorned by his fellow-citizens – busy seeking power, fame and fortune – who proudly insisted that the best life was lived by those powerful enough to rule over the weak. Socrates busied himself as a living rebuke to Athenians, arguing that self-knowledge – the psyche's life-long journey of self-discovery of the true purpose and rational knowledge of what it is to be a human being – was the most valuable thing. Such a life was at once the fulfilment of the human *telos* and the attainment of self-knowledge. It promised triumph over ignorance, ineffectual desire and the tribulations of bodily life. Ultimately it offered the soul's triumph over death.

Today Socratic and Platonic idealism may seem woefully naive. Perhaps philosophical idealism is all the more discredited because it was eventually adopted and elaborated in the spiritualism of Christian theology. Nevertheless, these ancient doctrines of moral idealism and spiritual transcendence are remarkably resilient ideas because Western politics and religion have always nurtured, and been nurtured by, a therapeutic 'care for the self'. The pre-eminence of the psyche – the soul, the spirit, the 'true self' – and its priority in individual reason, will and identity have remained bedrock beliefs in Western cultural mores. This has remained true even though some aspects of Western culture – especially modern science and historical relativism – have abandoned ancient philosophical and theological frameworks.

Consider the contemporary resonance of the words Shakespeare placed on the lips of Polonious, in *Hamlet*, when he pleads with his son Laertes to behave himself upon his return to university and the flesh-pots of Paris: 'This above all: to thine own self be true, and it must follow, as the night the day, thou canst not then be false to any man.' A strong and vivid thread of moral optimism runs from Polonious's admonition directly to New Age therapies of self-awareness, authenticity and personal autonomy. Modern therapeutic and self-help disciplines promise to their practitioners the ability to 'get in touch with the self' and 'discover your inner self' by 'opening up' and expressing from within things that could not be disclosed without the revelatory experiences of the therapies and the confessional settings in which they occur. Whether in the calm of a psychotherapist's study or the evangelical clamour of an Oprah Winfrey show, in lurid feature journalism or the cool minimalism of conceptual art, the aim is to 'confront' people with 'difficult material'. The adept soon learns that what one is really supposed to confront – fears, prejudices, shameful memories, extreme desires – *lies within the self*, that is, the psyche.

Whether New Age therapies rest upon assumptions that are less, or more, metaphysical than Plato's therapeutic political philosophy, the point is that in both ancient and modern visions strong ethical judgements are made. In each case the mode of deliverance from vice to virtue, sickness to health, is the same: self-disclosure is the path to self-knowledge. Illness, ignorance, immaturity, spiritual darkness, self-deception, cowardice, moral paralysis, deformity of personality, dependence and subjection – all of these are said to be traits of a person 'out of touch' with one's own 'self'. The enclosed self – locked and imprisoned – suffers stagnation, decay and death.

By contrast, self-disclosure in a safe and confidential setting, free from the intention to cause injury to others, is both healing and healthful. It is the enlightening, courageous, active and productive capacity of a liberated, autonomous, independent person capable of relating to others. Moreover, it is the transformative *process* of self-disclosure that is so highly valued. Self-disclosure is the vital behaviour of a healthy, well-adjusted, mature and skilful individual.

The Christian psyche

Although Christianity is not the only major world religion that emphasises inner awareness and self-knowledge, it has been the dominant exponent of these ideals in Western culture. Self-disclosure was central to the Judæo-Christian emphasis on a spiritual as well as a 'personal' relationship with the divine, as exemplified in the 'conversation' of prayerful confession (Kroger, 1994). Indeed, compared to other religions Christianity is especially concerned with practices to encourage 'opening the heart and soul' not only to God, but also to the community of believers.

In the Old Testament, the book of *Exodus* (33:11) records that 'the Lord used to speak to Moses face to face, as a man speaks to a friend' (Healey, 1990: 17). The religious experience as a self-disclosing personal relationship between man and God is described by Healey:

> It is possible to look at the story of the fall of Adam and Eve as a rupture in this relationship [between man and God], whereby shame and the need to cover up and hide come into being, thus introducing a burden upon humanity that did not previously exist.

The importance of disclosure and its attendant benefits, including forgiveness and a sense of liberation, are expressed in the *Psalms* (32:1-7):

Blessed is he whose transgression is forgiven, whose sin is covered.....
Blessed is the man...in whom there is no guile. When I kept silence, my
bones became old .... For day and night thy hand was heavy upon me.... I
acknowledged my sin unto thee, and mine iniquity have I not hidden. I said,
I will confess my transgressions unto the Lord, and those forgavest the
iniquity of my sin. For this shall every one that is godly pray unto thee in a
time when thou mayest be found.... Thou art my hiding place; thou shalt
preserve me from trouble; thou shalt compass me about with songs of
deliverance.

In the Roman Catholic tradition, self-disclosure as a means of spiritual
restoration takes its most direct form in the penitent's private confession to
a priest. Psychoanalysis has been described, often critically, as a modern,
secular version of the Catholic confession. Confession takes place in
absolute confidentiality, guaranteed by the priestly vow of secrecy of all
that is revealed in the confessional. The humbled penitent is urged to
confess both sinful deeds and equally sinful thoughts to priestly authority,
literally to a 'Father'. This confession, together with a show of contrition
and a commensurate penance of arduous prayer, is rewarded with
absolution and an exhilarating release from the guilt of sin.

Protestant Christianity has emphasised the value – indeed the
Christian's earthly goal – of the individual's public striving for
authenticity, truthfulness and prayerful contrition. The Protestant's zeal to
be 'pure in heart' by living a life puritanical in deed requires rituals of self-
condemnation. But the Protestant is encouraged to confess to all the
congregation the dreadful stains that befoul one's sinful heart and burden
one's body with the corruptions of desire. Rather than disclosure and
absolving contrition in the privacy of the confessional box, this is a form of
public self-exposure, a confession that invites both congregational support
and communal surveillance of the sinner's waywardness from the path of
righteousness. To this day, 'testimony meetings' and 'prayer meetings' –
wherein ordinary members express aloud their sins and private agonies to
the assembled faithful – are essential features of evangelical and 'low
church' Protestant worship.

Self-disclosure as an archetype of religious experience was enshrined
in early church history, liturgy and the sacraments. This was evident, for
example, in 'spiritual direction', a Christian religious discipline dating to
the early Church and monastic communities whose aims and techniques
have been compared to modern psychotherapy (Healey, 1990). Spiritual
direction was a relationship of guidance in prayer, meditation, purgation
and confession, establishing between the penitent and the director a trust
and intimacy that will 'help the individual keep honest in his or her search
to work continually at the process of unmasking, striving for inner freedom

and open-handedness in one's relationship with God' (Healey, 1990: 23; McCarty, 1976).

The therapeutic intimacy of this relationship is vividly expressed by St. John Climacus, a seventh-century ascetic who described the role of the priestly intermediary: 'Lay bare your wound to your spiritual physician. Without being ashamed say: "Here is my fault, Father. Here is my illness."' This emphasis upon the belief in the reformative powers of self-disclosure was earlier expressed by St. Basil, a fourth-century monk, who admonished a follower to 'reveal the secrets of his heart.... By practising such openness, we shall gradually be made perfect' (Nemeck and Coombs, 1985: 67-68).

These ancient religious aspirations for a spiritual identification and intimacy with God form a striking parallel with the modern aims of psychotherapy. Just as self-disclosure is the 'cornerstone and foundation' of spiritual growth, so it is the foundation of the deeper understanding of the self that is the goal of psychotherapy.

> Broadly speaking, psychotherapy is concerned with the growth and development of the individual to enable him or her to live more freely, unencumbered by the myriad maladaptive patterns that tend to restrict, confine and limit one's potential. In the psychotherapeutic process, self-disclosure promotes intimacy, which allows therapy to proceed (Healey, 1990: 21).

In the twentieth century, despite the emergence of a pervasive secular culture, the well-being of the psyche – variously translated in modern languages as mind, soul, spirit, ghost (*Geist* in German) – has, as we have seen, continued to be both a popular and a professional preoccupation. If anything, concern for the 'self' has given rise to more theories and disciplines of care, treatment and control than ever before, with sociologists speculating about a 'culture of narcissism' (Lasch, 1978). In the first half of the twentieth century, traditional religious discipline and the more recondite forms of deistic spiritualism gave way to 'scientific' caretakers of the human psyche through disciplines of medicine, psychology and psychotherapy. These have been rivalled in the late twentieth century by a resurgence of astrology, Satanism, pantheism, alchemy, psychic reincarnation and other frankly anti-scientific paths of spiritual 'recovery'.

Surprisingly, the popular assumptions, strategies and optimism about the psychotherapeutic benefits of self-disclosure are much the same as in Platonic and Christian beliefs. So far as the patient is concerned, the slow, painful process of self-disclosure is the prerequisite for recognition and catharsis. Only in this way can the patient be liberated from the repressive forces which had submerged traumatic experiences and produced neurotic symptoms. Whether or not articulated in this Freudian vocabulary, the entire range of 'mind healing' and 'self-help' therapies accept the reformative effects and curative powers of self-awareness, the imperative of self-exposure to the contents and affective influences of the unconscious mind, and the therapeutic consequences of this self-disclosure.

Conclusion

Self-disclosure – as a form of human expression and an ethically esteemed behaviour – *unites* the modern, secularised experience of psychoanalysis with ancient values and traditions in Western culture. Self-disclosure is not an absolute value, nor has it been accorded the status of an end in itself in religion, psychology and philosophy. Yet in all three spheres, a special ethical status has been attributed to self-disclosure as a path of escape from the silent tyranny of repression, the guilt of a sinful conscience and social alienation. Self-disclosure is good for you. It is an act of honesty to oneself and others. It is a deed of courage and a mark of humility. It is a means of taking responsibility for one's self, and thus an expression of emotional strength and maturity. As an articulation of the struggle to accept oneself – the acceptance of who you are, what you have been and what has fatefully, even tragically, befallen you – self-disclosure becomes a means of 'connecting' to others, at once to win, deepen and deserve good will and solidarity. It is to 'grow up'; but also, in desperate circumstances and personal failure, to 'own up', and thus initiate a recuperation of one's lost esteem and trust.

These value-laden terms of ethical judgement are, on the surface, at odds with aspirations to the scientific study of the mind. Nevertheless, on reflection we can see that such traditional moral estimations are related to – indeed practically must be the substance of – what a psychotherapist hopes to accomplish by the talking cure: the interpretation and resolution of debilitating repressions and the recovery of self-sufficient well-being.

Notes

[1] 'For now we see through a glass darkly; but then, face to face; now I know in part, but then shall I know even as also I am known' (I *Corinthians* 13:12).
[2] Wills (1999: 30), whose translation is used here, makes a special point of translating the title of Augustine's work as *The Testimony*, noting that in English '*Confessions*...has anachronistic connotations of criminal or sacramental confession', whereas Augustine's meaning is more faithfully rendered in his use of confiteri ('testify') and *testimonium*.

[3] Here Freud alludes to Goethe's *Faust* (Part I, Scene 3), in which Faust directly contradicts the biblical phrase, 'In the beginning was the word.'

[4] Freudian usage uses cathexis to refer to a substance 'force' – an instinctual drive or physically produced energy, as in the sexual energy of the libido – or the release or impact of that force. Catharsis refers to the release or discharge, during psychoanalysis, of emotional tensions. These include repressed, conflicting investments of energy – that is, symptomatic expressions of traumatic repression, 'resistance' and transference – that are identified, experienced and hopefully drained away in the 'work' of the patient's analytic experience (Freud, 1973: 14-15, 121).

[5] This debate has understandably been a matter of grave concern for the reputation of the profession and it raises difficult ethical issues that have been soberly and on the whole severely canvassed (Jourard, 1964; Weiner, 1978). Weiner frankly asserts 'the pitfalls of therapeutic openness' and insists that 'there are many possible misuses of self-disclosure' (1978: 89; 165-66). For a summary review of a variety of perspectives on therapeutic self-disclosure, see the concluding chapter by Striker (1990) in the comprehensive study by Striker and Fisher (1990).

[6] In a surprising paradox, those who boast that, theory aside, the talking cure 'works' or 'helps' adopt the pragmatic justification of behavioural psychology, the psychoanalytic tradition's greatest rival. Behavioural psychologists defend their methods of behavioural modification – by punishing and rewarding patients – on the simple ground that it works, leaving aside theories of the mind and its operations, and ignoring the problems of how one could ever know what it is to 'cure' or return to 'normal' something that cannot easily be shown to exist physiologically.

[7] Unease about the scientific status of 'the talking cure' is reflected in the uncertainty of its origins. It is certain that Freud's early collaborator, Breuer, used the term, but some scholars (Thom, 1981: 1) ascribe its origins to one of Freud's patients, 'Anna O' (Freud and Breuer, 1974: 95n).

[8] The famous allegory of the cave is in *The Republic*, Book VII, S. 514-19 (Plato (1945: 227-33).

References

Adams, J. and Williams, E. (eds) (1995), *Mimetic Desire: Essays on Narcissism in German Literature from Romanticism to Post Modernism*, Camden House, Columbia, South Carolina.

Barnlund, D.C. (1975), *Public and Private Self in Japan and the United States*, Simul Press, Tokyo.

Beier, E.G. and Young, D.M. (eds) (1984), *The Silent Languages of Psychotherapy: Social Reinforcement of Unconscious Processes*, 2nd ed., Aldine, New York.

Berman, J. (1995), *The Talking Cure: Literary Representations of Psychoanalysis*, New York University Press, New York.

Black, M. (1972), *The Labyrinth of Language*, Pelican Press, Harmondsworth.

Burck, C. and Speed, B. (eds) (1995), *Gender, Power and Relationships*, Routledge, London.

Chelune, G.J. (1979), *Self-Disclosure: Origins, Patterns, and Implications of Openness in Interpersonal Relationships*, Jossey-Bass, San Francisco.

Chomsky, N. (1976), *Reflections on Language*, Fontana, London.

Cornford, F.M. (1974), *Before and After Socrates*, Cambridge University Press, Cambridge.

Crews, F.C. (1995), *The Memory Wars: Freud's Legacy in Dispute*, New York Review of Books, New York.

Fisher, M. (1990), 'The Shared Experience and Self-Disclosure' in G. Stricker and M. Fisher (eds), *Self-Disclosure in the Therapeutic Relationship*, Plenum Press, New York, pp. 3-16.

Fitzpatrick, M.A. (1988), *Between Husbands and Wives: Communication in Marriage*, Sage Publications, Newbury Park, California.

Firestone, S. (1972), *The Dialectic of Sex: The Case for a Feminist Revolution*, Paladin, London.

Freud, S. (1970), *The Question of Lay Analysis* in *Two Short Accounts of Psycho-Analysis*, J. Strachey trans. and ed., Penguin, Harmondsworth.

_____ (1973), *New Introductory Lectures on Psychoanalysis* [1932-33], J. Strachey trans. and ed., Penguin, Harmondsworth.

_____ (1975), *The Psychopathology of Everyday Life*, J. Strachey ed. and A. Tyson trans., Penguin, Harmondsworth.

Freud, S., and Breuer, J. (1974), *Studies on Hysteria* [1893-95], J. and A. Strachey eds. and trans., Penguin, Harmondsworth.

Goleman, D. (1996), *Emotional Intelligence*, Bloomsbury, London.

_____ (1998), *Working with Emotional Intelligence*, Bloomsbury, London.

Greer, G. (1971), *The Female Eunuch*, Paladin, London.

Hale, N.G. (1995), *The Rise and Crisis of Psychoanalysis in the United States: Freud and the Americans, 1917-1985*, Oxford University Press, New York.

Healey, B.J. (1990), 'Self-Disclosure in Religious Spiritual Direction: Antecedents and Parallels to Self-Disclosure in Psychotherapy' in G. Stricker and M. Fisher (eds), *Self-Disclosure in the Therapeutic Relationship*, Plenum Press, New York, pp. 17-27.

Hillman, J. and Ventura, M. (1992), *We've Had a Hundred Years of Psychotherapy – and the World's Getting Worse*, Harper, San Francisco.

Jourard, S.M. (1964), *The Transparent Self: Self Disclosure and Well-Being*, D. Van Nostrand, New Jersey.

Kabat-Zinn, J. (1994), *Wherever You Go, There You Are*, Hyperion, New York.

Kennedy, E. (1975), *If You Really Knew Me Would You Still Like Me?*, Argus Publications, New York.

Klages, N. (1995), *Look Back in Anger: Mother-Daughter and Father-Daughter Relationships in Women's Autobiographical Writings of the 1970 and 1980s*, Lang, New York.

Kroger, R.O. (1994), 'The Catholic Confession and Everyday Self-Disclosure' in J. Siegfried (ed.), *The Status of Common Sense in Psychology*, Ablex Publishing, Norwood, New Jersey.

Langs, R. (1976), 'The Therapeutic Relationship and Deviations in Technique', *International Journal of Psychoanalytic Psychotherapy*, vol. 4, pp. 106-41.

Lasch, C. (1978), *The Culture of Narcissism: American Life in an Age of Diminishing Expectations*, Norton, New York.

Lum, W.B. (1988), 'Sandor Ferenczi (1873-1933) – Father of the Empathetic-Interpersonal Approach. Part I. Introduction and Early Analytic Years', *Journal of the American Academy of Psychoanalysis*, vol. 16, pp. 131-53.

Masson, J.M. (1984), *Freud's Suppression of the Seduction Theory*, Farrar Straus and Giroux, New York.

_____ (1986), *A Dark Science: Women, Sexuality, and Psychiatry in the Nineteenth Century*, Farrar, Straus and Giroux, New York.

_____ (1988), *Against Therapy: Emotional Tyranny and the Myth of Psychological Healing*, Atheneum, New York.

_____ (1991), *Final Analysis: The Making and Unmaking of a Psychoanalyst*, Harper Collins, London.

McCarty, S. (1976), 'On Entering Spiritual Direction', *Review for Religious*, vol. 35, pp. 854-57.

Mitchell, J. (1975), *Psychoanalysis and Feminism: Freud, Reich, Laing, and Women*, Vintage Books, New York.

Nemeck, F.K. and Coombs, M.T. (eds) (1985), *The Way of Spiritual Direction*, Michael Glazier, Wilmington, Delaware.

Smith, S. and J. Watson, J. (eds) (1996), *Getting a Life: Everyday Uses of Autobiography*, University of Minnesota Press, Minneapolis.

Pennebaker, J.W. (1990), *Opening Up: The Healing Power of Confiding in Others*, William Morrow and Co., New York.

Plato (1945), *The Republic*, F.M. Cornford trans., Oxford University Press, Oxford.

Rosenfeld, I. (1970), *Freud: Character and Consciousness. A Study of Freud's Theory of Unconscious Motives*, University Books, New York.

Sennett, R. (1978), *The Fall of Public Man: On the Social Psychology of Capitalism*, Random House, New York.

Shattuck, J. (1996), *The Talking Cure: TV Talk Shows and Women*, Routledge, New York.

Sifneos, P. (1991), 'Affect, Emotional Conflict, and Deficit: An Overview', *Psychotherapy and Psychosomatics*, vol. 56, pp. 116-22.

Smith, T.V. (ed.) (1965), *From Thales to Plato*, University of Chicago Press, Chicago.

Stricker, G. (1990), 'Self-Disclosure and Psychotherapy' in G. Stricker and M. Fisher, *Self-Disclosure in the Therapeutic Relationship*, Plenum Press, New York.

Stricker, G. and Fisher, M. (1990), *Self-Disclosure in the Therapeutic Relationship*, Plenum Press, New York.

Swiller, H.I. (1988), 'Alexithymia: Treatment Utilizing Combined Individual and Group Therapy, *International Journal for Group Psychotherapy*', vol. 38, no. 1, pp. 47-61.

Taylor, A.E. (1953), *Socrates: The Man and His Thoughts*, Doubleday, New York.

Thandi, H.S. (1993), *Self-Disclosure Perceptions among Students of Management*, Royal Melbourne Institute of Technology, Melbourne.

Thom, M. (1981), 'The Unconscious Structured as a Language' in C. MacCabe (ed.), *The Talking Cure: Essays in Psychoanalysis and Language*, Macmillan, London, pp. 1-44.

Toukmanian, S.G. and Brouwers, M.C. (1998), 'Cultural Aspects of Self-Disclosure and Psychotherapy' in S.S. Kazarian and D.R. Evans (eds), *Cultural Clinical Psychology: Theory, Research, and Practice*, Oxford University Press, New York.

Weiner, M.F. (1969), 'Nudity versus Neutrality in Psychotherapy', Paper presented to the First Annual Institute of the Golden Gate Group Psychotherapy Society, June 1969.

Weiner, M.F. (1978), *Therapist Disclosure: The Use of Self in Psychotherapy*, Butterworths, Boston.

Wills, G. (1999), 'Augustine's Magical Decade', *The New York Review of Books*, 6 May 1999, pp. 30-32.

Wolman, B.B. (1984), *Logic of Science in Psychoanalysis*, Columbia University Press, New York.

6 Applying the Gag

GREG McCARTHY

Introduction

In contemporary times disclosures abound. It appears as if anything and everything in the Western world can be revealed from the bathroom of the Oval Office to the bedrooms of suburbia. These disclosures take on multiple forms, from evidence given under duress in the Starr investigation into President Clinton to people clambering over others to confess on national television their innermost desires, predilections and tragedies. With this excess of disclosure the distinctions between life and art, fact and fiction, irony and double (or triple) irony, are left in an ambiguous state. Disclosing an unquestioned 'truth' about life and the human condition no longer seems possible. Instead, the contingency of truths has been revealed (Bauman, 1991: 242; Baudrillard, 1988: 166; Rorty, 1989: 2). The current penchant for personal disclosures also destabilises the modernist hierarchy of truth by uncovering that truth is referential and built on superior and inferior claims of disclosure. At the same time, it creates an opening to place truth in dialogue with hegemonic practice, whereby a dominant world-view prevails, 'gagging' alternative ideological perspectives.

These excessive disclosures reveal the ambivalent nature of truth. Individuals have responded to this revelation by turning to myths and ideologies which give shape to these disclosures, whilst acting as forms of closure on further disclosures. In other words, these myths and ideologies enter into an arena of discursive contestation where there is a battle to close off, or gag, some debates and elevate others to the status of universal truths. There are even attempts to gag, or muzzle, debate when a gag, in the sense of a joke, is made. Nevertheless, mass communication makes all these battles in and between discourses contingent. In this discursive realm of contingency, disclosures are subject to a variety of closures but the effectiveness of these gags has diminished. Concomitantly, those who seek to criticise these gags often find the resort to irony and comedy a more effective approach than claims to a higher truth (Eco, 1991: 68; Hutcheon, 1994: 8). With excessive disclosures, gags, in both senses of a joke and a closure, are flourishing.

This chapter addresses the issue of excessive disclosures and attempted hegemonic gags in the arena of popular culture. Through the study of popular culture it is possible to contemplate the complexities which exist not only within culture itself, but in the relations between what is disclosed, why it is disclosed, how it is received by those to whom it is exposed, and the relationship between these people and power. The terrain of popular culture is everyday life and people's lived experience. As such it stands in contrast to the equation of culture as the successive achievements of a particular civilisation in its march to a higher order (Williams, 1961: 57-88; Williams, 1976: 87; Hoggart, 1958: 22-24; Hall, 1980: 33-48). By addressing the question of culture as material and symbolic experience it is possible to consider the relationship between defined cultural products, or texts, and broader definitions of culture. Moreover, studies of popular culture embrace the multifarious character of audiences as well as the complex and, at times, contradictory means by which they receive and interpret a text (Ang, 1996: 13-15). A recognition of this pluralism can, however, be rather banal unless it makes reference to a larger social whole and to the issue of hegemony (Morris, 1990: 39-41).

In historical terms, debates over the meaning of the term 'culture', and what a 'culture' might disclose to an audience about society in general reached a critical intensity at a time when popular culture was becoming global. In the early 1950s, American culture as represented in films and television was having a profound effect on other Western societies. Reflecting on this phenomenon, Meagan Morris recalls how, as a young girl in Melbourne, Australia, the rambunctious Lucille Ball in *I Love Lucy* had a positive influence on her compared to the pervasive silence in her own household. For her, Lucy was in many ways a strong and admirable female character, which contradicted her father's depiction of Americans based on his war-time experience. In contrast to the traditional depiction of American television as a form of cultural imperialism, Morris's tale reveals its capacity from a feminist perspective also to have a positive effect (Morris, 1990: 16). Yet there was a far pervasive ideological influence in the 1950s that came from American popular culture, notably Hollywood, which acted to gag cultural expression and political debate in Australia and much of the Western world.

From both sides now

In the 1950s, Hollywood entered the Cold War debate clearly on the side of capitalism. Its representations were often crude, depicting communists as the enemy within and as having 'Un-American' attributes. The stereotype

'Commie' was someone who was sleazy, immoral, overweight, often an effeminate male, totally untrustworthy, and willing not only to betray his country but his family as well (Christensen, 1987: 89). According to the Hollywood of the McCarthy era, liberals and intellectuals were most easily duped by communism. The effect of this stereotype was the gagging of intellectual debate in the United States not only in terms of any possible merits of communism, but also over such matters as equality and the public provision of goods and services within a liberal-democratic society.

It is, therefore, with a heightened sense of irony that Woody Allen plays the role of a debunker of the communist witch-hunts in the 1975 movie, *The Front*, directed by Martin Ritt. *The Front*, a mild box-office success, was an unusual film for Allen as it was the first time he acted in a film without directing it. Allen, who often presents himself in his own films as a liberal intellectual, plays a character who turns the tables on those who were perceived as the enemy in the Cold War. In *The Front*, an overtly political film, Allen's character, Howard (representing the 'everyman'), acts as the front for three back-listed television writers. Through his willingness to take ten per cent of their income and all of their reputation he becomes aware of the horrors of the communist witch-hunt. Allen, nevertheless, subverts the political message of the film by inserting his familiar characterisation of a Jewish schlemiel pursuing his liberal girlfriend. He wins the girl and defends the good guys when he tells the House Un-American Activities Committee that he will not name names and 'they can all go fuck themselves'. As he is led off to prison to the strains of the nostalgic 'Young at Heart' sung by Frank Sinatra, the audience realises that Howard/Allen has not only stood up for good men against evil, but by doing so ensured that love is also triumphant (Sarris, 1978: 49).

Through its humour, *The Front* brought to audiences of the 1970s a critical perspective on the McCarthy period which had previously been expressed mainly in academic publications and dramatic representations. Here irony became the vehicle for the revenge of the blacklisted. The film included several of the blacklisted in its cast: Zero Mostel, Herschel Bernardi, Joshua Shelly, Martin Ritt and scenarist Walter Bernstein. Yet the moral of the film was muted as it turned the ideological debate into one of the persecution of good guys by ideological bovver boys.

As a film-maker, Woody Allen straddles the divide between high and low culture. His films have mass appeal and yet, despite lampooning himself, they are also intellectual exercises which have stimulated serious academic debate. Allen is ready to use gags both as openings and closures. For example, in *Star Dust Memories*, Allen, in the persona of the film director Sandy Bates pokes fun at his fame as a director and the tribulations which go with that fame. Bates is invited to attend a retrospective of his films, reproduced in the movie as avant garde parodies. In the symposium after the screening, Bates/Allen is asked by a member of the audience: 'Your films are always psychological never political, where do you stand politically?' Sandy Bates replies: 'What can I say to that, I am for total, honest democracy, you know, and I also believe the American system can work' (*Stardust Memories,* 1980). Thus a joke serves as Allen's tribute to democracy as well as an ambiguous assessment of the state of American politics.

Allen's films have layered and ambiguous meanings with the ability both to open up and close off debate. In many of his films Allen has taken the feminist catch cry, 'the personal is political', and used it to explore his own personal world from a variety of viewpoints. His success as a film-maker comes primarily from his comic anthologies of uncomfortably autobiographical disclosures of real-life love affairs with, at times, the very women who appear in his casts (*Annie Hall, Manhattan,* and *Hanna and Her Sisters*). In these films Allen shifted from his earlier character of the inept little guy to a philosophical lover and loser who draws distinctions between men and women, and by doing so recognises the superior wisdom of women. Yet, at the same time, it is Allen who always has the last word.

One of Allen's many skills is his capacity to turn a disclosed fact into a contested interpretation of truth. For instance, in a gag from *Annie Hall,* Allen plays with the notion that men and women regard the act of sex in different terms by juxtaposing the two lead characters' discussion with their psychiatrist concerning their relationship. When the psychiatrist asks Alvy/Allen how often he was having sex, he replies: 'Hardly ever, maybe three times a week'. Meanwhile, in a split screen, the same question is asked of the loquacious Annie (Keaton) who answers: 'Constantly, I'd say three times a week'. Thus Allen comically reveals the contingent nature of truth through their vastly divergent and subjective responses to an agreed fact.

Allen's films relegate any potential disclosures about American society, however, to a mere backdrop for his psychological and philosophical inquiry into the condition of 'modern man'. The film *Manhattan* is a prime example of Allen's tendency to open up a debate on society only to reduce it to a gag. In this film, Allen and New York City meld into one, simultaneously rich and shallow, pitiless and beautiful, romantic and hard edged, feminist and chauvinist. These dichotomies are evident from the opening lines of the film, with Allen, as the author Ike Davis, struggling to commence a novel set against vignettes of Manhattan while Gershwin's *Rhapsody in Blue* unfolds effortlessly as background music.

His attempts at authorship show the author/film director not only melding into the heart and soul of New York City, but also discloses Allen's tendency to collapse the political into the personal. For example, the voice of Ike narrates: 'He adored New York City, he idolised it all out of proportion...no, change that,...he romanticised it all out of proportion.' Beginning again, he muses: 'He was too romantic about Manhattan, as he was about everything else....' 'No [beginning again]: Chapter one. He adored New York City. To him, it was a metaphor for the decay of contemporary culture, the shallow lack of individual integrity.... No, it's too preachy.' Still unsatisfied, Ike reworks the opening lines to read: 'He adored New York City, although for him it was a metaphor for the decay of contemporary culture. How hard it was for him to live in a society degenerated by drugs, television, loud music....' Still dissatisfied, he tries again: 'Chapter One. He was as tough and romantic as the city he loved. Behind his black-rimmed glasses was the coiled sexual power of a jungle cat. I love this. New York was his town and it always would be' (*Manhattan*, 1979). In short, anxious political commentary about the decaying condition of modernity gives way to a gag on sexual prowess.

In the uncoiling of his sexual power, Davis/Allen has a series of love affairs, including one with Tracy, a seventeen year-old played by Mariel Hemingway. Again, Allen blurs the line between art and life, with his art disclosing moments in his own life. The closure of the film can be read as a representation of a purely romantic affair of the heart between an older man and a younger woman. But it also has the potential to be read as a justification for older men to exploit younger women. While Allen gives Hemingway the last line in the film, 'not everyone gets corrupted, you've got to have a little faith in people', this homily to the human condition is a mere echo of everything Ike has advised her during the film. Tracy's ventriloquist-like wisdom boomerangs back on Ike, evoking a response of pathos. Nevertheless, this pathos can be read as giving Allen the last gag and the last word, even if he does not say the lines. It is a clear instance of the double meaning of the term 'gag.' The joke is also a closure.

These readings were given a new dimension, moreover, when in 'real life' Allen's long-term partner, Mia Farrow, disclosed that he was having an affair with her adopted daughter. As the public dimension of Allen's private life colours the filmic depictions of his presentation of life from both sides, his previous feminist persona is now over-shadowed by a reading of his affair as male exploitation. Similarly, his elegy to Manhattan begins to lose its seductive and sexually charged edge when the prohibitive 'real' price of upper Manhattan real-estate is juxtaposed against its romantic, filmic appeal.

Disclosing nothing?

There is a certain irony in the fact that Manhattan is also the setting for the popular television series, *Seinfeld*. Sold as a series 'about nothing', it borrows heavily from Allen's obsession with the minutiae of everyday life and his use of a joke to gag debate. The four anti-heroes (Jerry, George, Elaine and Kramer) appear to be sophisticated Manhattanites always ready to put number one first and debate the trivia of life in New York while presenting it as the only place to live. This point is driven home when Elaine (Julia Louis-Dreyfuss) is given a new telephone number not designated for the Upper West Side. She is horrified and becomes pre-occupied with schemes to ensure that her number reverts back to the right area code, if for no other reason than to ensure her favourite Chinese take-away can be delivered to the right address. Similarly, George (Jason Alexander) portrays any visit to his parents in Queens as if he is going to the third world. Their obsession with themselves and New York is mediated only by a sense in which the four protagonists act in a familial manner to each other. Jerry (Jerry Seinfeld), for example, allows the others to use his fridge like family property and all counsel one another over their sequential failed relationships. The irony within the irony is that George and Jerry are depicted as striving to write a successful sitcom based on themselves and hence 'nothing', but can never convince a television studio of the commercial viability of the project.

The revelations in this program 'about nothing' are nevertheless shaped by a certain protocol of behaviour which takes its cue from a larger hegemonic position on the primacy of individualism constructed in the American dream within the boundaries of a dominant heterosexual norm. The four spend their leisure time at Jerry's place, or at Monk's Diner, or at the movies, where their self-disclosures are crafted to appeal to a wide audience, never straying from a commercially safe format. In an episode where Jerry and George are mistakenly 'outed' as gay, they are mortified. They regard homosexuality as completely at odds with their obsessive pursuit of women, but they temper this mortification with a politically correct rider: 'not that there is anything wrong with that' (being gay); a gag within a gag. The 'one liner' is employed to close off any suggestion of discrimination against gays, while simultaneously muzzling any suggestion that they are gay themselves. At the same time, in Jerry and George's exaggerated and paranoid reaction to the suggestion that anyone would ever think they could be gay, the episode reveals how 'politically correct', sophisticated Manhattanites are, behind this facade, uncomfortable with the issue of homosexuality.

The uncertain ideological positioning on homosexuality is reflected by poking fun at gay stereotypes. There are passing references to the 'odd couple' or gym room infatuations. Jerry gets tickets to the musical *Guys and Dolls* from George, who clarifies that it is not 'Guys and Guys'; Elaine gives him the collected works of Bette Midler; and Kramer (Michael Richards) presents him with a two-line telephone, a symbolic double entendre and a metaphor for the cross purposes of the accusation of gayness. Yet the position taken on the issue of homosexuality in this episode is a safe one within the discourse of the series. Everyone watching the show knows the sexual preoccupations of the two men. It is also a safe position for American sitcoms, in general, due to the perceived commercial danger of openly gay characters on television adversely affecting the sponsors' aim of reaching a large family audience. This commercial imperative was made most evident when Ellen DeGeneres 'outed herself' on her television program *Ellen*. Widely publicised as an affirmation of her lesbian 'real' life, this disclosure was followed by *Ellen* soon fading into sitcom history.

Seinfeld, like Woody Allen, also manages to deliver the final word in the form of a comic gag, in this instance in relation to politically correct rhetoric and being mistakenly 'outed' as gay. George's last lines in that episode are: 'All right, I'll tell you the truth. I'm not gay. My name's Buck Naked. I'm a porno actor'. Rather than having the desired effect of discouraging his girlfriend, however, this mocking fabrication only intensifies her interest as she replies, 'Really?' In his stand up comedy routine closing the show, Seinfeld quips: 'I'm not gay. I am, however, thin, single and neat. Sometimes when someone is thin, single and neat, people assume they are gay because that is a stereotype. They normally don't think of gay people as fat, sloppy and married. Although I'm sure there are, I don't want to perpetuate the stereotype' (*Seinfeld*, 1993).

The apparent openness of popular culture in depicting a variety of lifestyles is thus not without its gags. Disclosures have a certain contingency as one awaits the attempts at closure which follow. This contingency, it is often argued, is a characteristic of the post-modern condition (Lyotard 1983/1993; Jencks, 1978). Fredric Jameson pushes this sense of contingency further with his contention that it is impossible to discover aesthetic truths in an era when aesthetic images can only be representations. Due to the commodification of culture, the division between high and low culture is no longer sustainable and an all pervasive 'depthlessness' has invaded the space the avant-garde could once occupy to offer critical perspectives on society (Jameson, 1991: 7-19). For Jameson, it is not possible to disclose hidden power structures and think historically because, in the logic of late capitalism, the past has become a pastiche.

Post-modernism and popular culture occupy a similar theoretical terrain where disclosure is contingent and ambivalent because there is neither one historical past nor a defined agreement on a future. Instead, society is a complex, fragmented entity where everything is probable and little is certain. It is an arena dominated by representation rather than essence. According to Jameson, our ability to think of the past is destabilised by the presentation of the past in popular culture as a pastiche. Jameson sees the spate of nostalgia films (*American Graffiti, Star Wars, Chinatown, Raiders of the Lost Arc, the Conformist, Body Heat*) as examples of this pastiche. They are, for him, also reflections of a deep longing for a non-problematic past. This longing is presented in an inter-textual manner where the present and the past blend and dissolve historical meaning as the aesthetic style superimposes itself over 'real' history. In the film *American Graffiti*, for instance, there is a drag racing scene which is a direct allusion to the cataclysmic events in *Rebel Without a Cause*. Yet, in *American Graffiti*, the subversiveness of the Rebel (James Dean) and the attacks on the soullessness of suburbia are muzzled. The sub-conscious unease of teenagers in the nuclear family, portrayed by James Dean's character, is transformed in *American Graffiti* into a longing for an unproblematic past, a pre-Vietnam period of innocence. Jameson's revelations about these films and the predominance of them in recent years has struck a chord among many popular culture writers.

Other critics read these films from a different theoretical perspective and are not so keen to embrace Jameson's totalising schema. Barbara Creed, for example, agrees that Jameson makes incisive observations about the longing for historical innocence in these nostalgia films and their role as an act of closure on critiques of the American economic dream. But, from a feminist perspective, Creed argues that these films can be read as a disclosure of the pervasive, sub-conscious desire to restore a patriarchal order not just on the past, but also on the present (Creed, 1993: 405-407). Creed then notes, though, that her reading should not be counter-posed as a contest between Jameson's class truth and what she sees as her superior feminist truth. Instead, she maintains that disclosures, even feminist ones, can only ever be contingent and partial (Creed, 1993: 416).

Both Jameson and Creed regard popular cultural products, in this case films, as serious subjects which reveal to us important facets of contemporary society. They are equally concerned with the manner in which the past and present speak to one another through culture. They recognise that the Cold War with its totalising ideological closure has passed and cultural representations now saturate modern living. The question is how to make sense of all these disclosures and to identity the moments of closure. This era of excessive disclosures is pregnant with hope for those previously marginalised by ideological accounts of the progress of civilisation. However, as Vattimo argues, an excess of communication need not make society transparent, but can make it more complicated and complex, even chaotic (1992: 10). Mass media and popular culture have bombarded the audience with multiple voices, and given minorities and passed colonised people a presence and a voice. The sound of these many voices has both an emancipatory potential for marginalised groups like blacks, women, ethnic minorities and homosexuals, and equally a regressive potential by unleashing a backlash where their voices are gagged by powerful interests speaking on behalf of the 'silent majority' (Vattimo 1991: 141).

The gaggle of political correctness

The increasing depiction of diversity in the mass media nonetheless placed pressure on those in power, whether in government, business or the academy, to respond to social inequities. Here the issue of language and cultural practices became important to an understanding of how diversity had been suppressed. When minorities began to lift the gag on the expression of their exploitation, it was understandable that they would expose the way their community's dominant culture and language were ideologically loaded against them. These debates had a special poignancy and intensity in the fields of cultural and literary studies in universities. Particularly in the United States, discriminatory cultural practices became focal points on university campuses. Yet it did not take long before such efforts were attacked as being detrimental to free speech. It was claimed that self-appointed 'thought-police' sought to impose language and behavioural restrictions on the 'oppressed majority'. Thus the desire for greater recognition of diversity paradoxically became depicted as a move against free speech and the ideals of a democratic society.

Soon political correctness took on mythic proportions and was characterised as reverse discrimination against 'white' males who, according to this story, were being overlooked in favour of less qualified individuals. If media reports were anything to go by, it seemed as if the only way to get into university was to be a lesbian, black, single mother. Ivy League universities were stereotyped anew as bastions of black power and radical feminism, while English Literature had been swept aside by cultural studies. This revolution, the media warned, would soon sweep the country. In the face of this threat, white men, armed with the English canon of 'good books', had to take a stand against demands from minority groups on American campuses for the unthinkable: a more inclusive curriculum.

Men like P.J. O'Rourke, the satirist and feature writer for *Rolling Stone*, mounted their white chargers and defended the rights of men to be men. It was O'Rourke, for example, who took up the cudgel for the right of freshmen 'to put the make' on female students as a biological and cultural imperative (O'Rourke, 1994: 231). It was up to real men to return to nature and to bond naked in the woods in order to reassert their rightful place in society as hunters and not gatherers. But just as the victory flag was hoisted against the politically correct enemy, the campaign for 'real men' also became easy game for lampooning. Vice President Dan Quayle unintentionally opened the floodgates with his attack on the popular television character Murphy Brown (Candice Bergman). His criticism of the character as a bad role model because she was a single working mother was, for many, a gag of ludicrous proportions not only because he was jousting with a fictional creation but also because his criticism did not ring true for many divorced couples and double-income families. Attempts at closure can, at times, take on comical dimensions even, or perhaps especially, when solemnly asserted.

The campaign against political correctness revealed that when academics stood up for principles such as non-sexist language or a more inclusive curriculum, their claims were readily open to ridicule by the media as outside the 'mainstream'. As Grossberg (1997: 2) notes, progressive academics' righteous defence against charges of political correctness tended to be self-defeating. It just made them vulnerable to opponents who represented 'over-the-top' instances of political correctness as typical examples in scornful jokes. This is not to deny that the campaign against political correctness reflected ideological intentions to gag minority voices and reassert a more exclusive patriarchal agenda. It is nonetheless a good example of how satirical and ironic exaggeration is a two-edged sword (Ahluwalia and McCarthy, 1998: 79-82). Murphy Brown, after all, had the last laugh as Dan Quayle became a laughingstock and soon lost office.

Can bestiality lead to better literacy?

The cause of political conservatism is ironically subverted within the terrain of popular culture through a form of ridicule that takes political correctness to excess. A clear example of this trend is the program *South Park*. Here excessive disclosures are used to turn conservative dictates by the non-politically correct on their head. In this program, stereotypes are so black and white they become grey. For example, the 'black stud' stereotype in the form of Chef is readily enticed into the beds of the upstanding Mayor and other respectable women of the town. The single mother 'slut', Mrs Cartman, turns out to be a hermaphrodite. The schizophrenic school teacher, Mr Garrison, with his ultra-ego Mr Hat is 'outed' by the whole town and yet their homophobia is so extreme that it makes the 'outers' into the 'deviants'. Moreover, the stereotypes of respectable middle America are lampooned in the show for their hypocrisy and inability to discuss openly, as the children of the show do, such 'adult' topics as euthanasia, circumcision, bestiality, drug abuse and censorship. Thus the staunch defenders of the right to be politically incorrect are portrayed as narrow minded, ignorant and corrupt.

The question arises whether such programs as *South Park* act as a reinforcement for conservative views or, by lampooning them, lift the gag on debate. The answer to this question has to be equivocal as the relationship between representation and ideology is fluid. An episode of *South Park* on literacy, a consistent conservative theme in the criticisms of liberal reforms to education, is a case in point. The plot centres on the police chief Barbrady catching a 'chicken fucker', whom the children call a 'chicken lover'. As the plot unfolds, it turns out that officer Barbrady is illiterate and the Mayor sends him back to school. The denouement involves the revelation that the perpetrator of these acts of bestiality is the librarian who has left literary clues meant to encourage Barbrady to read. Upon capture, the hippy librarian gives the Police Chief a copy of Ayn Rand's *Atlas Shrugs*, which results in turning Barbrady off reading forever.

In this episode, the conservative cause of literacy is linked to sexual deviancy and the denigration of Rand's literary celebration of American capitalism. All of this is played out against an excessive number of quotations from popular culture, including a send up of 'real life' police shows (in this case called 'Cops'), *Dragnet*, the LA riots, day-time television talk shows and children's television programs, which are ridiculed by Terrence and Phillip in 'fart jokes'. Similarly, the debate over whether we can learn to read through television is alluded to in a crude literary test given to Brabrady by the English teacher, Mr Garrison, when the Chief fails to read the phrase, 'Oprah Winfrey has huge knockers'. In turn, it is later revealed in an equally derisory fashion that Mr Garrison does not know the plot of C.S. Lewis's *The Lion, the Witch and the Wardrobe*. According to this reading of *South Park*, the end, that is, the spread of literacy, is entirely subverted through the means of bestiality.

South Park, as a text, can be read at a number of levels but the discursive point of reference is that popular culture, as seen by the twenty and under generation, treats 'grown up' philosophical debates over the character of American society as a joke. *South Park* has become a commercial success with its associated merchandise sold across both the

Pacific and Atlantic. Although its reception in England and Australia, for example, will not be the same as in the United States or Canada, its references to a mountain town, akin to that in *Northern Exposure*, or its non-didactic morals contrasting with treatments in *The Simpsons* should be familiar to the television generation around the world. Whether South Park can have a counter-hegemonic influence similar to that which *I Love Lucy* had on Meagan Morris is yet to be seen. Its sexual politics is, however, deeply influenced by themes expressive of chauvinistic male culture. While *South Park* generally takes political correctness to excess to deride political conservatism, part of its 'radical' treatment of cultural issues depends upon the ambiguity of its daring to reinforce sexual stereotypes which marginalise and denigrate women.

So far I have argued that in an era of excessive disclosure negotiations between social, political and ideological forces over what is 'real' have become increasingly ambiguous. Hence the instability of popular culture's representations of the real has produced a shift in codes of revelation. What were once the dominant forms used to represent power have now been challenged and no longer have the same ability to gag debate. In the remaining sections of this chapter I will illustrate this shift through a series of representations of the myth that an American citizen may go from 'log cabin' to the White House. Concomitantly, my analysis shows how an enduring legend in American culture – the 'good' President who, like George Washington, would 'never tell a lie', or the stoically virtuous Abraham Lincoln – has been destabilised but not forgotten. Despite the lack of credibility for these myths by the 1970s, films concerning American politics still seek to persuade the audience that democracy is alive and well in the most powerful country in the world.

Who tells it like it is? Not the candidate!

In the 1970 film *The Candidate*, Robert Redford plays a liberal lawyer, Bill McKay, who is encouraged by a spin doctor to run for the Senate in California. Once he accepts this challenge his idealism and truthful answers on policy are depicted by the press as naïve, forcing McKay to play the electoral game and thus disclose nothing of substance. Although McKay is depicted as if he is becoming an automaton, he still manages to touch a chord with working men and women when he coins the line 'there has to be a better way'. Despite his selling out, the audience, like the people around him and even his estranged father and wife, want McKay to win. Irrespective of the campaign's shallowness, the audience roots for democracy. Just like the candidate, the voters are swept along by an election campaign in which all disclosures are constructed and unguarded comments are gagged. The candidate is victorious, but the hollowness of the victory is poignantly evident in the final frame of the film when McKay looks at his campaign manager and, in a stunned tone, asks 'What do we do now?' Here means and ends meld as winning the election is the means to office and victory the only objective. Nevertheless, the audience is left with the message that despite all closures on 'real' debate in election campaigns, being a candidate remains a valuable contribution to American democracy.

Who tells it like it is? The media!

The film, *All the President's Men,* also unveils electoral politics as deeply corrupt, but in this case democracy can be saved by the fourth estate, the media. The film champions the media as the bastion of truth and democracy in a system where power corrupts. More than a bastion of free speech, the media are credited with defending the entire American way of life. This 'whodunit' or, more accurately 'how-they-did-it', sends the moral message that only the two young reporters, Bob Woodward (Robert Redford) and Carl Bernstein (Dustin Hoffman), defend the truth by revealing that the Watergate break-in was only one part of a covert operation involving the highest office in the land. In short, the President might be immoral, but the free press still defends American democracy. This point is made loud and clear in the concluding exchange of the film where the two junior journalists tell their father-figure editor that 'everyone is involved'. In response, the editor informs them that the opinion polls are running strongly for Nixon and 'no one gives a shit' about Watergate. Then, in a voice inflected with journalistic cynicism and yet evoking Lincoln's high moral standing, he gives the instructive message of the film by telling the two young reporters that they must continue to do their job because there is 'nothing riding on this, except the First amendment of the Constitution, freedom of the press, and maybe the future of the country'. Concluding with Nixon's re-election victory, the film shows that even though the public can be gullible, the press will persist in revealing the truth so that good will ultimately triumph in the battle to preserve democracy.

All the President's Men was a seminal break in the filmic depiction of United States presidents. The god-like figure of Abraham Lincoln was relegated to a romanticised past no longer relevant after Nixon, the president who was a also a 'bad guy'. Although the public is duped by the electoral process, the film reassures the audience that they need not be too concerned because the moral fabric of American politics is defended by the fourth estate. A decade later, Ronald Reagan sought to persuade the American public that he was the embodiment of the American 'log cabin' dream. President Reagan by-passed 'reality' by deliberately modelling himself on the movie heroes he once played who were committed to God, family and country. At the same time, Hollywood was ironically subverting this myth by presenting presidents as mere mortals with both ordinary and extraordinary fallibilities: a widow in *Mr President*, being easily replaceable in *Dave*, and being revealed as a debauched murderer in Clint Eastwood's *Absolute Power*.

Who tells it like it is? The film-maker?

In *Primary Colours*, a film based on an incumbent president, the 'real' and the fictional blend into one. The President is flawed, and yet we are persuaded to support him. Although committed to fighting injustice, he is also a lecher. The film is based closely on the (un)anonymous (Joe Klein) journalistic account of Bill Clinton's rise to the White House. The movie portrays Bill Stanton/Bill Clinton (John Travolta) as both idealistic and cynical, manipulative and manipulated, a libertine and a family man, a consummate liar and a weaver of images of true Southern poverty and hardship. But while these dialectic disclosures appear to fit the 'reality' of Bill Clinton's history in office, from a post-modern perspective, 'President Clinton' has become hyperreal.

Like Clinton, Stanton has a larger than life appeal. On the one hand, he is able to evoke empathy for his sincerity towards the working poor, poignantly portrayed in a late night scene with a waiter in a diner, while on the other hand evoking disdain for his exploitation of women. The audience is presented with a two dimensional Stanton/Clinton, a sincere fighter against injustice and discrimination, and a serial womaniser who artfully deceives his own wife. Likewise, Hilary Clinton/Susan Stanton (Emma Thompson) is depicted as smart and savvy, but ever willing to forgive her husband's peccadilloes and work with steely determination to get him into the White House. She is, in short, both a strong woman and a victim for standing by 'her man'. Like her husband, Hilary Clinton has become a text, read in different ways by a mass audience and constructed by that audience. Before the Lewinsky affair, for instance, Hilary Clinton was unpopular in her own country for having over-stepped the role of presidential wife by engaging in policy debates. But since this recent sex scandal, her popularity has soared in her new public persona as the 'loyal wife' and victim of her husband's licentiousness. Filmic references bounce off journalistic portrayals as an active audience reads the text of public persons.

Yet, in terms of closure, the 'real' President Clinton's readiness to abandon his empathy for the poor against the bulwark of the Republican-led Congress when launching his bid for a second term is not even hinted at in *Primary Colors* (Walker, 1996: 183-184; Woodward, 1996: 195-196). The film's critique of Clinton, like that of the dominant media, is not from the left of politics. Criticisms focus on the disclosure of Clinton's sex life and not on the source of his election and re-election campaign funds, or how his support for welfare cuts could find any resonance with his supposed feelings for the downtrodden. Instead the film reproduces the idealised dream of the 'log cabin', albeit in this case with a deeply scarred character.

Through the vehicle of the narrator, Henry Burton (Adrian Lester), the film reveals Clinton's ability to rally support amongst the civil right leaders from the 1960s as well as prominent members of the anti-Vietnam generation. This point is reinforced by the role played by the trouble shooter, Libby Holden (Kathy Bates). As the idealistic defender of Stanton's reputation against scurrilous attacks, she evokes the hopes of the 1960s generation against corrupt party politics. She is steadfast in her determination to expose the dirty tricks of Stanton's opponents and is at the same time not prepared to follow Stanton to the White House unless he also renounces them. Indeed, when Stanton and his wife resort to such tactics and use the information she has gathered to smear his opponent, Libby responds by committing suicide. There is a double message in her suicide: first, that the idealism of the '1960s generation' is pointless without power, and yet gaining power corrupts the individual. Second, Libby's death eliminates the 'deviant' lesbian character in the film. These revelations about Clinton's supporters give the viewer a reference point to understand the hostility displayed toward him by many Republican politicians. The problem is not just his character as a man, but his connections with the anti-establishment ethos of the 1960s.

Who tells it like it is? No-one!

If *Primary Colours* is an attempt at a 'real-life-journalistic' account of a presidential campaign, *Wag the Dog*, subtitled *A Comedy About Truth, Justice And Special Effects*, is an irreverent attack on elections, the media and Hollywood. The film, moreover, gained greater poignancy by its timely release, uncannily matching the 'real life' tale of President Clinton and Monica Lewinsky's affair then being revealed to the public. The opening scene sets the political tone for the film, with the television news breaking a story, just eleven days before the election, that the president has been accused of having an illicit sexual liaison with a teenage girl who was visiting the White House. The Opposition's candidate is quick to release a commercial showing the White House with a voice-over asking rhetorically, 'has the president changed his tune?' to the tune of 'Thank Heaven For Little Girls'. The media, the music and commercial are referential signs: the woman in the childlike body of Audrey Hepburn, who is the object of Maurice Chevaliar's ode to romance, set in more innocent times, hints at presidential paedophilia.

In response, the president's re-election campaign committee hires trouble shooter Conrad Been (Robert De Niro) to orchestrate its damage control strategy. When confronted with a strategic issue, Been's favourite phrase is always: 'I'm working on it'. His 'working on it' leads him to confide to his somewhat naïve but quick learning assistant, Winifred Ames (Anne Heche), that he intends to produce a fake war against Albania. He heads off to Hollywood to hire a famous movie producer, Stanley Motss (Dustin Hoffman), to manufacture the phoney war. When Motss (the 't' is silent) queries the strategy, Been informs him that all the American public can remember about the Gulf War was the 'smart bomb, down the chimney' and 'that image was manufactured in Virginia. Even if it was not, who would know, or could tell?' Motss is convinced by this example and sets out with his entourage of irreverent but professional image makers to construct a fictional war against Albania.

Once on board, Motss marshals all the image-making power of Hollywood to facilitate his fabrication. Whenever there is a hitch in the scheme he responds with the quip that 'this is nothing' compared to making a movie. He quickly sets up a shoot of an Albanian girl (Kirsten Dunst) escaping from Albania while carrying a bag of chips through war torn streets and across a bridge to freedom. For a more homely effect, the chips later have a computer enhanced white kitten super-imposed over them. Then there is the theme song dutifully arranged to complement the image by song meister Johnny Green (Willie Nelson). The first theme song is a patriotic hymn, called 'Guard the American Dream', an ironic jibe both at the Cold War and the 'We are the World' phenomenon. When tactics change, this tune is replaced by 'Courage Mom' with Willie Nelson copying a Bruce Springsteen clip. It is all image and self-referenced: there is no real war, just aesthetic creations.

Nor is the irreverent tone of the film tempered by moralism. For example, when the conspirators, travelling in an ubiquitous limousine, muse over the implications of misleading both the press and the public to ensure the re-election of an immoral president, Been states that one just needs to take '[p]ride in a job well done'. Still with a hint of naiveté, Winifred Ames intervenes that it was not 'just a job well done' as there is also the 'gratitude of your party and your president' to be had at the end of the day. Agreeing with Been, Motss adds: 'We did a good job. You know you can't save the world, you can only try'. The ironic dimension that all politics is hyperreality is played out over Willie Nelson's patriotic hymn to the United States.

In the penultimate scene of the film, however, Motss begins to consider that there is a higher meaning to their production as it represents his finest hour as a producer. This phoney campaign even surpasses his acclaimed production of *Moby Dick,* 'from the point of view of the whale'. Motss thus demands the credit for his production. Although Been counsels him against such dangerous thinking, Motss's hubris gets the better of him when he sees a television debate on the election in which an academic commentator, pontificating on the official television campaign, concludes that the 'President is a product' sold via commercials. Motss is doubly offended because, in his artistic view, the official campaign featuring the slogan, 'you don't change horses in mid-stream', is 'hicksville'. He is outraged that a 'dick-head from film school...some limp dick film school ponce takes the credit: I want the credit'. Motss's demand is a running gag throughout the film as he bemoans the fact that 'there is no academy award for producers'. Ultimately, his demand for recognition for producing the 'real' campaign seals his fate and the film ends with his funeral. Thus, the gag placed on the disclosure of a truth is again set within a gag: the joke that the campaign was based on a fictional war must never be revealed to the public who must continue to believe in American democracy.

This Barry Levinson film (he previously directed *Disclosure*) reveals how the media are manipulated by political spin-doctors, and while Hollywood does not produce the truth, people still want to cling to the myth of a healthy democracy. Levinson cleverly draws the audience into rooting for the fabricators, defending their lies and deceptions against a supposed enemy. We want them to win and carry the deception through to the end, even if it means the murder of Motss. The implication for Clinton, as the presiding president, is that people readily defend him even though they know his flaws. The people want democracy to win. They also, as portrayed in the *Candidate,* want the president to win against what many (if opinion polls are any guide) see as a less worthy opponent and, in Clinton's case, a vengeful Republican-led Congress.

From courting to completion

Disclosures are always ambiguous. Even when the creator of a disclosure has a specific intent, it is open to multiple interpretations and to having its meaning re-shaped by other events (McRobbie, 1994: 13*)*. The author is alive, but has lost control over the reading of his or her revelations. Thus the satirical intent of *Wag the Dog* took on an entirely new meaning with the exposé of President Clinton and Monica Lewinsky's affair. Then, its meaning took on another dimension with the attack on Iraq by the United States and British Air Forces, conveniently executed at the very time Congress was moving to impeach President Clinton. The obvious question for the press to pose was whether Operation Desert Fox was also a fictional war designed to divert public attention away from the impeachment hearings: indeed, was life reflecting art?

Let us look at another example where the disclosure takes on a different meaning when it becomes a point of reference for another disclosure. In this case the disclosure is concerned with different subjective definitions of sex, in particular the distinction between what was once called 'heavy petting' and sexual intercourse, and the new twist accorded to this distinction by the revelations about President Clinton and Ms Lewinsky contained in the Starr Report.

In the 'grunge' movie *Clerks,* sub-titled *Just Because They Serve You Doesn't Mean They Have To Like You*, the director, Kevin Smith, presents a snap shot of his own life but with references to popular culture which are familiar to the 'twenty-somethings.' The main dialogue is presented in the form of a Socratic dialogue and is imbued with the theological musings of the thirteenth-century poet, Dante Aligheri. The film was independently produced but rose to prominence when it won an award at the Sundance Film Festival. The setting for the film is a Quick Stop convenience store in New Jersey where the store clerk and college drop-out, Dante Hicks (Brian O'Halloran), engages in scabrous banter with the video clerk next door, Randal (Jeff Anderson). In this instance, Dante's indifference to his customers is counter-posed with Randal's treatment of them as brainless morons, deserving no pity.

The technique used by Smith to wed popular culture with philosophy turns a conversation, usually about sex, into a revelation of hypocrisy, double standards, and the gulf between men and women over identity and the past. Smith's dialogue moves from profound insights to obscenity, and back to philosophy, without missing a beat. The consistent theme in his films is the deep insecurity and angst of young men, especially when confronted with women who have a clearer sense of direction and identity. It is a tale about philosophical subjectivism in a post-modern age in which the debate over identity has taken a prominent place and where there is a loss of innocence over something as natural as dating.

Censor's warning: classified section for mature adults only

For those readers who want to retain their innocence they might prefer to skip the following dialogue. In a discussion with his girlfriend, Veronica (Marilyn Ghigliotti), Dante muses over sexual techniques and asserts that it is easier for men to come than women. In response, Veronica quips that perhaps his 'broad generalisations' are merely 'generalisations about broads'. This gag leads to an interchange about their past sexual experiences. When Veronica asks him 'how many different girls have you slept with?' Dante replies in an off-handed but boastful manner, 'twelve'. She then inquires, 'does that include me?' Dante answers, 'twelve including you'. Veronica retorts that 'you [referring to men in general] would sleep with anything that will say yes'. Dante then asks her how many men she has had sex with. Veronica says that she has 'slept with three men', adding the rider, 'including you'. Dante thus feels confident and secure that he is more experienced than her. But this interchange is about to be turned on its head.

. An old acquaintance of Veronica enters the shop and the two of them exchange pleasantries about the 'greatness of love'. After his departure, Veronica remarks that he is known for his sexual preference of wanting a 'snowball'. Dante asks her what a 'snowball' is. Veronica informs him: 'It is a blow job thing', saying that her friend Sylvia told her about it and it means that 'after he gets a blow job he likes to have it spit back into his mouth while kissing...it is called snowballing'. Dante is horrified and berates Veronica over what he thinks her girlfriend did. For Veronica, however, it is a matter of personal choice, just something that particular guy 'gets off on' and, by the way, it was not Sylvia but herself who performed the task as she discloses: 'I snowballed him'. Dante is mortified, attacking Veronica with the tirade: 'You sucked that guy's dick...you said you only had sex with three guys?' Veronica responds by saying that she had only 'slept with three guys', that is, only 'had sex with three guys', which 'doesn't mean that I didn't go out with guys', 'I went with guys'. Dante's insecurity turns to aggression as he belligerently asks 'how many dicks have you sucked?' Veronica stops to think and replies, 'something like thirty-six'. Dante retorts, 'does that include me'? She replies, 'thirty-seven'. The gag has been turned full circle. In classic subjectivist style, Veronica defends her position by insisting that sleeping with a guy, that is, sexual intercourse, is her definition of sex and it is quite different from a 'blow job'. Oral sex is only dating or fooling around. Thus, she says: 'I went down on a few guys...going down is no big deal'.

The dialogue produces a clever shift in the positioning of the characters' sexual experience and provides a nuanced debate about definitions and meanings of sex and love. But the issues raised in these gags took on a far greater significance when placed in the context of the public disclosure of the Clinton-Lewinsky affair. In defence of President Clinton's claim that he 'did not have sex with that woman' his lawyers resorted to both biblical and legalistic definitions of sexual intercourse. The Starr Report, by contrast, asserted that all forms of sex are akin to sexual intercourse and dismissed the President's nuanced distinction between intercourse and oral sex, which coincidentally held a remarkable similarity to Veronica's definition in *Clerks*. Starr provided evidence from his cross examination of Ms Lewinsky in an attempt to prove their encounters were, indeed, sexual exchanges. Describing their first 'encounter', Starr claimed: 'While the President continued talking on the telephone she [Ms Lewinsky] performed oral sex on him.... In her recollection: "I told him that I wanted to complete that. And he said that he needed to wait until he trusted me more. And then I think he made a joke that he hadn't had that in a long time"' (Starr, 1998: 43).

Starr then recorded that in their second sexual encounter, after they had kissed, the 'President touched Ms Lewinsky's bare breast with his hands...according to Miss Lewinsky, "he unzipped his pants and exposed himself" and she performed oral sex. Again, he stopped her before he ejaculated' (Starr, 1998: 40). In the final 'encounter', in which President Clinton later admitted to having had 'inappropriate contact' with Ms Lewinsky, it would appear he did somewhat reluctantly come. The disclosure in Ms Lewinsky's evidence to Kenneth Starr goes like this:

> ...'I continued to perform oral sex on him and then he pushed me away, kind of as he always did before he came and then I stood and said I care about you so much.... I don't understand why you won't let me...make you come, it's important to me; I mean it just doesn't feel complete, it doesn't seem right'.... Ms Lewinsky testified that she and the President hugged, and 'he said he didn't want to get addicted to me, and he didn't want me to get addicted to him'. Then saying that 'I don't want to disappoint you' the President then consented...for the first time, she performed oral sex through completion (Starr, 1998: 68).

From this act of completion, Ms Lewinsky's blue Gap dress bore the semen stains of the President.

Conclusion: Oh! For the sound of silence!

The disclosure here is so pregnant with irony that it must surely be artificial in its presentation. Here a God-fearing President does not think sex is being performed unless he exchanges bodily fluids, a self-disclosure which matches his claim that he smoked marijuana but did not inhale. Ms Lewinsky, moreover, seemingly thought that her 'relationship' with the President would be somehow more complete with his completion. And Kenneth Starr believed that by exposing this sexual exchange he was doing Congress and the American public a service. The use of science, via DNA testing, proved an 'ultimate truth' about Bill Clinton. Yet it is a truth that was either well known or irrelevant to many people, that is, that Clinton is a womaniser and a compulsive liar. Moreover, through Starr's exposé, disclosure has been taken to such an excess that the majority of people are calling out for the gag to be applied.

There is more going on here than just the humiliation of Bill Clinton and Monica Lewinsky. The disclosure has become both the source of a political battle between the Republicans and the Democrats on Capital Hill, and a re-living of the ideological battles of the 1960s over the promiscuous society. It is also a contest by the Evangelical Right for control over the Republican Party and to regain a Christian ascendancy over the dominant ideology in American society. It is a disclosure in which the American dream has become contingent, with the President regarded as morally flawed, but with limited criticism of the reality of American Presidential politics. Instead, Clinton is depicted either as somewhat of a 'bad apple' on a healthy democratic tree, or as a politically and economically sound President but a morally defective leader. Moreover, the impeachment trial's cacophony of sound is in stark contrast to the gag placed on formal political discussion of the polarisation of wealth in the United States (West, 1993: 216). In this climate, it is no wonder that only thirty-five per cent of the eligible voters in America voted in the November 1998 Congressional election. If you listen intently enough you can hear the sound of the American public calling out for the sound of silence.

In conclusion, contemporary culture can be characterised as producing an overwhelming excess of disclosure. Everything appears open, as if anything can be said. Yet disclosures are contingent and ambivalent, grabbing our attention while we fail to notice the silencing closures. A comic gag can also serve to gag debate. Moreover, in a culture of excessive disclosures and increasingly receptive to the contingent nature of truth, comic gags have been accorded an elevated status. As Woody Allen muses, 'we live in a society that puts a big value on jokes, you know. If you think of it this way, if I had been an Apache Indian, those guys didn't need comedians at all, right? So I'd be out of work' (*Star Dust Memories*, 1980).

A gag is never innocent: it is a joke shaped by a specific world-view. Each world-view is negotiated through disclosures and closures which express and reflect competing sources of power in society. Popular culture is a key arena in modern Western society in which such contests are fought because it can represent what is 'real' and in so doing shape the 'real'. In this arena, gags in both senses of the term are in abundance. Comic perspectives operate as ideological forces to elicit, but also to shape, our responses to disclosures. Thus gags are both intellectually amusing and potentially dangerous. Although comic gags have the appearance of revealing and opening up debate, they can just as readily be used as the final word on a matter to gag, or close off, further debate.

References

Ahluwalia, P. and McCarthy, G. (1998), 'Political Correctness: Pauline Hanson and the Construction of Australian Identity', *Australian Journal of Public Administration*, vol. 578, no. 3, pp. 79-86.

Ang, I. (1996), *Living Room Wars: Rethinking Media Audiences in a Postmodern World*, Routledge, London.

Baudrillard, J. (1988), *Selected Writings*, Polity Press, London.

Bauman, Z. (1991), *Postmodernity, or Living with Ambivalence*, Cornell University Press, Cornell.

Christensen, T. (1987), *Reel Politics: American Movies from Birth of a Nation to Platoon*, Basil Blackwell, Oxford and New York.

Creed, B. (1993), 'From Here to Modernity: Feminism and Postmodernism' in J. Natoli and L. Hutcheon (eds), *A Postmodern Reader*, State University of New York, New York, pp. 398-419.

Eco, U. (1984), *Postscript to the Name of the Rose*, Harcourt Brace, Florida.

Grossberg, L. (1977), *Bringing It All Back Home*, Duke University Press, Durham.

Hall, S. (1986), 'Cultural Studies: Two Paradigms' in R. Collins *et al*, (eds), *Media, Culture and Society: A Critical Reader*, Sage, London, pp. 33-48.

Harvey, D. (1989), *The Conditions of Postmodernity*, Blackwell, Oxford.

Hoggart, R. (1958), *The Uses of Literature*, Oxford University Press, Oxford and New York.

Hutcheon, L. (1994), *Irony's Edge: The Theory and Politics of Irony*, Routledge, London.

Jameson, F. (1991), *Postmodernism or the Cultural Logic of Late Capitalism*, Verso, London.

Lyotard, J.F. (1993), *The Postmodern Condition: A Report on Knowledge*, The University of Minnesota Press, Minnesota.

McRobbie, A. (1993), *Postmodernism and Popular Culture*, Routledge, London.

Morris, M (1990), 'Banality in Cultural Studies' in P. Mellencamp, (ed.), *Logics of Television: Essays in Cultural Studies*, Indiana University Press, Bloomington, pp. 15-44.

O'Rourke, P.J. (1994), *All the Trouble in the World*, Pan Macmillan, Sydney.

Rorty, R. (1989), *Contingency, Irony and Solidarity*, Cambridge University Press, Cambridge.

Sarris, A. (1978), *Politics and Cinema*, Columbia University Press, New York.

Starr, K. (1998), *Clinton: The Starr Report*, Orion, London.

Vattimo, G. (1991), 'The End of (Hi)story' in I. Hoesterey (ed.), *Zeitgeist in Babel: The Post-modernist Controversy*, Indiana University Press, Indiana, pp. 132-141.

Vattimo, G. (1992), *The Transparent Society*, Policy Press, London.

Walker, M. (1996), *Clinton: The President They Deserve*, Vintage, London.

Williams, R (1976), *Keywords*, Fontana, London.

Williams, R. (1961), *The Long Revolution*, Penguin, London.

Woodward, B. (1996), *The Choice*, Simon and Schuster, New York.

7 Silence

PAUL CORCORAN

> Still-born Silence! Thou that art
> Floodgate of the deeper heart.
> Richard Flecknoe, *Miscellania* (1653)

Introduction

Why conclude a study of the concept of *disclosure* with *silence*? If disclosure *breaks the silence*, revealing what had been quietly hidden, it would seem that disclosure and silence are mutually exclusive opposites. Yet silence is profoundly revealing. It is eloquently expressive of human will, especially when we stubbornly refuse to speak. Silence may be violently imposed or bought at a price. In either case silence is a complex communicative process. It involves subtle, private and intimate dispositions, even when one is 'beaten into silence' in a violent relationship or by frustrating years of being ignored. Silence is the 'mystery' experienced in the act of *not telling* or the condition of *not knowing*. It energises the disequilibrium we feel, and others exploit, in both secrecy and gossip. Thus silence – the wilful or imposed absence of speech or other sounds – is far from meaningless or incomprehensible. Silence is often described as profound, conspicuous and eloquent.

This chapter explores how silence in both interpersonal and public contexts discloses dramatically expressive and psychologically powerful meanings. Even when 'golden silence' is sought as a retreat, or is imposed as a discipline upon children, women or other groups, the context of gestural and symbolic meanings exposes moral commitments, political strategies and institutional subordination. Silence involves resistance, tension and opposition. Yet we also find that silence is advocated as a right. Whether afforded or denied, the 'right to silence' discloses how constitutional regimes acknowledge spheres of individual privacy and spiritual convictions and protect us from coerced self-incrimination.

The experience of silence

Silence, like many familiar things variously experienced, is not easy to define. Key (1975: 128) notes how 'the comforting, companionable silence between people in equilibrium...must be distinguished from the negative, disturbing silence of anger, fear, or hate.' Hedges and Fishkin (1994: 3), summarising Tillie Olsen's (1979) groundbreaking study of the role of silences in literature and literary culture, distinguish 'natural silence' – periods when the creative life lies fallow – from 'unnatural silences' imposed on people due to circumstances of class, race, sex, educational disadvantage 'or the demands of nurturing.' Cheung (1993; 1994: 113) explores the notion of 'attentive silence' represented in the work of Asian novelists, and discusses how in Western languages the meaning directly opposed to silence is speech or speaking, whereas in Japanese, the opposite of silence is noise or disorder.

Silence is a common experience. Sometimes we withdraw to it as a haven. We may stubbornly choose to be silent or be humiliated and disarmed by having it imposed upon us. In different circumstances, we enjoy it, build and insulate to secure it, yearn for it, fall asleep with it and fear it. It may be something we hope and plan for, even though at other times we do our best to abolish it with amplified music and anxiously contrived conversation. There are times when silence seems a treasured luxury with its gifts of peace and reflection, even though in a crowded lift, at a dinner party or in a classroom silence can be embarrassing and a genuine discomfort.

On the surface, it might seem that silence is the antithesis of disclosure, which is always an act of communication, or at least an attempt to reveal facts, opinions, or oneself to others. Disclosure normally presupposes an opening, a yielding, a bearing forth of hidden recesses of meaning, whereas silence suggests a closed door carefully locked.

There is a sense in which we imagine and speak of silence as if it were an inner space, a quiet back room in which we might shelter, hide in failure or simply wait. In the experience of it, silence has dimensions in time and space. A 'minute of silence' as a ritual of respect at a great public gathering has an unmistakable intensity and seems endless. Its powerful tendency to turn our consciousness inward is almost oppressive.

Reviewing these common experiences is useful merely to underscore the point that silence is not simply the opposite of speech or noise. It is not an absence or void. Silence can be described physically and acoustically. Psychologically, it has an existential valence. Silence, between friends or in music, has emotional registers. In the sound studio it is measured as a 'signal to noise ratio.' In drama, music, bedtime stories or in ordinary conversations, silence has an unmistakable elocutionary force. Indeed, silence may be a strategic exercise of power, or a resistance to it.

'Don't just stand there! Say something!'

Such an injunction might be spoken by a parent to an obstreperous child in a contest of wills. It might be a lover's poignant plea to her desperate partner. In either case, silence is a communicative act in a threatening situation. Disclosure – that is, the demand for it, or the lack of it – is precisely what is at issue.

A 'domain' of silence is presupposed by the concept of disclosure. The very absence of speech creates a pressure, a damming up of things that need to be revealed. One cannot break through the wall of silence if it is not there to breach. The hidden recess is conspicuous and tantalising. In the public realm, especially in modern bureaucracies, a complex regime of secrecy and privileged information is used to consolidate power and expand state control (Rourke, 1961: 21-23). For the individual, silence may be the domain of intimate privacy, the preserve of status or a costly commodity bought and sold. In tragic circumstances impenetrable silence is the mute enclosure of the psychotic or autistic self.

Inevitably, silence is a problem. One is 'confronted' by it. More troubling still, silence poses a question about whether confrontation and, by implication, resistance are really at issue. Not knowing constitutes the issue. When a public figure replies 'No comment' to a journalist, does that mean the person has nothing to say, or does it mean the person has much to say and chooses silence to hide it?

Silence, especially when it is contested politically or legally, is easily interpreted as a sign of partisan interests, opposition and calculation. It is not the lack, but rather the suppression, of intelligible sounds. Perhaps an interested observer can tell the difference. However, ignorance or uncertainty engendered by this silence is itself a problem: not just a gap but a privation. This in turn offers an opening to suspicion, conspiratorial fantasies, paranoia and other types of delusion. Yet silence, official or otherwise, may reflect ignorance, apathy, fear and incompetence – in other words, actual social and communicative dysfunction.

In either circumstance, silence is certainly not devoid of meaning or a forfeiture of communicative intention. Silence has a rich and dramatic repertoire of meaning that is felt, heard and keenly interpreted. On the receiving end of 'the silent treatment', whether you are an investigative journalist or a lover, you know you are getting the cold shoulder.

Speech and the loss of silence

Silence and disclosure do not form a 'binary pair.' The one is not the antithesis or the overcoming of the other. They are not simple, mutually exclusive opposites. Silence is not the opposite or the absence of speech, but a part of it. Nevertheless it remains tantalisingly true that disclosure is an utterance brought forth to others, an embrace of language. Yet if disclosure is an act, so is non-disclosure. Confessions may be courageous, bold and dramatic, but the same may be said of obstinate silence. Silence as well as disclosure may be eloquent, moving and powerfully expressive. Silence is not only the background of revelation; when carried forward and prolonged, it reveals a withholding, a denial, a resistance – an act of courage or, perhaps, relentless sedition.

Silence is the profound starting point, the origin of expressive meaning. As the philosopher-poet Norman O. Brown (1966; Hassan, 1967: 201) declared: 'Silence is the mother tongue.' Human speech and its evolving patterns of meaning may be conceptualised as having sundered the 'primordial silence' pre-dating human consciousness. The 'Word' is both the symbol and the instrument by which humanity has distinguished itself from other beings, even if this distinction has been at the price of our increasingly complete and painful alienation from an ineffable spiritual union with nature and the divine. In the mundane world of noise and 'messages', only rarely do we recapture moments of awed silence before sublime nature or images of the divine. With necessary irony, a few modern writers and playwrights have memorialised the loss of the silent Eden and rebelled against humanity's condemnation to the futile, divisive labour to build the noisy cities of Babel.[1]

These richly symbolic interpretations of the Promethean powers of language presuppose that the unity, spiritual integration and undisturbed bliss of silence is divine: 'In the beginning was the Word, and the Word was with God, and the Word was God' (St. John, 1:1). The book of Genesis records humanity's first conversation, not between Adam and his wife, but between Eve and 'the serpent' – a paradigm of the seductive power and the fatal pitfalls of speech. The silence now fatally broken, the forbidden fruit thus eaten, neither innocence nor virtue, much less spiritual union, survived. Though language was a gift of God enabling Adam to 'give names to all cattle, and the fowl of the air, and to every beast of the field,' modern philosophers from the time of Hobbes have signalled the fatal 'Fall' into language, humanity's vain and quarrelsome alienation from ineffable nature. Noisome humanity, in this view, will endure until the Apocalypse, an ancient revelation contemporary readers might well envisage as a quiet, cold nuclear winter in the aftermath of the final earsplitting explosions: 'The rest is silence; after the last judgement, the silence' (Brown, 1966; Hassan, 1967: 218).

From this apocalyptic perspective of an ultimate revelation, self-disclosure seems almost a form of venal pride, a wish to be like God, to 'become known as we are known.' Yet speaking oneself to others – revealing ourselves as an 'open book' for others to 'read' – requires us to cross that seemingly unbridgeable gulf of inner silence that looms even between close friends. We sense a jarring, even violent, implication in the phrase, 'breaking the silence'.

Neither those who valorise communication as beneficial nor critics who condemn the numbing effects of vulgar rhetoric give the whole story. It may well be a noisy world, with 'chat' rooms, 'talk-back radio' and the frantic din of the mass media, but our confinement in such a world has not made silence impossible. The primordial silence may have been broken, but its looming presence remains. Silence always threatens to close in and envelop speech within the interior of the individual mind. Silence, for a time, or in a special place, may also be a welcome resort. It often serves as a bond, or a safety zone, between ourselves and others. Silence remains, always, as in music, the background against which sounds may be distinguished.

Regimes of silence

In recent years, there has been a great deal of talk about the 'silencing' of disadvantaged groups. Presumed to be an act of suppression by powerful groups against those who are thereby 'disempowered', silencing is considered an effect of unequal power relations. Thus feminist scholars argue that women are 'silenced' by men and by society's pervasive patriarchal institutions.[2] In turn, some argue that they are being silenced by newly entrenched bastions of 'political correctness.' Post-colonial theorists describe how individuals and entire cultures are silenced not simply by rules or naked force but by images and stereotypes, such as 'Orientalism.' Cultural theorists claim that the imagery of literature, popular entertainment and the mass media relegate non-white, non-Western, non-Christian populations to the margins of 'Otherness.' They are not seen or heard except when they are used to evoke the imagery and voices imposed upon them by European and American cultural hegemony.

In such studies, silence, far from meaning a background condition – the absence of sound or a state of unbroken spiritual union – has been promoted from a noun to an oppressive active verb. Silence is understood as an act of power which stifles and dominates. Thus silence is conceived as a discriminatory and repressive project, presumably a difficult one that requires power to achieve because of a natural inclination to speak and be heard.

St. Paul used his authority in the early Christian church to advocate such a project. Writing to the Christian community in Corinth, where there was apparent confusion about moral issues, liturgical practices and the questionable relevance of Judaic law and precepts, he advised in no uncertain terms:

> Let your women keep silence in the churches: for it is not permitted unto them to speak; but they are commanded to be under obedience, as also saith the law. And if they will learn anything, let them ask their husbands at home: for it is a shame for women to speak in the church (I *Corinthians*, XIV: 34-35).

In a letter to an apostle, Paul returned to this theme:

> Let the woman learn in silence with all subjection. But I suffer not a woman to teach, nor to usurp authority over the man, but to be in silence. For Adam was first formed, then Eve. And Adam was not deceived; but the woman being deceived was in the transgression. Notwithstanding she shall be saved in childbearing, if they continue in faith and charity and holiness with sobriety (I *Timothy* II: 11-15).

Eighteen hundred years later Jane Austen (1966: 105), with perhaps a confident spice of irony, advised women that it was prudent to impose a degree of silence on themselves:

> Where people wish to attach, they should always be ignorant.... A woman, especially, if she have the misfortune of knowing any thing, should conceal it as well as she can.

Scholars of all kinds today are keen to 'subvert' the meaning of texts, or at least 're-read' them with irony. Opposition, if not deconstruction, is the rule of thumb. So when we read passages such as the ones above, we know that the real concern is not silence but its very opposite. St. Paul is not directly interested in silence in the church at Corinth. He is concerned about noise, that is, the sound of the female voice.

St. Paul's advice about silencing women reveals that early Christian practices were a disturbing challenge to traditional Hebrew forms of worship. There was a growing clamour and his irritated tone tells us unmistakably that it was the clamour of women. In Jewish temples, women had not only been silent but were sequestered behind screens. They were barely spectators of a service in which they did not participate. But in the motley, multi-cultural Christian communities adherence to Judaic law was being questioned in many respects. The old Hebrew practices and prohibitions were breaking down. The Sabbath was questioned. The admission of gentiles – non-Jews – to Christian communities was opposed by traditionalists, but strongly supported by Paul. What, then, to do about the rabbinical traditions, the baptism of uncircumcised males and the laws regulating hygiene and food? What was to be done about the presence and active participation of women, even unmarried women, in communal worship? Christ himself had famously treated widows, the poor and even harlots with particular sympathy. Clearly St. Paul thought that a line must be drawn. If women were to be admitted into communal worship and included in the celebration of the Feast of the Last Supper, at least the old ways should be respected by prohibiting women from proclaiming (*prædicare*, preaching) the good news (in old English, *godspel*, from the Greek *evangelion*). Otherwise, where would it all end?

Remarkably, the debate today about this prohibition is still divided over St. Paul's proposition. Over the centuries it has undeniably silenced women in the church, even though no one could doubt that their faithful presence, silent prayers and tangible offerings have sustained the church from the beginning. For two thousand years there have been few women evangelists and, in the Roman Catholic Church, no female priests, although now there is open dissent from St. Paul's advice. In the Protestant tradition the record has been much the same until this century. St. Paul's views, as well as his anxieties, were certainly reflected in two tracts by the celebrated seventeenth-century English divine, George Fox (1661): *Concerning Sons and Daughters, and Prophetesses Speaking and Prophecying in the Law and the Gospel* and *Concerning Women's Learning in Silence and also Concerning Women's not Speaking in the Church*. Such works reveal that the voices of women were a troublesome concern in the dissenting and reformed churches of England. The late twentieth-century dispute over the clerical and, in the Anglican Church, the episcopal ordination of women has now returned to a level of noise over issues nearly identical to the Corinthian problems that St. Paul encountered on his travels throughout the Mediterranean world.[3]

Wherever there is a rule about silence, you know immediately that there is a problem. The problem is noise, unruliness and controversy. Who may speak, who should not, and in what circumstances? Austen acknowledged this as a danger for women, and offered them a pragmatic rule of thumb for peaceful domestic coexistence: pipe down.

Silence, or the lack of it, is no less a concern in any other assembly, particularly those of a political nature. A parliament is supposed to be about speaking, as the word signifies – from the French *parler* and its Anglicised *parley*. However, the rules of 'parliamentary procedure' focus on rigorous but normally unsuccessful strategies to keep silence in the house. One person 'has the floor' to speak. All other speech is 'out of order' – that is, disorder and noise – unless special permission is given to interject. In the British House of Commons, there is a quaint but apparently effective means whereby the Speaker may return order to chaos and pandemonium. The Speaker, in a symbolic but no less shocking ultimatum, puts on his or her hat. Though rarely resorted to, it is meant to bring stunned silence to the House. It signifies that the Speaker is on the brink of departing, and in that event the sitting is adjourned.

It is worth reflecting on the fact that there are many rules aimed at imposing silence, in the home, at school, in church, and even in some games and spectator sports. Indeed, contemporary feminists have argued that patriarchal social structures throughout society are aimed at silencing women in particular, although the present scope of argument suggests that the silencing of women is part of a larger and more pervasive social tension. The process of 'silencing' is, after all, also the process of 'being heard.' At every level of discourse, it is the establishment of order: the sequence, hierarchies and alternations in which some voices are heard while others are not. Inevitably this involves silencing those who are 'ruled out of order.' Feminists no less than advocates of other disadvantaged groups are, therefore, rightly concerned when entire classes – for example, the 'silent woman' in traditional cultures or indeed in the artistic traditions of Western culture (Key, 1975: 127-29) – are silenced as a matter of cultural practice or legal principle.

Here again one needs to apply the rule of opposition in analysing the social relations of silence. Systematic 'regimes' to impose, maintain or recover silence are an indication of how difficult the task is. Radical disciplines – a police state or a monastic order's vow of silence – may be employed but, one often suspects, against the odds and not very successfully. Following this line of opposition suggests a surprising implication: that regimes of silence stand ever in opposition to the 'norm' of speech, noise, laughter, shouting, singing, chanting and reverberant disorder. Despite the pompous rhetoric and grandiloquence of the political arena, speakers struggle to be heard against a constant din of cheers and jeers, bickering, hisses and boos.

Nevertheless political rhetoric aims to 'master' the throng, bringing them to rapt attention and rendering them spell-bound. Rhetoric may be, as Arendt (1958: 180) suggests, either 'mere talk' or a display of public self-enactment, but only a few of us do it while the many listen passively or turn away in apathy. Silence in such cases is a sign of apparent compliance or at least quiescent order. Lyndon Johnson boasted of achieving this among his cabinet colleagues with a firm metaphorical grip on their lower anatomy. Shakespeare (1953: 652) allowed Mark Anthony a more civil idea: 'Friends, Romans, countrymen, lend me your ears!' Obedient attention, in a school classroom or the army, is the first law of civil order. Unless everyone is quiet, nothing can proceed. 'Order in the court' means 'Shut up!'

Chosen and imposed silence

The value placed upon silence, or indeed its necessity for disciplined cooperation, raises important questions about human communication. Is noise – a discordant freedom with a potential for occasional harmony – 'natural'? Is silence, enforced if not freely chosen, a prerequisite to social and political life? Do we fall silent, or must we be pushed?

I suspect that noise *happens* – as parents of a new-born infant will attest – and that is why we tend to think of noise as spontaneous and disorderly. Silence must be imposed. Public assemblies have bailiffs, sergeants at arms and rules of order; schools have masters and prefects; some parents slap and spank their loud and sassy offspring. Despite the many cases of enforced silence that spring to mind, there are times when it is self-imposed. Rigorous disciplines of silence are required by some religious orders. We might make a vow of silence to keep a friend's secret. But we occasionally welcome a moment of quiet retreat or the pleasure of an undisturbed daydream.

Nevertheless, the idea that noise is somehow 'natural' whereas silence is 'governed' by social power would appear to have a significant bearing upon disclosure. Do we – naturally, ordinarily, all things being equal – express, reveal and expose ourselves, whereas silence is a detour, a postponement, a defeat? In fashioning an answer to that question, we will find that silence is not only a condition imposed by repressive power but may also be a strategy for powerful resistance to authority.

Silence *versus* communication

Scholars of communication generally take for granted that vigorous communication is a 'norm' and a 'good.' It is an additive virtue. The more communication the better. In democratic theory, speaking out is the ideal of rational, moral, competent, virtuous human behaviour. As the ancient Roman maxim expressed it – *Vox populi, vox dei* – the voice of the people is the voice of God. Jean-Jacques Rousseau described this voice as public opinion, and personified it as the queen of virtues. Following in these ancient footsteps, modern political theorists have argued that speech is a paradigm of political action, the very means by which political life is articulated both formally and informally (Arendt, 1958; Corcoran, 1989; Dallmayr, 1984a, 1984b; Habermas, 1984, 1987; O'Barr and O'Barr, 1976).

However, also from ancient times there has been a contrary view that formal politics is 'all talk and no action'. The problem is not with rhetorical display as such, which can be entertaining and uplifting. Nevertheless political speech-making has long been regarded as a lot of egotistical hot air: a deceptive but empty substitute for 'real' action. A fearful implication of such a view is that political decisions are actually made behind closed doors where the debates, if any, do not reach the ears of the public. Rhetoric is deployed to hide rather than reveal those private deliberations.

Arendt (1958: 178-80), however, makes an important distinction between genuine rhetorical 'self-enactment' and what she calls 'mere talk'. The latter is public speech pressed into service for politicians' competitive struggle for victory at all costs. It is a form of verbal combat between allies and enemies in which strategic conquest, rather than self-disclosing enactment, is the goal. In Arendt's sense, 'mere talk' is not a substitute for political action, but to the extent that rhetoric is deceptive and empty – where speech lacks 'the disclosure of the agent in the act' and persuades without regard to the truth – such efforts weaken and subvert the common enterprise for the public good.

> In these instances, which of course have always existed, speech becomes indeed "mere talk," simply one more means toward the end, where it serves to deceive the enemy or dazzle everybody else with propaganda; here words reveal nothing, disclosure comes only from the deed itself... (Arendt, 1958: 180).

There is, however, an unmistakable cynicism in the popular castigation of politics as 'all talk' which goes much farther than Arendt's critique of 'mere talk'. For example, the commonplace phrase – 'actions speak louder than words' – strongly implies that 'talk' is inferior to, or indeed the opposite of, 'political action.' Flights of rhetoric, especially in the political arena, are easily dismissed as 'dilatory tactics', 'ego-tripping' or a veil of hypocrisy to disguise self-interested deeds. These popular criticisms of political speech, however, sharply deviate from ancient understandings of the justly constituted political order and also profoundly underestimate the formative power of language.

To say that politics is 'all talk' implies that it is not brute force and violence. Indeed, a politics based upon talk is precisely what emerged in the Athenian constitution as a form of open, precariously democratic government based upon persuasion rather than noble lineage or superior force of arms. The antecedents to the 'power of persuasion' were despotism, intrigue, violent coercion, and plain murder – all forms of action quite consistent with public silence. One need not idealise the actual practise of the Athenian democracy in its Periclean form to affirm that its ideals and some part of its experience were based upon a vigorous dialogue among citizens of diverse interests and social status who were nevertheless engaged in free self-rule. Indeed this was the context in which even critics of democracy such as Socrates and Plato were able to debate theories of justice in dialogues with their disciples, philosophical rivals and fellow citizens.[4] Statesmanship, even for Plato's ideal philosopher-king, was conceived as 'dialectic' – the art of learned discourse – in which the city-state was to be governed by laws formulated and administered through oral communication rather than the force of arms.

From this classical perspective the dismissive view that 'politics is all talk' is both sophistic and cynical. It implies an impatience with democratic life. It deprecates the possibility of an informed citizenry and the efficacy of popular government. This betrays a preference not simply for action but for the silent intrigue of despotic action. Even tyranny, by contrast, can be forcibly popular and is often based upon eloquence and charisma: more talk.

It is important to understand that the solemn, or vain, rhetorical combat in the political arena is not the only 'game' in town. There are language games of all kinds, from occasional instances of revelatory self-disclosure to the competitive struggles with chosen sides, rules, winners and losers. Such is the noisy 'playground' for a healthy society's many voices. Outsiders, or those who are for whatever reason unappreciative, will hear cacophony, disorder, noise. They may feel that uniformity, silence and attention to a single authoritative voice should be the order of the day. Implicit in such a predilection is the notion that 'politics' cannot begin until everybody is quiet, even the politicians. However, those who value the play of language will see 'free speech' itself – the noisy, absorbing spectacle of political combat, rabble-rousing dissent and even the pompous sonorities of elected officials – as the sound and substance of what democratic politics ought to be. Of course the audience is an active part of this spectacle, and when for whatever reason they are silenced or rendered passive, the 'play' becomes a dumb show and the audience a mere mass of obedient or sullen onlookers.

Communicative action

So far I have speculated that nature inclines us, from the moment of birth, to a noisy hue and cry and that the hurly-burly of communicative behaviour is a healthy sign of civil society. Elsewhere in this book it is suggested that open, honest communication is an essential virtue between intimates. If 'giving voice' is both a natural trait and a civil virtue, this would seem to go a long way toward establishing a moral case against silence.[5] However, as we have already seen, there is a case to be made for silence that also seems psychologically grounded and deeply embedded in social values and concepts of human dignity. To be perfectly honest, a lot of talk is a pain in the neck. It is an annoyance that most people like very much to be relieved of. Within earshot of the din of radio, television, a campaign speech or a popular restaurant on Friday night we might well feel that 'silence is golden.' Is silence, then, also a virtue? Swinburne (1924: 289) seemed to think so:

> For words divide and rend
> But Silence is noble till the end.

In a purposely far-fetched analogy, we might compare skilful communication, which requires knowledge, a lot of practice and a certain amount of style, to the practice of going regularly to the gym. Vigorous exercise is hard work. It is a nuisance, and so are most of the people who are really fit and have great bodies: hard, impressive, affronting. The rest of us – flabby, sullen, intimidated (that is, silent) and anxious about our envy – have a bad conscience. We know that exercise would be 'good' for us. But the effort is difficult to fit into our daily routine. So it is easy to be suspicious about the joy and ideals of all those healthily sweating, aerobically articulate, beautifully toned bodies.

These reflections do not obviously suggest an allusion to Jürgen Habermas's notion of an 'ideal speech situation.' Nevertheless, entertain for the moment the idea that the society envisaged by his elaborate theories of 'communicative rationality' and 'communicative action'[6] is like a busy fitness centre, where there is an unusually high concentration of colourfully leotarded, tautly sculpted bodies all going hell for leather in coordinated, enthusiastic, orderly unison. Mostly these beautiful bodies are counting, chanting, urging themselves on to greater pain and sacrifice. They are doing and saying things so inane and repetitive that disagreement or opposition would be pointless. Their speech is not 'strategic' or 'instrumental' in the nasty, manipulative, exploitative way that Kant or Habermas would eschew. Rather, the communication is voluntary and consensual, individuals actively engaged in communal cultivation. Everyone should be in it. It is easy to imagine that the sweat, noise, empowerment and adrenaline rushes, rather than health and fitness, are ends in themselves.

Analogies pushed this far begin to exude an acrid odour. A reader's appreciation of that pungent metaphor, and of my analogy between the racket in a gym and the hubbub of public discourse, is in fact a nice illustration of the point Habermas makes about the relationship between speech behaviour and rationality:

> Actors are behaving rationally so long as they use predicates such as "spicy," "attractive," "strange," "disgusting," and so forth, in such a way that other members of their lifeworlds can recognize in these descriptions their own reactions to similar situations (Habermas, 1981: 16-17).

Robust communication – in political campaigns, parliament, the pub or at home, as well as at the gym – may require a high level of pressure, intensity and routine. Such speech may indeed cultivate certain skills, discipline and muscle. As a consequence one will also have to tolerate a lot of hot air. Is this good? Will more communication always be better? This purely quantitative (summative) ideal – talk, as it were, for the pleasure of the exercise, the more the merrier – may run up against the same qualitative objections that John Stuart Mill opposed to the utilitarian pleasure principle (Mill, 1961: 50-51; 332, 336). Mill concluded that some pleasures were finer than others, and usually came at the cost of some pain. Is a really good speech, then, worth a lot of silence? Is a lot of happy noise an acceptable substitute for 'superior' communication?

Downwind, the opportune response might be to escape the noise and seek the solace of silence. However, it is worth remembering that Rousseau's model of direct democracy rejected the idea of delegating our voices to a representative who will 'speak for us'. It is a forfeiture of our true interests and duties to a corrupting public silence (Rousseau, 1968: 141).

Revising Habermas, the moral dimension of social action may not run from bad (strategic) to good (cooperative) communication, but from silence to speech. Perhaps a democracy is worth a lot of hot air and solemn monologues. But at the level of personal experience, if we are profoundly happy, do we need to talk about it? Would many want to listen in good faith? For a very long time? If we are experiencing profound sorrow or humiliation, might we not choose and need silence? These questions will surely attract differing answers. For example, many women find talking a nurturing, strengthening experience, whereas many men would attribute these benefits to silence. Yet even these differences point out how there may be times when the 'ideal speech situation' is pure silence. Some cultures, at a time of pleasure or sorrow, adopt the meditative and consensual 'mark of silence.' This is a practice of Australian Aboriginal people when greeting each other after periods apart, or when convening around a campfire. A similar occurrence, perhaps, is the 'knowing silence' in a novel – a 'conspiracy' established when the reader understands what the 'silent woman' does not say – that female novelists have endeavoured to represent in their female characters (Laurence, 1994).

In the rhetorical gymnasium, people who talk a lot probably get a lot of good out of it. One thinks of people who teach, run for office, preach or, in the extreme, lie. Very elderly people are reputed to talk incessantly, repeat themselves constantly. This may well be, for them, a way of keeping the battery charged, the old grey cells pumping, active, alive. What is it for others?

There are many deprecatory terms for describing incessant speech: garrulous, voluble, prolix, verbose, gossip, tattle-tale, talkative, boring. Women have been saddled with the stereotype, 'chatterboxes', while men have been traditionally compared to Hollywood's 'strong, silent type.' In recent years the 'sensitive New Age guy' – rather ambiguously characterised as one who loquaciously 'gets in touch with his feelings' – has discovered his 'feminine side' just as some feminists have dismissed this effort as an 'essentialist' error or a masculinist fetish of Lacanian 'lack.' Clearly the 'gendered' view of silence is troubled and uncertain. Postmodern, feminist and post-colonial defenders of the 'silenced Other' have widened the 'margin' to the point of effectively 'deconstructing' – that is, silencing – any voice that might represent the centre.

Silence as a human characteristic is often characterised as a powerful, peaceful, good and 'golden' thing: calm, quiet, tranquil, resolute, stoic, dignified and unyielding. Silence is highly regarded even in reference to mechanical things. A smooth engine runs quietly; it is a mark of excellence, and a marketing exaggeration, when a machine is said to run 'silently.' Yet silence has a number of negative connotations: mute, incommunicative, closemouthed and taciturn.

All of these synonyms suggest that silence is highly revealing of attitude, character and self-possession. Silence, then, can be a powerfully gestural mode of communication in its expressive or repressive enactment of important meanings and values. The experience of silence can be electric. It is like being tuned in perfectly to a powerful radio station from which an audio signal but no program content is being broadcast: it rivets your attention and conveys a sense that something is wrong. Simply being silent can be evocative, eloquent, even explicit to those in its presence. In a sense 'withdrawing into oneself' is more embodied than speech itself. Anxiously, husband and wife, teenager and parent or two lovers feel something is terribly wrong when absolute silence is the only 'sign.' Abused children tend to 'go silent'. In such situations there is a haunting, conspicuous unity of the sign and the signifier.

Silence, then, is highly emotive. The silence of others, as mentioned above, may evoke fear, sorrow or contempt. It can be insistent, assertive, defiant, proud and arrogant. Yet the evocativeness of silence may be entirely private. Silence enables us to conjure up images and feelings in a contemplative quiet that requires even our own voice to be still. It has a sharpening effect on the senses, enabling us to listen for subtle things around us and even see things we might not otherwise observe. Silence is especially needed to activate and furnish the inner landscape of our memories, imagination and waking fantasies. Clearly silence is not simply the circumstance, but the necessary condition and discipline, for meditation and many religious exercises.

Silence may be eloquent, but it is not always articulate. Silence forces the 'listener' to participate, supply meaning, fill in the blanks.[7] In this way it has an aesthetic power. Indeed, silence is like a cartoon with no punch line or balloon of words. One is compelled to enter into it, to read, speak and hear the humour and pathos.

Silence in some circumstances will oblige a response. Indeed, it may be a response. In this sense silence is actively communicative. It can play a part in a dialogue. Silence operates within the normal syntax and grammar of conversation as visual and aural punctuation. It can be a full stop, a comma or an ellipsis – each with its distinct and easily read meanings. As a form of punctuation, silence gives order and structure to communication, rendering meanings in spatial, sequential and even 'logical' ways.[8] The 'no comment' phrase in political and diplomatic discourse is the most obvious example, but actual silence – a mute bowing of the head, the look of stubborn defiance, the 'pregnant' pause – may reveal far more complex, subtle and easily understood (or purposely ambiguous, easily misunderstood) meanings.

The right to silence

Considering the complex psychological and gestural meanings of silence, and of silent persons, it is not surprising that 'non-disclosure' and formal silence have been the subject of careful and more or less narrowly circumscribed legal and juridical speculation. The 'right to silence' as a legal precept is specifically identified in modern times with constraints in police investigation and interrogation, pre-trial judicial proceedings and criminal trials. However, as Susan Easton (1991: 1-2) notes with respect to Britain:

> in the law of evidence generally the right is much more broadly conceived as both a right and a privilege, a privilege against self-incrimination which developed in the late sixteenth and seventeenth centuries. The privilege in this broader sense embraces both the right of the defendant not to testify at his own trial and also the decision of third party witnesses not to disclose self-incriminating evidence....
>
> The privilege against self-incrimination gained acceptance in the seventeenth century in response to the forced interrogations and arbitrary power of the Star Chamber, the prerogative Court of the King, Charles I, and to the ecclesiastical court of the High Commission. Methods used by the Star Chamber included torture, mutilation, the pillory and imprisonment.... Both courts [were] abolished in 1641 and by 1660 the common law courts had established their supremacy. It was in this political context that the privilege against self-incrimination developed (Easton, 1991: 1-2).

This privilege, born in reaction to arbitrary power, violent religious intolerance and barbarous methods of obtaining confessions in the seventeenth century, was reworked and strengthened by the new practice of allowing legal counsel for the accused in the late eighteenth and early decades of the nineteenth centuries.[9] These procedural changes were part of the wider social and political reforms in the period and also a response to a massively expanded constabulary. Yet the right to silence evolved slowly and reluctantly in the complex system of law courts in Britain. Originally meaning nothing more than that a man was not compelled to make the initial accusation against himself, the idea gradually extended to a prohibition of all compulsory testimony by a defendant in the investigatory, pre-trial and trial stages of prosecution.

In fact the English common law tradition has not been in the vanguard of advocacy for human 'rights', except those relating to property and physical liberty. The legal principle of silence as a *privilege* in judicial procedure was finally, in the Criminal Evidence Act of 1898, accorded the status of a *statutory right* to silence in police inquiries, pre-trial proceedings, and at trial (Easton, 1991: 3-7). However, silence against self-incrimination has never been granted the exalted status of a human or constitutional right. Eric Barendt (1985: 64), for example, still prefers the precision of the traditional formula, 'the common law privilege against self-incrimination.' The exercise of this privilege by professional groups during investigation or as trial witnesses is, as he notes, very different from the American case he cites, and even further removed from a criminal defendant's right of silence at trial:

> Doctors, priests, journalists may refuse to give evidence or to help police on the ground of professional privilege, and the press may use the argument that if it is not allowed this privilege, its sources of information will dry up.... Such an immunity is very far removed from the right not to speak established by the [U.S. Supreme] Court in the *Barnette* case, and the contrast may shed some light on the scope of this latter right (Barendt, 1985: 64).[10]

Asserting this right or privilege in Britain – that is, remaining silent under charge or examination – heightens the jeopardy of those who do so. At various times and places, judge and jury have been free to comment upon and infer, if they choose, that 'silence implies consent' (Easton, 1985: 7-9). In recent years in Britain the entitlement to silence in pre-trial inquiries and the protection from adverse comment in court in relation to a defendant's silence have been weakened by trials involving the prosecution of persons accused of terrorist activities in Northern Ireland and England.[11] These developments have been established in statutory law by the Criminal Justice and Public Order Act 1994, which specifies the types and extent of adverse inferences that may be drawn and commented upon in court in relation to the accused's failure or refusal to account for being present at a particular place, or the failure to account for possessing 'an object, substance or mark' incident to an offence (Bell, 1995: 172-76).[12]

Interestingly, this begrudging approach to a person being conceded the privilege of remaining silent in the face of accusations, incarceration and the weight of official power did not evolve in terms of a presumption of innocence, or any human or procedural 'right.' Rather, the *nemo debet prodere se ipsum* principle – that one should not be required to testify against oneself – arose from the idea of *incompetence*. The principle evolved by analogy with the ancient assumption of the legal incompetence of a child or a woman, or the mentally deranged, to give true, reliable, independent, rational evidence in a court of law. Since such evidence must be inherently tainted, there was no reason to hear it. Thus it was safe to assume that evidence elicited from a defendant would be similarly tainted: as a witness he would be 'incompetent'; his testimony could not be relied upon by the court to be truthful, independent, objective evidence against himself if he were guilty. Hence the concession of a privilege that J.H. Wigmore (1961: 292) described as 'creeping' into English law rather than being heralded as a landmark of liberty or a bulwark against arbitrary government.[13]

In the American legal tradition dating from the late eighteenth century, the right to silence was effectively declared from the outset in the U.S.

Constitution and the Bill of Rights in the Constitution's first ten amendments. The Fifth Amendment guarantees defendants as well as witnesses in a court of law the 'right against self-incrimination.' In recognition of this right, both federal and state jurisdictions have established procedures and even legislation which prohibit the trial judge from commenting in any respect on the accused's silence when instructing the jury. Some states have even prohibited the discussion of the defendant's silence in the private deliberations of the jury (Easton, 1991: 3).

Nevertheless, attempts to strengthen the right of silence in criminal proceedings tend to inflame common prejudices about guilt and innocence because such protective measures run against powerful moral assumptions about individual and social obligations. Should a suspect's rights be zealously protected, or should they be subordinated to vigorous and intrusive efforts to apprehend and prosecute lawbreakers? If silence against self-incrimination be accorded the status of a privilege or a right, this inevitably places a high premium on social tolerance and commitment to rules of fair play. It is not surprising that attempts, especially in appellate judicial rulings, to strengthen and expand the defendant's rights against self-incrimination and invasive surveillance have led to popular reaction and legislative moves to undermine or narrow these rights. The rhetoric of this reaction proclaims that the hands of the police should be 'untied' in accordance with their duty to apprehend and prosecute. Stronger enforcement, it is argued, must 'tip the balance' of rights in favour of the victims of crime and the police, not the accused.

There is, of course, a certain common-sense basis for the *prejudice* against according a suspect or a criminal defendant a right of silence. It may be costly and time consuming for police and prosecutors; it has demonstrably led to expansive interpretations of privacy, extending to prohibitions upon surveillance or seizing evidence. It is also costly, difficult, and ultimately impossible for the state to prevent adverse inferences about those who exercise the right of silence. Again, it seems to fly in the face of common sense. By refusing to answer questions relating to one's actions, whereabouts and knowledge of a crime, a suspect, defendant or witness seems to betray some degree of culpability, either as a perpetrator or an accomplice. It seems apparent that this person has something to disclose, but will not. Although to draw that inference is, strictly speaking, a kind of prejudice, it rests upon a rather pragmatic and mature assumption that if someone is innocent of a crime, that person will honestly say so and freely disclose evidence to that effect. If the person will not say so, and will not give evidence, then there is a compelling reason to believe that the person is somehow caught up in the crime and has interests served by invoking a right of silence to suppress the truth.

On the other hand, to *coerce* one who is 'on trial' seems to fly in the face of both logic and common decency, since forced self-incrimination effectively aborts the very issue that is being 'tried.' For Thomas Hobbes, 'inviting' self-incrimination, even by force, is an ultimately futile attempt to violate the 'right of nature' that had priority over all other laws of nature:

> The Right of Nature…is the liberty each man has to use his own power, as he will himself, for the preservation of…his own life; and consequently of doing anything which, in his own judgment and reason, he shall conceive to be the aptest means thereunto (Hobbes, 1958: 109).

Comparing Hobbes's justification of naked self-interest with the civilised, rather delicate and fragile 'right to silence' proffered to the accused shows how the latter concept is perhaps psychologically deficient. Notwithstanding the majesty of the law and the court's blind presumption of innocence on behalf of the accused, in the final analysis it is impossible to prevent suspicions being formed against suspects whom the police and prosecuting attorneys have taken pains to charge, indict and try.

If silence were *not* in some way allowed as a basis of inference it would impose an even greater burden upon credulity and the appearance of fairness in judicial procedure. It would be tantamount to arguing that silence is a perfect defence, on the patently absurd grounds that if a man is guilty of a crime he will surely admit it. A juror does not need to *talk* to other jurors to make such inferences, and steps to prevent such thoughts would be both draconian and a travesty of fair trial.

Historically, the doctrines of legal silence in English common law and American constitutional law may be distinguished from each other. The English idea of 'privilege' granted to incompetency is based on a strong scepticism about an individual's ability to give evidence that will jeopardise one's liberty and interests. The American doctrine of silence is also based on scepticism, but in this case a scepticism about the competency of government. The individual's constitutional – not statutory – rights against self-incrimination presuppose the state's propensity, in its pursuit of incriminating evidence, to abuse coercive powers.[14] This is not only a right to silence but, as secured in the Fourth Amendment, the right of citizens to be 'secure in their persons, houses, papers and effects, against unreasonable searches and seizures.'

In the twentieth century, with the rise of extensive police forces and more intrusive means of surveillance and recording of evidence, landmark Supreme Court cases such as *Gideon v. Wainwright* (1963) and *Miranda v. Arizona* (1966) ruled that criminal defendants have a constitutional right to counsel. A lawyer will, in effect, speak for them and safeguard their defence by advising, in private, how the defendant's interests will be served by remaining silent. Police methods which thwart or undermine the right to silence and the protection against self-incrimination – coercive police interrogations, unreasonable search and seizure, the extraction of evidence by force, entrapment or invasions of privacy – have also been constitutionally prohibited on other grounds.[15] The right against self-incrimination was directly expanded and strengthened in two other cases in the 1960s when the Supreme Court extended this Fifth Amendment right by prohibiting prosecutors from using as incriminating evidence a person's subpoenaed testimony before official commissions and court-sanctioned inquiries (*Malloy v. Hogan*, 1964; *Murphy v. Waterfront Commission*, 1964). In recent years, American courts, both state and federal, have amplified and consolidated the right of silence (Wigmore, 1998: 940-44).

In an earlier and separate line of constitutional reasoning, the Supreme Court recognised an 'inferred' right of silence in its broader interpretations of First Amendment rights concerning freedom of speech. This implicit right of silence was asserted against legislative attempts to compel oaths and symbolic speech or to require citizens to disclose opinions or memberships. In the *Barnette* Case (Jackson, 1943), the court protected the refusal to salute and swear the oath of allegiance to the U.S. flag by school children from families espousing the faith of the Jehovah's Witnesses. The court characterised West Virginia's law which prescribed this ceremony as 'requir[ing] the individual to communicate by word and sign his acceptance of the political ideas it thus bespeaks. Objection to this form of communication when coerced is an old one, well known to the framers of the Bill of Rights' (633). The court made it clear that it was not disposed to 'say that a Bill of Rights which guards the individual's right to speak his own mind, left it open to public authorities to compel him to utter what is not in his mind' (634). Justice Robert Jackson, in the majority opinion, firmly rejected the 'validity of the asserted power to force any statement of belief or to engage in any ceremony of assent to one' (634), and ruled that any such action 'invades the sphere of intellect and spirit which it is the purpose of our Constitution to reserve from all official control' (642).

What is at issue in this idea of a right to silence is much deeper than the common law principle of a privilege, conceded on the grounds of presumptive 'incompetence', that exempts the accused from being compelled to testify against himself in a criminal case. Justice Jackson's defence of silence, in an opinion delivered in the midst of World War II, not only limits the state's power of forcing speech but recognises and protects what is essentially an unlimited political 'freedom to differ' on matters central to the framework and values of society:

...freedom to differ is not limited to things that do not matter much. That would be a mere shadow of freedom. The test of its substance is the right to differ as to things that touch the heart of the existing order.

If there is any fixed star in our constitutional constellation, it is that no official, high or petty, can prescribe what shall be orthodox in politics, nationalism, religion, or other matters of opinion or force citizens to confess by word or act their faith therein. If there are any circumstances which permit an exception, they do not now occur to us (Jackson, 1943: 642).

It is clear that silence is a morally charged concept. Silence is not just a backdrop, or the absence of speech. As an expressive behaviour, it has a powerful rhetorical potential as symbolic communication. It may be a refusal to communicate, but it cannot be a denial of meaning. Just as the spoken word is capable of concealing as well as conveying information, so silence is powerful in each of these capacities. In a card game, a 'poker face' is not essentially a skilful blanking out of meaning. It is a careful strategy to beat you with a weak hand and clean you out with a strong one. In court you can beat the wrap.

The effects of silence

A careful examination of the evolving patterns of disclosure in political and social communication in ancient and modern Western culture reveals that 'disclosure' is a linguistic performance for purposes, and with effects, that may have a profound impact on both speaker and audience. We acknowledge this when we say of a speaker that he has 'exposed himself' and 'laid himself bare.' Standing in opposition to disclosure is confidentiality, secrecy, silence. If disclosure is an opening, an affirmation, a revelation, then non-disclosure is a refusal, a resistance and a protective enclosure.

Yet *silence is also a revelatory enactment*. It has important personal and social effects. From the point of view of noisy political discourse, or at least in the view of its most vocal participants, silence might seem a nullity, a void or hiatus. But even the briefest reflection calls to mind how hard it is to keep quiet – the courage and strength it may require, as Austen suggests, and the impact of 'maintaining silence' on one's self and others.

Silence is not innocent. It is not existentially or morally neutral, nor is it necessarily a communicative default or withdrawal. A refusal to disclose is a kind of denial. It has a negative but powerful valence. There is the assumption of the unspoken, the hidden, the dividing up between those who don't know and those who aren't talking. The dramatic paradigm for this is the defendant who 'won't talk'. Here the unspoken takes on the force of sedition, conspiracy, the insider who remains silent in the quiet eye of the storm.

For these reasons, as noted at the beginning of this chapter, disclosure and silence do not form a simple dichotomy. Just as disclosure is a dramatic and often complex linguistic performance, so too is silence. Both are revelations made for reasons and purposes. Secrecy, silence, confidentiality and other forms of non-disclosure are interruptions, breaks, estoppals, embargoes. Such acts of omission are *interventions* in public discourse. They often serve as powerful constraints on the operation and effectiveness of political institutions.

Silence is nevertheless a troublesome matter in modern democratic societies. There is a presumption that it must be subversive of the democratic political process, whereas openness, citizen representation, advocacy and vigorous and noisy public debate about large and small issues are the lifeblood, the very substance of democracy. Groups that work silently or behind closed doors are presumptive violators of the ethical standards of popular elections and parliamentary government. Similarly, an accused who does not testify faces – despite the formal 'presumption of innocence' – prejudice, doubt and suspicion, even (or especially) when afforded a *privilege* to remain silent and a *right* to refuse to divulge things that the police, the courts, statutory inquiries and the press most want to know.

There are, then, powerful legal or political pressures upon individuals to 'disclose' themselves in the interests of open, fair, equitable and well informed public debate. This is compounded by the seeming imperatives of the 'information age' in which credit cards, passports, electronic files and other 'private' information are increasingly exposed to official and unofficial access. Moreover there are increasing therapeutic pressures to reveal one's medical condition or to 'open up' and 'relate' to professionals, workmates or 'fellow sufferers' of a 'condition.'

These pressures for disclosure constitute, however, a serious paradox in a democratic society, where personal freedom and human dignity are closely allied with the values of individual privacy, security against intrusion and the right to silence. The widely recognised 'goods' of individual privacy – in one's body, one's beliefs, one's pleasures, one's choice of seclusion or association – stand in serious tension with the also widely recognised virtues and benefits of 'full disclosure.'

Self-revelation

Speech is the voice of contingent, proximate, experimental representations of our thoughts, our mind and feelings, our knowledge and memory. If in various ways we always have, in our everyday lives, a 'right to silence', there is also the sense in which we are 'on trial' every time we speak: at a dinner party, in the classroom or tutorial, or surrounded by friends and others in the workplace or at the pub. If what we *say* is judged by others, so too is our silence judged, and not only by others. The inward, invisible, inaudible dialogue of our mind and conscience performs a constant surveillance on what we say and refrain from saying. This inner forum of the conscious mind is so ineffable that there seems not to be one term to classify, much less judge, the layers and cross-purposes of intentions that determine every instance of speech and silence.

At the same time, despite the amorphous inner dialogue, public speech is the skill that enables even small children to make and use marvellous representations – fanciful tales, wonderful other worlds and creatures – with great agility and creativity. Children also, with alarming precocity, attain skills of lying and dissimulation. Young children can also keep things hidden and fearfully repressed, while at the same 'innocently' disclosing things both mundane and bizarre.

Of course adults as well as children always say less and more than they consciously intend: both less and more than they know. Everything we 'know', even before we speak, is thought and formed into possible utterances within the enclosure of a native tongue. So we inescapably say things to some persons and *not* to others. Silence is the reflex of speech. Silence does not just 'happen': it is a communicative process in a speech community. It is not simply what some do to others, but what inevitably occurs when some speak, others listen, and others still do not understand.

Conclusion: noisy and silent worlds

In the contemporary culture of publicity and celebrity there remain powerful forces of silence. I refer not only to regimes of formal political power, but to other institutions – both in Western and non-Western societies – which quietly endure and have so far lived on in defiance of an age and culture won over to the easy virtues and promiscuous pleasures of disclosure. Consider, for example, the teenage boy in India who, in 1999, was arrested, convicted and imprisoned for kissing his girlfriend in public. All around the world seemingly impenetrable redoubts of religion, traditional morality and familial patriarchy thrive in which privacy, bodily modesty and piety are sacred values. Invisible, barely audible crevices of specialised, hidden, largely inaccessible discourses survive in which this one speaks and that one listens in silent obedience.

In the noisy world at large, only with difficulty in the West can one hear the silence emanating from the great mass of the world's population. It is so difficult, in fact, that a generation of theorists, both Eastern and Western, have 'constructed' a silence. Here I refer not only to the 'silenced Other' as conceived by feminists, critics of Eurocentrism and other sophisticated exponents of the marginalised, dark and silent masses, as they tend to be described even by non-European 'post-colonial theorists' (Chow, 1998: 31).[16] There are also silent communities in Western society in remote mountain and rural areas, anonymous urban sub-cultures and minor religious sects, as well as the unvoiced lives of suburban middle-class mass murderers and inarticulate youth suicides. The issues and ideas championed by righteously indignant theorists are mainly foreign and incomprehensible to those on whose behalf they are being urged. Indeed it is unlikely that even the alleged perpetrators of 'Othering' – the vast sprawl of trades, arts and professions improbably characterised as white, male, Protestant and living in either Hollywood or Fifth Avenue – would comprehend, much less accept, the indictment.

In many nations, cultures and religions, in the West as well as the East, silent obedience is not necessarily explicable by such simplistic dichotomies as nature *versus* nurture, freedom *versus* slavery, or male *versus* female. The ancient spiritual ideal of reverence and self-abasement before the divine certainly cannot be reconciled with the notion that silence signifies oppression and cowed defeat. If contemporary scholarship is enamoured of a 'multiplicity of voices' and defiant 'interventions', there are others who attend to the significance of contemplative silence, the unspoken, the conspicuous and profound 'absences' in artistic and spiritual discourse (Kane, 1984; McGuire, 1985).

Silence, then, need not be a 'sign' of defeat. As we have seen in this chapter, silence often signifies power, inward strength, resistance and meaning. Consider again Jane Austen's prudential pragmatism in recommending that a woman's quiet concealment of opinions, interests and superior intelligence will enhance her dignity and life chances in society (Laurence 1994; Hedges and Fishkin, 1994). Was Austen's observation simply an unwitting, or indeed a cowed and worshipful, capitulation to patriarchal hegemony? It takes a good deal of 'nurturing' in the discipline of literary theory to enable one to read Austen's counsel as simply a desperate and humiliating plea for mercy by those who have been abased and woefully damaged by their father-captors (Johnson, 1988: 40; 112-113). On such readings, it may be Austen herself who is being 'silenced.'

Silence remains in many parts of the world an unquestioned reflex to the acknowledged command of the patriarch and a profound reverence to the Almighty. It is a devout conformity to what are believed absolutely to be divine powers and universal laws. That such beliefs 'survive' in the modern world confounds the Western world-view. This enigma to Western minds seems by and large to be a proud and happy fact to traditionalists in the 'silent world' whose views, for one reason or another, come to notice. Traditionalists also know that the noise of modernity stealing in on invisible electronic wavebands threatens the timeless silence and the structures of authority which depend upon reverential silence. Loudspeakers have been usefully deployed in many ancient temples and mosques to amplify ancient prayers. The muezzins may not know, or care, that their voices have been electronically 'sampled' to produce 'world music' intended to celebrate the post-modern world.

Silence, however, is not the distinguishing criterion between East and West, male and female, rich and poor. Silence – diverse, complex, psychologically indeterminate as language itself – is a universal mode of human expression. When we resort to silence, we mean something by it. Silence embodies a message in a way that other people try to understand simply because of the urgency of the range of possible meanings: anger, distrust, terror, courage, peace, piety, contentment or adoration. Thus we understand why 'silence implies consent' is a claim fraught with powerful interests. To accept such a claim might involve, for example, the costly performance of a contractual obligation, the culpability of criminal complicity or the condoning of rape.

Silence, however, is not only a domain of urgency and tension. Silence is also associated with cooler and more relaxed connotations, calling to mind what is passive, calm and quiet, or the meditative, even hallucinatory, stillness of absolute silence. There are moments of ecstatic silence when we are 'speechless', and our surprise is 'beyond words.' Although this chapter has emphasised the urgency and sublimity of silence as an expressive concept and a cultural phenomenon, it is worth remembering that silence is nevertheless readily available to practical experimentation. Stop talking, turn off the television, do not answer a friend's question, close the door, retreat to the wilderness. People will notice, and so will you. You may find that silence is difficult to achieve but it will not escape the notice of others that you are making a statement.

Notes

[1] Hassan (1967: 203-04) argues that Miller and Beckett are 'prophets of silence' whose anti-art returns to silence by striving for 'absolute zero, an ideal state': 'When the civilized world is wiped out, as Miller pretends to believe, men will walk the earth as gods, and the inner harmony, the peace they will achieve, will possess the quality of silence.' Compare (Sontag, 1969: 7): 'The exemplary modern artist's choice of silence is rarely carried to this point of final simplification, so that he becomes literally silent. More typically, he continues speaking, but in a manner that his audience can't hear. Most valuable art in our time has been experienced by audiences as a move into silence (or unintelligibility or invisibility or inaudibility); a dismantling of the artist's competence, his reasonable sense of vocation – and therefore as an aggression against them [i.e. the audience].'

[2] Using 'silence' as a keyword in searching a university library catalogue or a database of periodical literature will discover that a preponderance of the references are to studies of women who are 'silenced.' For example, A. Clark (1987), *Women's Silence, Men's Violence: Sexual Assault in England 1770-1845*, Pandora, London; C. Luke (1994), 'Women in the Academy – the Politics of Speech and Silence', *British Journal of the Sociology of Education*, vol. 15, no. 2: 211-230; L.C. Olson (1997), 'On the Margins of Rhetoric: Audre Lorde's *Transforming Silence into Language and Action*', *Quarterly Journal of Speech*, vol. 83, no. 1: 49-70; H. Afshar (1996), reviewing K. Makiya, *Cruelty and Silence – War, Tyranny, Uprising and the Arab World*, *Women's History Review*, vol. 5, no. 2: 300-01. Many references to *silence* deal with domestic violence, crime and illicit or conspiratorial acts.

[3] One other example will suffice to show that the silence of women was a matter of interest from ancient times, and not ony in the Hebrew and Christian communities. Aristotle (1960: 1260a) not only endorses the importance of women remaining silent but quotes the Sophoclean play, *Ajax*, as an authority: 'A modest silence is a woman's crown.' Aristotle's point is that this is true for a woman, but not for a man, in whom a disposition to silence brings no honour. In Book V (1313e) of the *Politics* Aristotle implies that their propensity to talk makes women useful as informers to a tyrant, whose despotic rule cuts him off from public sources of information; but elsewhere (1314d) he points out that 'the insolence of women has often been the ruin of tyrannies.'

[4] Although Socrates was tried, convicted and executed in 399 BC on trumped up charges of impiety and subverting the youth because of his incessant questioning of Athenian morality, the trial was carried out before a jury of five-hundred citizens, Socrates spoke in his own defense, made a second speech to the jury to propose a sentence, and continued to communicate with his friends to the very end.

[5] If, as some have argued, males normally exhibit less communicative behaviour than females, does this mean that silence for men is a virtue? Or a deficiency? These questions would seem to beg an answer whether 'normal' be defined in terms of congenital or social factors.

[6] 'This concept of communicative rationality carries with it connotations based ultimately on the central experience of the unconstrained, unifying, consensus-bringing force of argumentative speech, in which different participants overcome their merely subjective views and, owing to the mutuality of rationally motivated conviction, assure themselves of both the unity of the objective world and the intersubjectivity of their lifeworld' (Habermas, 1981: 10, 285-86).

[7] One powerful form of silence, paradoxically the most 'disquieting', is crying. When speech 'breaks down', the voice is at a physical and emotional impasse. Choking sobs and tears replace the fluency of words. Speaking becomes difficult or impossible. Both the one who cries and the listener are overtaken by emotions, and both may be rendered mute.

[8] In the 1970s I saw a play in London about a married couple with a communication problem. The wife had spoken to an uncommunicative husband for many years. He sits, legs crossed, reading the paper or watching television. His only response to her incessant nagging and chatter is to twitch his foot up and down, or side to side, in alarm, disagreement or indifference. The play's comedy arises from the fact that the wife has actually adjusted to the silence by directly addressing his foot, effectively carrying on a 'normal' conversation that the audience also gradually accepts.

[9] Langbein (1994) argues that the evolution of the defendant's 'right to silence' as a procedural principle in English courts is less a reaction of conscience against the seventeenth-century Star Chamber excesses than a by-product of the late eighteenth and nineteenth-century emergence of having the accused represented by counsel. This led to procedural reforms in which the accused was now afforded the *right* to speak in his defense (having earlier been excluded under the *nemo debet* rule of 'incompetence') or the right to remain silent. See *infra*.

[10] The context of Barendt's discussion seems to suggest that he means the *extreme* 'scope' of the reasoning underpinning the right to silence enunciated in *Barnette*. See *infra*.

[11] This has been described (Keane, 1996: 365-71) as "a major curtailment of the 'right to silence.' Thus although the accused retains his 'right' to remain silent both at the trial and under interrogation, 'proper' inferences may be drawn from his failure to give evidence or his refusal, without good cause, to answer any question at the trial (s 35) (ii) his failure to mention certain facts when questioned under caution or being charged and (iii) his failure or his refusal to account for objects, substances or marks (s 36) or his presence at a particular place (s 37)."

[12] For a detailed account see Morgan and Stephenson (1994: 18-38 and pp.141ff). For a discussion of Britain's 'right to silence' law in the context of United Nations conventions, international law and the European Convention, and in particular the European Commission's report (10 May 1994) on *Saunders v UK* and the 'privilege of non self-incrimination', see Eriksen (1996: 55-61).

[13] 'The privilege, thus creeping in by indirection, appears by no means to have been regarded in England as the constitutional landmark that the later American legislation [*sic*] has made it' (Wigmore, 1961, vol. 8: 292).

¹⁴ In Australia, another common law country more consistently influenced by English common law, the 'right of silence' is discussed with a somewhat more resolute tone. However, when a recent Chief Justice of the High Court, Mason C.J. (1991: 131 *et seq.*), opined that it is 'a fundamental rule of the common law', he seemed more comfortable in defining it as an 'entitlement' that is 'subject to some specific statutory modifications', including restricted comment by counsel and judge, and permissible inference. For a concise exposition of the Australian law on the silence of the accused and permissible inference and a comparison with other common law jurisdictions – in particular distinctions from British judgements and legislation in response to prosecutions in Northern Ireland, see New South Wales Law Reform Commission (1998: 15-35).

¹⁵ The landmark cases in these matters are *Rochin v. California* (1952) and *Mapp v. Ohio* (1961). For a brief discussion of these cases see Abraham (1967: 90-99).

¹⁶ Edward Said (1994: 235) is perhaps the best authority to support such a reflection: "only recently have Westerners become aware that what they have to say about the history and cultures of 'subordinate' peoples is challengeable by the people themselves". However, what he immediately goes on to say provides a telling illustration of how even the originator of 'Orientalism' (Said, 1978) as a critical concept betrays a rather simplistic, if not arrogant, presumption on behalf of Western culture. He summarily describes these 'subordinate' nations as 'people who a few years back were simply incorporated, culture, land, history, and all, into the great Western empires, and all their disciplinary discourses.' This simple 'incorporation' would be astonishing news, one imagines, to the many peoples of cherished ancient cultures he thus relegates.

References

Abraham, H.J. (1967), *Freedom and the Court: Civil Rights and Liberties in the United States*, Oxford University Press, New York.

Aristotle (1960), *The Politics*, E. Barker ed. and trans., Oxford University Press, Oxford.

Austen, J. (1966), *Northanger Abbey*, Zodiac Press, London.

Arendt, H. (1958), *The Human Condition*, University of Chicago Press, Chicago.

Barendt, E. (1985), *Freedom of Speech*, Clarendon Press, Oxford.

Bell, C.D. (ed.) (1995), Criminal Justice and Public Order Act 1994 (c 33), §§ 408-11, *Cracknell's Law Student's Companion: Evidence*, 2nd ed., Old Bailey Press, London.

Brown, N.O. (1966), *Love's Body*, Random House, New York.

Cheung, K-K. (1993), *Articulate Silences*, Cornell University Press, Ithaca, New York.

_____ (1994), 'Attentive Silence in Joy Kogowa's *Obasan*' in Hedges and Fishkin (eds) (1994), pp. 113-29.

Chow, R. (1998), *Ethics after Idealism: Theory, Culture, Ethnicity, Reading*, Indiana University Press, Bloomington.

Corcoran, P.E. (1989), 'Language and Politics' in D.L. Swanson and D. Nimmo (eds), *New Directions in Political Communication*, Sage, Newbury Park, Calif., pp. 51-85.

Dallmayr, F.R. (1984a), *Language and Politics: Why Does Language Matter to Political Philosophy?*, University of Notre Dame Press, Notre Dame.

_____ (1984b), *Polis and Praxis*, M.I.T. Press, Cambridge.

Easton, S.M. (1991), *The Right to Silence*, Avebury, Aldershot.

Eriksen, M. (1996), 'European Convention: The Privilege Against Self-incrimination in Criminal Cases and the *Saunders* Case', *The Company Lawyer*, vol. 17, no. 2, pp. 55-61.

Fox, G. (1661), *Concerning Sons and Daughters, and Prophetesses Speaking and Prophecying in the Law and the Gospel* and *Concerning Women's Learning in Silence and also Concerning Women's not Speaking in the Church*, 'Printed for M.W.', London.

Gideon v. Wainwright (1963), 372 U.S. 335.

Habermas, J. (1981), *The Theory of Communicative Action*, vol. 1, *Reason and the Rationalization of Society*, T. McCarthy trans., Beacon Press, Boston.

_____ (1987), *Moral Consciousness and Communicative*, M.I.T. Press, Cambridge, Mass.

Hassan, I. (1967), *The Literature of Silence: Henry Miller and Samuel Beckett*, Knopf, New York.

Hedges, E. and Fishkin, S.F. (eds) (1994), *Listening to Silences: New Essays in Feminist Criticism*, Oxford University Press, New York.

Hobbes, T. (1958), *Leviathan*, Bobbs-Merrill, New York.

Jackson, Justice R. (1943), *West Virginia State Board of Education v. Barnette*, 319 U.S. 624.

Johnson, C. (1988), *Jane Austen: Women, Politics and the Novel*, University of Chicago Press, Chicago.

Kane, L. (1984), *The Language of Silence: On the Unspoken and the Unspeakable in Modern Drama*, Fairleigh Dickinson University Press, Rutherford, New Jersey.

Keane, A. (1996), 'Inference from an Accused's Silence or Refusal to Consent to the Taking of Samples' in *The Modern Law of Evidence*, 4th ed., Butterworths, London, pp. 365-71.

Key, M.R. (1975), *Male/Female Language*, Scarecrow Press, Metuchen, New Jersey.

Langbein, J.H. (1994), 'The Historical Origins of the Privilege Against Self-Incrimination at Common Law', *Michigan Law Review*, vol. 92, pp. 1047 *et seq.*

Laurence, P. (1994), 'Women's Silence as a Ritual of Truth: A Study of Literary Expressions in Austen, Brontë and Woolf' in Hedges and Fishkin (eds) (1994), pp. 156-67.

Malloy v. Hogan (1964), 378 U.S. 1.

Mapp v. Ohio (1961), 367 U.S. 643.

Mason, C.J. (1991), *Petty v Regina*, 102 *Australian Law Reports*, 129.

McGuire, P.C. (1985), *Speechless Dialect: Shakespeare's Open Silences*, University of California Press, Berkeley.

Mill, J.S. (1961), *The Philosophy of John Stuart Mill*, Modern Library, New York.

Miranda v. Arizona (1966), 384 U.S. 436.

Morgan, D. and Stephenson, G.M. (eds) (1994), 'The Right to Silence Debate' and 'Abolition of the Right to Silence' in *Suspicion and Silence: The Right to Silence in Criminal Investigations*, Blackstone Press, London.

Murphy v. Waterfront Commission (1964), 378 U.S. 52.

New South Wales Law Reform Commission (1998), *The Right to Silence*, Discussion Paper 41, N.S.W. Law Reform Commission, Sydney.

O'Barr, W.M. and O'Barr, J.F. (1976), *Language and Politics*, Mouton, The Hague.

Olsen, T. (1979), *Silences*, Delta, New York.

Rochin v. California (1952), 342 U. S. 165.

Rourke, F.E. (1961), *Secrecy and Publicity: Dilemmas of Democracy*, Johns Hopkins University Press, Baltimore.

Rousseau, J-J. (1968), *The Social Contract*, Penguin, Harmondsworth.

Said, E.W. (1978), *Orientalism*, Pantheon Books, New York.

_____ (1994), *Culture and Imperialism*, Vintage, New York.

Shakespeare, W. (1953), *Julius Caesar*, III: 2 in *Twenty-Three Plays and the Sonnets*, T.M. Parrot ed., Charles Scribner's Sons, New York.

Sontag, S. (1969), *Styles of Radical Will*, Farrar, Strauss & Giroux, New York.

Swinburne, A.C. (1924), *Atalanta in Calydon* [1865] in *Collected Poetical Works*, 2 vols, William Heinemann, London, vol. II, p. 289.

Wigmore, J.H. (1961), *Evidence in Trials at Common Law*, 10 vols, rev. ed., J.T. McNaughton, Little, Brown, Boston.

_____ (1998), *Evidence in Trials at Common Law, 1998 Supplement*, Arthur Best (ed.), *Aspen Law & Business*, Denver, Colorado.

Index